BlackBook List

New York

2006

Restaurants, Bars, Clubs, Hotels

WWW.BLACKBOOKMAG.COM

The BlackBook List is your covert guide to New York City's shining culinary stars, dimly lit dive bars and everything in between. Whether you're searching for a strong pour to soothe your nerves, a romantic enclave with that perfect corner table or somewhere to indulge in a night of unprecedented debauchery, these listings offer a variety of select restaurants, bars, clubs and hotels to choose from in every price range.

*Disclaimer: The contents of this manual may be hazardous to your health. Always employ discretion when heading out into the night. Proceed with caution. Good luck.

ISBN # 1932942106 $9.95
© 2005 BlackBook Media Corp.
678 Broadway, 2nd Floor
New York, NY 10012

This handy manual is an expanded edition of the cult classic Little BlackBook List published
inside of *BlackBook* magazine since 1997, covering nightlife around the globe.

The editorial content, voice, and integrity of the BlackBook List is 100 percent unadulterated. All content & design in this book are the explicit property of BlackBook Media Corp. All possible steps have
been taken to ensure that the information in this book is accurate. New York's restaurants and
nightspots have the shelf life of your average carton of milk, so some information may have changed.
If this is the case, please visit our website at www.blackbookmag.com for accurate listings.

BlackBook List

CREATIVE

SENIOR EDITORS
Andrew Bangs
Fernando Cwilich-Gil

ART DIRECTOR
Tamara Wiesen

CONTRIBUTING WRITERS AND RESEARCHERS
Cindy Augustine, Liz Bangs,
Andrew Paine Bradbury, Sloane Crosley,
Conrad Dornan, Nathan Heiges, Scott Indrisek,
Madhu Puri, Daria Brit Shapiro, Hadley Tomicki

PROOFREADER
Yamana Sozen

PRODUCTION DIRECTOR
Amy Steinhauser

SPECIAL THANKS
Regina Anderson, Jess Holl, Clifford, J3, Nello, Irv Louis,
Hudar, Ava Lib, Meg Thomann, Hadley Tomicki, William Tomicki

BLACKBOOK MEDIA CORP.

678 Broadway, 2nd Floor, New York, NY 10012
CEO Eric Gertler
President Ari Horowitz
Publisher Jyl Elias
Executive Assistants Candice Naboicheck, Serena D'Arcangelo
Editor in Chief Aaron Hicklin
Art Director Eddie Brannan
Senior Editor Jordan Heller
Managing Editor Jess Holl
Photography Director Stephanie Waxlax
Fashion Director Elizabeth Sulcer

To purchase a copy of the *BlackBook List*,
send $9.95 via check or money order to:
BlackBook 678 Broadway 2nd floor
NYC, NY 10012.

Want your restaurant, bar, club, or hotel to be considered for the
BlackBook Lists? Submit your information at www.blackbookmag.com

To purchase a copy of the *BlackBook List* online
or subscibe to *BlackBook* Magazine:

WWW.BLACKBOOKMAG.COM

Table of Contents

How to use

BlackBook = BlackBook List Editor's Pick
☆ = recent opening

Listings are arranged alphabetically by neighborhood. The dollar amount after each listing represents the average cost of a two-course meal and a drink. A plus sign (+) before the number means your bill may be north of that figure. A minus sign (-) means you may have cab money home.

THE DIRECTORY

New York City Information 311

Learn the rules to the Big Apple, if you want your piece of the pie.

EMERGENCY & ESSENTIAL DIGITS

Ambulance-Fire-Police 911 Flavor Flav finds it funny.
Animal Bites (212) 566-2068 tell 'em Sigfried sent ya.
Belleview Hospital Center (212) 562-4141 The voices are asking you to call.
Child Abuse (800) 342-3720 Help capture the Friedmans.
Crime Stoppers Hot Line (212) 577-8477 Snitch is such a harsh term.
Crime Victims Hotline (212) 577-7777 Welcome to New York
Doctors on Call (718) 745-5900 Ladies, strapping medical professionals come to your rescue!
Elder Abuse (212) 442-3103 If an old dude beats you up…or the other way around.
FBI (212) 335-2700 If you think your neighbor Al is really Qaeda
Food & Hunger Hotline (212) 533-6100 See also Ford Models in the yellow pages.
Help & Crisis Center (212) 532-2400 Black Book magazine has this on speed dial during deadlines.
Lead Poisoning Hotline (212) BAN-LEAD Mmm…delicious paint chips.
Metropolitan Hospital Center (212) 423-6262
Metropolitan Transportation Authority NYC Travel information (718) 330-1234 Great source of excuses when late for work again.
Missing Persons (212) 374-6913 Is that lil' Lizzy Smart?
Non-Emergency Information 311 Old ladies making noise complaints.
NYC Office of Emergency Management (OEM) (212) 477-3574 or (212) 477-3598 When your emergencies need to be properly organized.
NYPD Hotlines (866) 856-4167 or (212) 741-4626 Just hope it's not the 70th precinct.
Poison Control (212) 340-4494 If you ate street meat after leaving the club.
Power Failure (Consolidated Edison) (212) 683-0862 Let's make black out babies!
St. Vincent's Hospital (212) 604-7285 Pool tables in some rooms!
Suicide Prevention (212) 673-3000 Jessica Simpson makes more money than you. Eat the pills.

LIBRARIES

Brooklyn Public Library (Central) at Grand Army Plaza (718) 230-2100 Where Brooklynites get their edjamacation.

NY Public Library for Performing Arts 40 Lincoln Center Plaza (212) 870-1630 Find that rare Balanchine video

NY Public Library for Humanities and Social Sciences 5th Ave. (42nd St.) (212) 930-0830 An architectural gem since 1897

NY Public Library for Science, Industry, and Business 188 Madison Ave. (34th St.) (212) 592-7000 Aeron chairs!

NY Public Library for Schomburg Center for Research in Black Culture 515 Malcolm X Blvd. (212) 491-2200 Feeling hoodwinked or bamboozled?

PARKS & GARDENS

Battery Park 1,9 Subway to South Ferry Station Cool sculptures, great river views, jogger and sunbathing yuppies. Take a stroll up to the trapeze school.

Brooklyn Botanical Gardens 1000 Washington Ave. (718) 623-7220 Sakura in springtime.

Bryant Park 40th to 42nd Sts. (5th & 6th Aves.) Big lunchtime, wi-fi Conde Nasties. Movies Mondays in summer, Fashion Week epicenter.

Bronx Zoo Southern Blvd. (182nd St.) 2 or 5 Subway to East Tremont Ave./West Farm Sq. Station The fences are to keep the 'hood out of the zoo.

Central Park 59th to 110th Sts. (5th Ave. & Central Park West) Roller skaters, joggers, tanners, Summerstage, gets packed; a yuppie-muggers paradise. Strawberry Fields forever.

Coney Island Surf Ave. (Atlantic Shore) Technically you can go in the water. Peep the massive collection of freaks and guts. It's not St. Tropez, but you ain't Brigitte Bardot, either.

Fort Tryon Park Riverside Dr. to Hudson River (W. 192nd to Dyckman Sts.) Epic sunsets.

Prospect Park Prospect Park West, (Flatbush, Parkside and Ocean Aves.) Olmstead's more rugged version of Central Park, harkens back to Breukline days. Check the aggro thesbian softball scene and the stoller/small dog mafia. Shout out to the black cowboys.

Prospect Park Zoo 450 Flatbush Ave. (718) 339-7339 Price: $2.50; $1.25 seniors; 50 cents kids. 50 Cent takes his kids.

Tompkins Square Park 7th to 10th Sts (Aves. A & B) Squatters are gone, needles quasi-cleaned up, still not the place for your toddler to frolic in the grass

Union Square Park 14th to 17th Sts (Broadway and Park Ave. So.) Huge protests, big lunch scene, farmers market on weekends. Skaters and assorted others after dark.

Washington Square Park W. 4th St. and Waverly Pl. (MacDougal St. & University Pl.) Dirt weed, NYU kids, storied hangman's tree. Avoid the raids. Performances in the fountain. Shout out to Albert Owens, Master Lee and Diarmuid.

MUSEUMS

Brooklyn Museum of Art 200 Eastern Pkwy. (718) 638-5000 Rudy's favorite for feces-based art!

The Cloisters at Fort Tryon Park Riverside Dr. to Hudson River (W. 192nd to Dyckman Sts.) (212) 923-3700 Getting medieval on your ass. Catch Pacino lost and looking for his horse, easily one of the most beautifulest locations in the city.

DIA Chelsea 535 W. 22nd Street (212) 989-5566 Great rooftop make-out spot.

El Museo del Barrio 1230 Fifth Ave. (104th St.) (212) 831-7272 Spanish Harlem cultural hub. Fun events, underrated.

Frick Collection 1 E. 70th St. (5th Ave.) (212) 288-0700 Time warp a hundred years ago. How a lonely steel mogul spent his fortune.

Guggenheim 1071 5th Ave. (89th St.) (212) 423-3500 F.L. Wright's masterpiece overshadows whatever exhibit happens to be there.

Metropolitan Museum of Art 1000 5th Ave. (82nd St.) (212) 879-5500 It's free, it's incredible, and it's one of the world's best museums. Check out the Egyptian wing, the Grecos, the exhibit du jour. Wander for hours or days…chill on the rooftop with a drink on summer days.

MoMA 11 West 53rd St. (212) 708-9400 Visiting MoMa is no longer an outer-borough experience. The museum is back in its former midtown Manhattan digs.

Neue Gallery 1048 5th Ave. (86th St.) (212) 628-6200 The latest werk from Stuttgart, mon lieb.

New Museum of Contemporary Art 538 Broadway (Prince & Houston Sts.) (212) 219-1222 Out with the old, in with the Dario Robletos.

Tenement Museum 90 Orchard St. (Delancey & Broome Sts.) (212) 431-0233 Lower East Side homage to immigration. Get ice cream at il laboratorio on the way up.

PS 1 Contemporary Art Center 22-25 Jackson Ave. (46th Ave.) Long Island City (718) 784-2084 LIC is blowing up, son. Incredible spaces, emerging artists, big summer parties draw art stars, name djs and euro dancers.

Whitney Museum of American Art 945 Madison Ave (74th & 75th Sts.) (212) 570-3676 Modern masters, busy biennial, cool design, expensive.

CAR SERVICES

Delancey Car Service (212) 228-6666 Lower East Side's fastest car service, covers the rest of downtown too. Good mini-vans, but they charge you extra.

Tel Aviv Car & Limousine Service (212) 777-7777 or 212-666-8888 Hard to forget the number, even when blazed and headed to JFK. Reliable, clean, efficient.

Allen Car Service (212) 226-8999 If Delancey is slammed.

Princess Limousine (212) 684-6227 Town cars and limos.

STADIUMS & CONCERT VENUES

Aqueduct Race Track 110-00 Rockaway Blvd. Jamaica, Queens (718) 641-4700 Blow your paycheck, play the ponies.

Belmont Park Race Track 2150 Hempstead Turnpike Elmont, NY (718) 641-4700 if the OTB's too much of a bummer. Belmont Stakes.

Giants Stadium New Jersey(201) 507-8900 The swamp. The house that Parcells built. Broadway Joe Namath. And of course, Jimmy Hoffa. Nets tickets always available next door.

Hammerstein Ballroom at the Manhattan Center 311 W. 34th St. (212) 485-1534 Good sound system, bands, events.

Irving Plaza 17 Irving Pl. (15th St.) (212) 777-6800 Smallest of the commercial venues, where all LES bands aspire to play.

Keyspan Park 1904 Park Surf Ave. (W. 17th & W. 19th Sts.) (212) 307-7171 Brooklyn Cyclones, sporty hipsters, insane characters, NY's true local team, cheap beers.

Lincoln Center 62nd & 65th Sts. (Columbus & Amsterdam Aves.) (212) 875-5030 World-class cultural epicenter: opera, ballet, recitals, gala events, highbrow entertainment. Check the free summer concerts and dance classes in the plaza. Watch for Julitards.

Madison Square Garden 7th & 8th Aves. (32nd & 33rd Sts.) Home to the Rangers and the Knickerbockers.

Prospect Park Bandshell Prospect Park West, (Flatbush, Parkside and Ocean Aves.) Feel-good world music events, positive rap, multi-culti couples and strollers.

Roseland Ballroom 239 W. 52nd St. (Broadway & 8th Ave.) (212) 247-0200 Cool midtown midsize music mofo. Hit Russian Vodka Room or Russian Samovar to get loaded before the show.

Shea Stadium 123-01 Roosevelt Ave (126th St.) (718) 507-8499 Price: See event listings. Take the 7 train to watch the Mets or Andy Roddick win it next door.

Yankee Stadium River Ave. (161 St.) Bronx bombers. House that Ruth built. Come October, this is where you have to be, next to Billy Crystal. Or in the bleachers with all the drunk rabble-rousers.

AIRPORTS, BUS STATIONS, TRAIN STATIONS, HELIPORTS AND MARINAS

Grand Central Station 42nd St. & Park Ave. (212) 340-2210 Gorgeous building, good bars and restaurants before heading back to Connecticut with your lawyer commuting buddies.

Helicopter Flight Services (212) 355-0801 Really the only way to get around these days.

Hoboken Ferry Pier A at Battery Park 1-800-53-FERRY The chillest way to commute from New Jeru.

Islip Airport 100 Arrivals Ave. Ronkonkoma, NY (631) 467-3210 String Island, small planes.

John F. Kennedy Airport Jamaica, NY (718) 244-4444 Named for skirt-chasing prez, biggest and most convoluted airport in this fair city. Nothing says "welcome home" like buying the NY Post right after landing.

La Guardia Airport Queens, NY (718) 533-3400 Named for weed-loving mayor. Good food court.

Newark Airport Newark, NJ (973) 961-6000 The Bricks. Take the train to the plane.

Port Authority Bus Terminal 8th Ave. (40th & 42nd Sts.) (212) 564-8484 All roads lead to Port Authority. Pre-Rudy, the epicenter of Times Square sleaze. Now cleansed and sanitized so you can lug that shelf from the Ikea bus. Go bowling.

Staten Island Ferry Battery Park to Staten Island (718) 815-2628 Great views of the harbor for free.

Teterboro Airport Teterboro, NY(201) 288-1775 Goin' back to Cali with Young Hov in the Lear.

"If a man can live in New York, he can live anywhere." —Arthur C. Clarke

TOP 5 Best Developments in NYC Nightlife

(Sleep is for the daytime)

1. **Increasingly Lax Enforcement of the Smoking Ban**
   Puff, puff pass
2. **Rampant Promiscuity**
   More girls than boys means stiff competition
3. **White Girls with Ass**
   It's a new phenomenon, says Ludacris
4. **shamelessrestaurants.com**
   Find out who's screwing who over
5. **The Failure of Bin Laden's Plot to Poison Our Coke**
   Our smack, on the other hand...

TOP 5 Best Bartenders

(No mixologists, dammit)

1. **King Cole Bar**
   All class, plus they invented the Bloody Mary
2. **Employees Only**
   Have their own bartending school
3. **Passerby**
   Toby makes the best gin and tonic ever
4. **Angel's Share**
   Cool cylindrical ice cubes
5. **Sushi Hana**
   Tiny hands make better drinks

TOP 5 Discrete Bathrooms

(Bring your keys…)

1. **The Park**
   Girls love the private roof deck bathroom
2. **Bungalow 8**
   Always a line
3. **Cain**
   Why bother with the bathroom, though?
4. **Passerby**
   Spacious, for group fun
5. **Butter**
   Multiple uses for that Amex Noir

TOP 5 Old School Bars

(What NY was like before PR and implants)

1. **Campbell Apartment**
   No jeans allowed, sailor
2. **Bemelman's Bar**
   Carlyle gem
3. **Ear Inn**
   Has seen it all, check the photos
4. **King Cole Bar**
   St. Regis style
5. **Old Town Bar**
   Big burgers and beers

TOP 5 New Kitchen Talents

(The next Wolfgangs, Jean-Georges and Marios)

1. **Marco Canora, Hearth**
   Formerly at Craft, Tuscan master
2. **Jodie Williams, Gusto Ristorante e Bar Americano**
   Making us love Italian food all over again
3. **Shea Gallante, Cru**
   Bouley prodigy, redefining American cuiz
4. **Patrick Nuti**
   Gave us Petrosino, now at coming-soon Osteria del Circo
5. **Josh DeChellis**
   At W. Vil's Sumile, learned from the best

TOP 5 Places To Spit Game To A Supermodel

(So...what do you do?)

1. **Upstairs at Cipriani**
   Carmen
2. **The Park**
   Kate
3. ▬▮▬
   Daria
4. **Double Seven**
   Karolina
5. **Groovedeck at Bed**
   Filipa

TOP 5 Places to Punch a Hipster

(…in the head)

1. **Supreme Trading**
   Like a Napolean Dynamite convention some nights
2. **Luke & Leroy**
   Asymmetrical hairstyles abound
3. **Union Pool**
   Low key on weekdays, obnoxious on weekends
4. **Dark Room**
   Hipstasi underground torture cell
5. **Sway**
   Especially on Sundays: Moz Night

TOP 5 Places to get into a "Best Pizza Argument"

(Shhh…the secret is the water they use in the dough)

1. **Grimaldi's**
   Defend Brooklyn
2. **Lombardi's**
   Big lines of tourists
3. **John's**
   Bleeker St. classic
4. **Nick's**
   Queens' best-kept secret
5. **Pepperoncino**
   The Slope's recent entry

TOP 5 Boldest Names

(Where celebs attempt to get into Page Six)

1. **Nello**
   It's Al Sharpton talking to Isiah Thomas, talking to Ed Koch...
2. **Cipriani Downtown**
   In it's own orbit
3. **Da Silvano**
   And the food's actually great
4. **Koi**
   A bit of LA in NYC
5. **Nobu**
   Rappers, NBA players and their sizable posses

TOP 5 Media Bistros

(Not the best place to talk off the record)

1. **KGB**
   One actual novelist for every 25 wannabe novelists
2. **Elaine's**
   Old school, still packs in the heavy hitters
3. **Langan's**
   NY Post after-work hangout
4. **Michael's**
   For when you score that book deal
5. **Siberia**
   Teeth-grinding, bottom-dwelling gossip columnists

TOP 5 Plastic PR Chicks Per Square Foot

(So…like, when can we expect coverage?)

1. **Sushi Samba**
   Lil' Grubmans
2. **One**
   PMK posse
3. **Park Avalon**
   Nadine Johnson's minions
4. **'wichcraft**
   Susan Blond Inc. clones
5. **Dos Caminos (Park Ave. So.)**
   Rubenstein round up!

TOP 5 Day Clubs

(Where the city's fabulously unemployed text and stare at each other)

1. **Coffee Shop**
   Be waited-on by non-working models
2. **Café Habana**
   The drug models love
3. **Café Gitane**
   Bring points for outdoor seats
4. **Nello**
   Home of the seven hour lunch
5. **Pastis**
   Is it 5pm already?

LOWER MANHATTAN (map p. 189)

Times they are a-changin' in the oldest part of the city, once the meeting place of our forefathers and the blessed site of many a brothel. The narrow streets teem with brokers, hawkers of knock-off bags and label-whores headed to **Century 21**. Tourists trawl the **South Street Seaport** for suitable souvenirs, while we stroll along the waterfront and ponder our fate, dodging seagull poop and careening strollers. But when 5pm hits, the ties loosen up and the bras get thrown into the air at **Jeremy's Alehouse**. While your boss savors a luscious slab of meat at **Delmonico's**, plot corporate mutiny at the revolutionary **Fraunces Tavern**. Wade through the sea commuting suits to **Coast** to drown your stock market sorrows in a blue cosmo, the color of a toxic ocean. This hood was once a sad site for nightlife, but party people now flock to clubs like **Remy Lounge**, for a night they'll never remember. If you don't score a honey at **Romi**, end your evening with boobs, beers and Bon Jovi tunes at **Pussycat Lounge**.

RESTAURANTS Lower Manhattan

Bridge Café 279 Water St. (Dover St.) (212) 227-3344 American. Oldest NYC restaurant location since 1794, sleeps at the foot of the BK Bridge. Looks like the site of a nautical murder mystery and is rumored to be haunted by ghosts of sailors and whores, like your parents' bedroom. Here's to hoping the famous buffalo steak levitates into your mouth. $30

Coast 110 Liberty St. (Trinity Pl. & Greenwich St.) (212) 962-0136 Seafood. If you're a "man over-bored", this is the spot to kick off your loafers and head out to sea. Wood and green interior with a long, modern bar. Glowing blue cosmos that look like windex to clean your guts after a pile of fish n' chips. $25 ★

Delmonico's 56 Beaver St. (So. William St.) (212) 509-1144 Steakhouse. Handsome, dark, mahogany wood dining room with glowing chandeliers. Quenching your insatiable bloodthirst since '28. That's 1828! Steakhouse staples come perilously large and juicy, justifying legends. Slabs of steak, big burgers, raw bar for Exchange regulars and huge salads for the skirts. $65

14 Wall Street 14 Wall St., 31st fl. (Broad St. & Broadway) (212) 233-2780 French. Power lunch at J. Pierpont Morgan's old aerie. Young bucks and old-time pros with that well-scrubbed pink look come to his private dining room to guffaw over their filet mignon. Pretend to listen to your boss rattle on, while you take in the fantastic views of Liberty Harbor. $50

Fraunces Tavern 54 Pearl St. (Broad St.) (212) 968-1776 American. Opened in 1762, former meeting place of Revolutionary War heroes has recently undergone a 2 mill. renovation to better serve the American Way. Stately interior befits both Generals and stock-traders. We recommend the filet mignon with lobster mash. George Washington gorged on Beef Wellington within these walls- now you can too! $45

Gigino 20 Battery Pl. (at Wagner Park) (212) 962-0136 Italian. Sweet, modern spot tucked under the stone arches in Wagner Park. Sit outside on the patio and burn calories watching the cute rollerbladers by the river. Like an expensive picnic served by strangers. Delicious homemade pastas and rustic Italian fare. $35 **BlackBook**

Harry's at Hanover Square 1 Hanover Sq. (Pearl & Stone Sts.) (212) 425-3412 Steakhouse. Over 1,000 bottles to choose from, feel free to get loaded on lunch break. Lest you have trouble finding red meat in the testosterone-saturated financial district, here's a winner from Harry, who never seems to lack VIPs replenishing with booze n' beast. $50

Ise 56 Pine St. (Pearl & William Sts.) (212) 785-1600 Japanese. Past the nondescript, empty dining room, lies a modern sushi bar Babylon with the freshest fishies this side of Fulton. Best spicy tuna handroll is swimmingly good. Forget the menu, let the chef hook you up with some creative raw dishes, but be prepared for the big bill. $40

Les Halles Downtown 15 John St. (Broadway & Nassau St.) (212) 285-8585 French. Tony may be busy eating oddities on TV, but his master meaterie hasn't suffered. Sexy bistro looks, soft glowing lights. Endless assortment of moules frites, but the beef's all magic: dopest cuts of cote du boeuf and other delights that make you go "Moo." $45

Quartino 21 Peck Slip (Water St.) (212) 349-4433 Italian. Cozy spot under the B Bridge aside the E River, packed with cute Italians. An airy dining room where we munch on organic pizza, pasta and seafood. Freshly baked oil-infused focaccia and chickpea farinata, creative salads rock fare like parmigiano and walnuts. Great prices, beautiful surroundings. +$30

Spice Grill 19 Murray St. (Broadway & Church) (212) 791-3510 Indian. Big, sexy orange interior, that's usually empty on weeknights. We don't know why, the food is soul-strengthening. Stunning presentation of dishes like samosas with feta and pomegranate. Lamb Saagwala is tender fenugreek love. Some of the best Indian in the city. Eat a frankie with Johnny. $30 **BlackBook**

Vine 25 Broad St. (Exchange Pl.) (212) 344-8463 American. Dine inside chilly old bank vaults on typical snooty nouveau French-American fare. Attentive waitstaff serves up steaks and fish galore, with requisite items like grilled sea bass or salmon. A veritable wonderland of Wall Streeters closing deals over mounds of meat. $45

NIGHTLIFE Lower Manhattan

Dakota Roadhouse 43 Park Pl. (Church St. & W. Broadway) (212) 962-9800 Retired fireman and aspiring alcoholics at this pseudo-Chuck E. Cheese for the older set. Grab-the-lobster mechanical claw to satisfy your sadistic streak. Pool tables that host geeky leagues and Foosball to recapture your childhood. Cheap and yummy bar eats, unsurprisingly grease-laden.

The Full Shilling 160 Pearl St. (Wall & Pine Sts.) (212) 422-3855 Drink at the Full Shilling for a measly farthing. Elegant structure, big wood bar is over 100 years old, shipped from Belfast on a steamer. The stowaways are now pouring plenty of cold brews, slinging whisky and friendly banter. Perfect if you need a magically delicious evening.

Jeremy's Alehouse 228 Front St. (Peck Slip & Beekman St.) (212) 964-3537 The folks at Jeremy's swear by the "hair of the dog": "red-eye special" happy hour from 8am-10am. Eves packed with brokers chugging 32 oz. beers from styrofoam cups. The Brooklyn Bridge backdrop starts to sway and your cheap date adds her bra to the festive collection dangling from the ceiling.

Pussycat Lounge 96 Greenwich St. (Rector & Carlisle Sts.) (212) 349-4800 She works hard for her money, honey, at this veteran establishment. Where Bon Jovi is king and the patrons and strippers both seemingly having a ball with no one getting hurt, so drink up and rock out. Check out the upstairs lounge. You are guaranteed not to run into someone you know.

Romi 19 Rector St. (Greenwich & Washington Sts.) (212) 809-1500 Brought to you by Soho's Naked Lunch crew. Corporate singles converge for mergers aplenty at this huge 2-story bar. Tall ceilings with wood beams, mod sofas and candlelit corners. Balcony for cleavage-gazing. Ladies love the yummy Romi Martini, a pineapple cosmo with a kick. ☆

Remy Lounge 104 Greenwich St. (Rector & Carlisle Sts.) (212) 267-4646 Huge slick space with velvet couches, candles and cuties. Mixed crowd, mixed music. Latin ritmo up top, street beats boom below. Salsa Saturdays bring in ambitious singles with gelled hair and butt crack-baring jeans.

Swan's Bar and Grill 213 Pearl St. (John & Fletcher Sts.) (212) 952-0266
Nothing graceful about this swan. Here comes a regular, smelling like six nights ago.
Fun for colorful run-down characters and those who adore the type of wild drunk sto-
ries you can only hear in AA or Las Vegas.

"You cannot stop New York City." —*Anonymous note at WTC site*

TRIBECA (map p. 190)

Known for its elegant restaurants like **Bouley** and sophisticated residents such as the **late JFK Jr.** and **50 Cent**, Tribeca is a cluster of contradictions that's harmoniously hip and glamorous. The TRIangle BElow CAnal is home to NYC's finest industrial architecture, all presided over by **de facto mayor Robert DeNiro** and his fledgling empire of restaurants and nightlife spots. Packed with mid-century design shops, galleries and trendy boutiques, Tribeca was formerly a ghost town for nightlife. With the inception of the Tribeca Film Festival in 2002, the perpetual allure of the **Church Lounge** and the arrival of buzzing nightspots like **Dekk** and **Sugar**, the dead zone has transformed into a hotbed of celebrities, models, moguls and the hipsters who love them. Many refer to this unique little triangle as the **Hollywood of the East**. When Tribecans throw on their Marc Jacobs and leave their light-filled lofts for a night on the town, they stay local. This 'hood is the perfect locale for a delicious and debaucherous night on the town. Kick off the evening with a rose petal cocktail at **Azafran**, followed by a luscious steak frites at **Le Zinc**. Replenish your zen with a saketini at **Megu's Kimono Bar** and by 2 am, you'll be studying your impending hangover at the **Brandy Library**.

RESTAURANTS Tribeca

Arqua 281 Church St. (White St.) (212) 334-1888 Tuscan. Lofty corner space with soaring ceilings, glowing sconces and enormous windows to make the passerbys jealous of your endless piles of prosciutto. Chef Leonardo Polito's menu rocks the rustic Italian flavor with artichoke lasagna and a seasonal risottos. +$40

Azafran 77 Warren St. (Greenwich & W. Broadway) (212) 284-0577 Spanish. Glowing purple lights lured us to this sleek, minimal spot for inventive tapas. Order your sweetie an Azafran cocktail garnished with rose petals. Chefs imported from Spain masterfully whip up Brocheta de Gambas (skewered shrimp with dates) or the ham croquetas. Muchos besos to the sexy barstaff. +$25

Bouley 120 W. Broadway (Duane & Reade Sts.) (212) 965-2525 French. Two romantic dining rooms, choose your poison: Red Room if you're saucy, White Room if you're sweet. Superstar chef David Bouley can do no wrong. Start with the Seared foie gras served over foie gras terrine (pinch yourself, it's real). We're lovin' on the lobster in a passion fruit port wine paprika sauce. +$55 **BlackBook**

Bouley Bakery & Market 130 W. Broadway (Duane & Reade Sts.) (212) 608-5829 French. Bouley's tri-level food temple. The Cellar Market explodes with local produce, artisinal cheeses, dry aged beef which beckons. At street-level, pizzas prepared in the wood-burning oven. The top floor is a café with awe-inspiring cocktails alchemically mixed by mysterious brothers. Prepare to be converted. +$20 ☆

Bread Tribeca 301 Church St. (Walker St.) (212) 334-8282 Italian. Lofty space that buzzes late into the night. Start with the fritto misto (Italian for "fried goodness"). Watch the stellar staff navigate the maze of tables to present you with a rib eye steak from the wood-burning oven, served on a cutting board. Owner directed Jackson's "Beat It" video. $35

Bubby's 120 Hudson St. (N. Moore St.) (212) 219-0666 American. Rib-stickin' southern cookin'. They come by the droves for celeb-spotting at Sunday brunch-expect a wait. The dining area is sparse, wooden and white, but it's the food that counts. Fried chicken or tender pulled pork served with a side of mac 'n cheese or collard greens just like yo mama never made. $30

Casse-Croute 73 W. Broadway (Warren & Murray Sts.) (212) 693-2212 French. Chat with the charming owner Jackie, while her minions prepare your succulent sandwich. The homemade quiches are unbeatable, and we're willing to throw-down for the savory duck tart. This place is strictly take-out, so prepare to cuddle up with your lunch in City Hall Park. $15

Capsouto Freres 451 Watts St. (Washington St.) (212) 966-4900 French. Tres romantique, open for 25 years and going strong. A airy space with crisp white tablecloths, glowing candles. Try the Souffle Bar: an entire menu dedicated to the delicate dish. If you're feeling savory, try the wild mushroom and cheese, or if you're sweet, praline with hazelnut creme anglaise. Fluffy and fabulous, like your perfect hairdo. +$55

Chanterelle 2 Harrison St. (Hudson & Chambers Sts.) (212) 966-6960 French. Elegance done to perfection at this legendary spot for romantic foodies. The city's best spot for food orgasms is celebrating its 25th year with a menu cover designed by Rauschenberg. Try the prosciutto wrapped roast or the grilled white tuna. Karen and David posted their artsy menu covers on the wall as a reminder of their excellence. +$60

Churrascaria Plataforma Tribeca 221 W. Broadway (White St.) (212) 925-6969 Brazilian BBQ. Perfect for the Paleolithic dieter. Atkins cavemen dressed as hotshot execs devour delicious meat on sticks. Don't waste space on veggies, dive into flank steak or short ribs. Dramatic space that echoes our collective sigh as a bar on wheels visits the table like a souped-up Mr. Softee truck. Wear loose-fitting clothes. +$50

City Hall 131 Duane St. (Church & W. Broadway) (212) 227-7777 American. Big, wood dining room lined with old-school photos of the LES. We are reminded of our poor immigrant roots while we devour Delmonico Steaks smothered in roquefort. Outstanding wait staff, bordering on psychic, delivers goodies from the raw bar and decodes the mind-boggling wine list. $40

Danube 30 Hudson St. (Duane & Reade Sts.) (212) 791-3771 Austrian. Bejeweled, bedazzling Art Nouveau interior behind velvet curtains. Looks like you've walked into a Klimt painting, with diners in the throes of ecstasy, all composed by David Bouley. Traditional Austrian cuisine is spiced-up, try the venison in huckleberry sauce, finish off with caramel strudel, then taxi home and rent Amadeus. -$50

Della Rovere 250 W. Broadway (Beach St.) (212) 334-3470 Italian. Elegant space with tall ceilings and a sexy mahogany bar. We're dazzled by 100 choices of by-the-glass wines, smitten with the attentive service and seduced by the amazing array of oysters. For dinner, order the osso bucco tortellini or the succulent pancetta wrapped duck breast. Maintain some decorum and try not to lick your plate. +$45 ✯

Dominic 349 Greenwich St. (Harrison & Jay Sts.) (212) 343-0700 Italian. Formerly Pico, this offbeat spot on the main drag attracts Tribeca residents able to find a babysitter. Quirky chandeliers, exposed brick, and yellow walls feel homey. Get the Almond Crusted Lamb and daydream in the cozy back garden with your date. For dessert, toss your own zeppole. +$40

Duane Park Café 157 Duane St. (W. Broadway & Hudson St.) (212) 732-5555 American. Named after the first park in NYC, which is about the same size as the restaurant. Sedate, elegant, white tablecloths and stately illumination. Delectable seafood-start with the ginger-miso lobster rolls, then roll on to the Chilean sea bass. Heavyweight Bouley looms nearby, but DPC is doing just fine, thank you very much. +$45

Dylan Prime 62 Laight St. (Greenwich St.) (212) 334-4783 Hip steakhouse that attracts hot thirtysomethings: definitely not your typical meat and potatoes.. Juicy, incredible cuts in all sizes and descriptions (the steaks and the crowd) including five types of dry-aged Omaha steaks. Sleek, candlelit space with a clever glass-walled wine cellar pleases the eye, and the pallet. There's a kickin' single scene at the bar, too. +$45

Edward's 136 W. Broadway (Thomas & Duane Sts.) (212) 233-6436 American. Sweet space with brasserie looks, so you can check out the competition on the mirrored walls. Awesome moules frites that rivals their neighbor, Petite Abeille. Cute, model-y barstaff offer an impressive wine by-the-glass list and shake up some seriously salacious cocktails into the wee hours. You'll become a regular. $20

Flor de Sol 361 Greenwich Ave. (Franklin & Harrison Sts.) 212-366-1640 Spanish. Our Tribeca amigos say this is the best sangria in the 'hood. By the size of the crowd that packs this sexy Spanish tavern, we believe it. An extensive tapas menu, highlighted by sole in banana sauce or lobster stuffed with crabmeat. Great place for loud groups or boring dates that have nothing interesting to say. +$30

Fresh 105 Reade St. (W. Broadway & Church St.) (212) 406-1900 Seafood. Curvaceous walls that conjure the belly of a ship. Bright, open kitchen lures foodies to this big, modern fishmonger to the stars. A special contract allows chef Daniel Angerer get the pick of the day's catch before anyone else, so you know it's the freshest. We liked the grilled Nantucket strawberry bass. $45

The Harrison 355 Greenwich St. (Harrison St.) (212) 274-9310 American. Tribeca grandeur defined, you half expect Tyrone Power to waltz in and casually order a martini. Seductively beautiful space defined by dark wood, a long bar, soft lighting and gleaming white tablecloths. Classic entrees with a twist- we like the pork tenderloin. +$35

Kitchenette 80 W. Broadway (Warren St.) (212) 267-6740 American. When you walk through the squeaky screen door, you've entered your mama's country kitchen. Replete with all sorts of gingham and rickety, mismatched chairs, the 50's charm packs 'em in for weekend brunch. Order the Hudson Valley omelette and finish with a slice of cherry pie. $20

Kori 253 Church St. (Franklin & Leonard Sts.) (212) 334-4598 Korean. Like Koreatown minus the hectic streets. A tranquil, modern spot with amazing Korean BBQ and ginger kamikazes. Rust colored walls and flickering candles. Has garnered some serious praise for its crazy array of hot-pots and the excellent waitstaff. After your BBQ feast, indulge in a fantastic chocolate dessert. +$35

Landmarc 179 W. Broadway (Leonard & Worth Sts.) (212) 343-3883 American. This is Tribeca dining defined. No reservations taken at chef Marc Murphy's haven for straightforward foodies. An industrial looking space with an open brick oven keeps us warm. We love the marrowbones and goat cheese profiteroles. Choose from five types of steak, served with kick-ass french fries. Great deal, open late. $45

Le Zinc 139 Duane St. (Church St. & W. Broadway) (212) 513-0001 American Bistro. Restaurant's casual cousin may be approaching classic status. Walls plastered with art exhibition posters, dimly lit, large but intimate space with a few sexy booths. Service is spotty but you're enjoying your food too much to notice. Steak au poivre and teriyaki salmon burger are favorites of devoted regulars. +$35 **BlackBook**

Megu 62 Thomas Street (Church & W. Broadway) (212) 964-7777 Japanese. Koji Imai's dramatic, bi-level Zen-modern fortress. Celebs hide in cozy booths, mesmerized by the life-size ice Buddha melting into a pool of rose petals. The confusing menu yields huge flavors in teeny tiny portions. Try the Toro steak in white truffle oil or the Kobe beef cooked in sake. Not for the faint of heart…or wallet. +$75

Montrachet 239 W. Broadway (Walker & White Sts.) (212) 219-2777 French. Drew Nieporent's heavy hitter has been here twenty years, still has plenty of shine. The dining room is packed with modern art and a sophisticated crowd. 40 wines under 40 bucks sauce you up while you tackle the cote de boeuf with marrow or the Chilean sea bass. You can't go wrong at this Tribeca classic. +$40

Nam 110 Reade St. (Church & W. Broadway) (212) 267-1777 Vietnamese. The door to this hipster haven is flanked by bamboo stalks miraculously growing out of the sidewalk. Only in Tribeca. Inside is an intimate, elegant space, glowing an eerie green, with interesting B&W photo-portraits in round light boxes. Diners whisper over candles to their cute dates, sharing their ca chein snapper or pho bo. Delicious, excellent deal. +$25

Next Door Nobu 105 Hudson St. (Franklin St.) (212) 334-4445 Japanese. Nobu's hot little sister is still our favorite sushi in the Triangle. Essentially the same food as Nobu Senior (see below), with lower prices, a hipper crowd and no reservation hassle. Order rock shrimp tempura then yellowtail sashimi. Gets slammed on weekends, but that doesn't deter the assorted rappers and models in attendance. +$45

Nobu 105 Hudson St. (Franklin St.) (212) 219-0500 Japanese. Though nearby Megu gives Nobu a run for its bling, Matsuhisa-san still brings the culinary ruckus. South American-inflected Japanese cuisine that's incredibly varied, inventive and delicious. For an epic experience, try the Omakase dinner: multiple courses of the chef's choice. Order plenty of sake to soften the sting of the bill. +$75

The Odeon 145 W. Broadway (Thomas & Duane Sts.) (212) 233-0507 French Bistro. In case you slept or snorted your way through the 80s, allow us to remind you: this place rocks. Spacious dining room lined with mirrors emanates an energetic buzz. American Psychos chow down on incredible salmon and steak frites while arguing over business cards. The summer sidewalk scene is the place to be seen in Tribeca. +$35

Petite Abeille 134 W. Broadway (Thomas & Duane Sts.) (212) 791-1360 Belgian. Cute and neighborly bistro with enough room to park your stroller. Thursday's all-you-can-eat moules with frites and a Stella is your best bet. Brush up on your

Belgian athletics in the WC. Ye Olde Tribeca Standby for consistently good eats like Chimay cheese croquettes and monstrous burger with "special sauce." $25

Scalini Fedeli 165 Duane St. (Hudson and Greenwich) (212) 528-0400 Italian. Occupying the former home of Bouley, Scalini lives up to its "location location location". Lemony walls, vaulted ceilings and plush carpeting that muffles the sting of stilettos. Romantic enough to play footsie under the tablecloths. Prixe fixe menu with awesome choices like pignoli crusted salmon and a bad-ass veal chop. +$65

Shore 41 Murray St. (Church St.) (212) 962-3750 Seafood. The down to earth sister of Fresh. Faux New England clam shack with Tribeca prices. Feels like you're in the belly of a ship, drink enough wine and it will start to sway. Everything at the raw bar is fresh and delicious, plus excellent lobster and shrimp. Fried stuff in paper dishes eaten with silver cutlery.$35

66 241 Church St. (Leonard St.) (212) 925-0202 Upscale Chinese. Baby, you could be famous. Just hang at Jean Georges V's sprawling and dynamic scene maker. With a central communal table, Meier's modern design is ultra-clean, so make sure your shoes have non-marking soles. The Shanghai Surprise is that The South Beach Diet now endorses the crispy foie gras roll and the lobster e-fu noodles, right? +$55

Sosa Borella 460 Greenwich St. (Desbrosses & Watts Sts.) (212) 431-5093 Argentine & Italian. A steady lunch crowd revels in bizarre combinations for extreme sandwiches. A modest space of white walls and exposed beams serves as setting for sculpturally complex, but delicious dishes. The pizzas are delish, props for the strip steak with chimichurri. Gauchita! That's Sosa for hamburger. $40

Thalassa 179 Franklin St. (Greenwich & Hudson Sts.) (212) 941-7661 Greek. That evening, Ulysses and Calypso dined on shellfish saganaki and snapper spatslota. Self-proclaimed gods and goddesses ate their weight in fish by the pound. The stars twinkled as the celebs mingled. Ouzo flowed as only ouzo could, Calypso got loaded and Ulysses got lucky. The greatest drama of our time. Class dismissed. +$45

Tribeca Grill 375 Greenwich St (Franklin St) (212) 941 3900 American. Cavernous space, exposed brick walls with big modern paintings. Where DeNiro reigns over his three-sided fiefdom. Hearty slabs of meat and grilled fish define the menu. Start with the Peekytoe crab salad. We adore the sea scallops with morels and pancetta. Doubles as a de facto Miramax cafeteria, LA confidential meets NY quintessential. $50

VietCafe 345 Greenwich St. (Harrison St.) (212) 431-5888 Vietnamese. Lan Tran Cao's Viet-thrilla is all the rage with the Tribeca tribe. A modern bamboo laden interior sets the scene for yummy eats. Warm, buttery mood lighting makes everyone look sexy. We're in the mood for roast duck and it's rumored that the shrimp goes 2 ways. Is it hot in here? $25 ✭

Walker's 16 N. Moore St. (Varick St.) (212) 941-0142 American. English pub with American fare, legendary in the land of Burgerdom. Unpretentiously cozy like American Werewolf in London. A bloody satisfying experience. Hit the back room for off-the-hook burgers with bleu cheese and a side of mashed potatoes. Big with everyone from firemen to Nathan Lane, not together, of course. $20

Zutto 77 Hudson St. (Jay & Harrison Sts.) (212) 233-3287 Japanese. Wooden, quiet and downright Zen. Sit at the colorful glass-tiled bar, or nestle in at an intimate table. Eclectic lanterns illuminate your scrumptious seaweed salad and white tuna sashimi. Secret hideaway for low-key celebs without makeup. Like a Buddhist mountaintop retreat outside bustling Tokyo, sits just steps from clamorous Nobu. Oishi-so. $30

NIGHTLIFE Tribeca

Anotheroom 249 W. Broadway (Moore & Beach Sts.) (212) 226-1418. Brought to you by the owners of room and otheroom, duh. Kick out the jams in this industrial steel, slate & cement singles mecca. Indie rock fills the uncomfortable silence with your date and rotating art exhibits hang above the velvet benches. Secure the highly coveted window seat and you're good to go. Packed on weekends.

Brandy Library 25 North Moore St (Varick St.) (212) 226-5545 The Encyclopedia Britannica of booze. Upscale sophisto-lounge with deep mahogany tones, leather banquettes, Sherlock Holmes style. Classic cocktails done to perfection- masterful Mint Juleps. Don't order a whiskey sour or you'll be hopping the next Sidecar to anotheroom. ✭

Bubble Lounge 228 W. Broadway (White St.) (212) 431-3433 Sophisticated, sexy champagne bar for top-notch headaches and hangovers. Plush couches, vintage Tattinger posters set the mood for the best night you'll never remember. Sexy downstairs, and the largest, most diverse bubbly selection in the country. Get krunked in the Krug Room- a VIP wine cellar.

Canal Room 285 W. Broadway (212) 941-8100 From Marcus Linial, a nicely planned and lit multi-leveled lounge space with a bangin' system and the occasional awesome DJ. The scene of ridiculous music industry parties. Draws 'em from every corner of the Garden State with too-tight jeans and one-shoulder shirts, fighting over their place in line. In the morning, step over stray hair extensions on the sidewalk.

Church Lounge at the Tribeca Grand 2 6th Ave. (White & Walker Sts.) (212) 519-6600 Recently renovated, super-chic Grand lobby hotel bar. Models mingle with hotel guests- (it's included in the hefty room rate). Lounge on soft leather sofas and dark wood chairs, with musical atmos provided by lounge-oriented DJs. Velvet rope on weekends, so wear your Saturday Best.

Dekk 134 Reade St. (Hudson & Greenwich Sts.) (212) 941-9401 Bi-level space with exposed brick and white tiles, draws in a serious crowd on weekends. Regular movie screenings act as a backdrop for your worst pickup lines. Quickly becoming a neighborhood favorite for creative cocktails and indie flicks, interesting bar food. Fun Wednesday night parties on the lower Dekk. ✮

Grace 114 Franklin St. (Church St. & W. Broadway) (212) 343-4200 One of the best spaces in Tribeca, with a gorgeous long bar, high ceilings and cozy back room. Gets packed with Wall Streeters, most weekdays are a big, oxford shirt n' khakis pick up scene. Try not to spill beer on Brad's topsiders. Good news for conservative Triangle dwellers: kitchen stays open til 4am.

Kimono Bar 62 Thomas Street (Church & W Broadway) (212) 964-7777. The upper level bar in Megu, where we enviously peer over the balcony. Intensely gorgeous and calm space, with walls decorated in kimono fabric. Intimate booths where Megu bestows its Blessing upon you: a house cocktail with vodka, strawberries and pomegranate juice. Be careful, bar tabs can be ohm-inous.

Knitting Factory 74 Leonard St. (Broadway & Church St.) (212) 219-3055 Consistently cool venue for indie heavy-hitters and avant-garde shows as well as quirky parties. Interesting multi-leveled space with jazzy bar downstairs and a cozy street-level bar ideal for stepping out of the noise for a frothy draught. Check the weekly listings, some shows sell out quick.

Liquor Store 235 W. Broadway (White St.) (212) 226-7121 The Ear Inn of Tribeca. Old fashioned oak bar staffed by super-friendly bartenders. Low-key crowd seeking sanctuary from the suits. One of the best jukeboxes around. Escape to feel anonymous, share a sidewalk table with a perfect stranger.

M1-5 52 Walker St. (Broadway & Church St.) (212) 965-1701 Sophisto Tribeca swank mixed with low-key East Village candor, part loft, part local pub. Similarly mixed crowd orders stylish cocktails, plays darts and billiards in back. Great place to throw a birthday party. We love the discounted prices for local artists, does origami count?

Sanctum at the Tribeca Grand Hotel 2 6th Ave. (White St.) (212) 519-6600 Where everyone is pretty, or at least trying to be. Sophisticated design of oak and metal, interesting and creative cocktail menu, lots of hip off-duty staff from nearby boutiques and designer furniture stores. Celeb-fueled scene has cooled off a bit, err…but I'm a model!

Sugar 311 Church St. (Lispenard & Walker Sts.) (212) 431-8642 Pour some ____ on me, c'mon fire me uuuup! Actually, don't. We'd rather kick back in a slick booth with a $12 cocktail and admire all the pretty people. 1950's Palm Springs meets Danish modern décor- and it somehow works. Nice downstairs lounge with occasional screenings on the gigantic TV and a hot staff make for a sweet spot.

Tribeca Rock Club 16 Warren St. (Church St. & Broadway) (212) 766-1070 No longer a boarded up pee-spot for dogs and drunk guys. Straightforward bar space with no frills. Cheap drinks. Draws some impressive guitar-driven rock, blues and country acts, for that escape from Tribeca evening with Escape from Alcatraz types.

"New York's such a wonderful city. Although I think of the Army today. The guys are very rude.

I said, 'I'd like a card.' He says, 'You have to prove you're a citizen of New York.'

So I stabbed him." —Emo Philips

CHINATOWN

(map p. 191)

Um, this neighborhood is ok, but can we maybe fit in a couple thousand extra people into that empty square inch of space over there? We think we see an opening between the bizarre space vegetable and that poor duck hanging in the window. **Yes, Chinatown is one messy, cramped and often malodorous experience**. And that´s precisely what makes it so much fun – **it´s like a field trip to a different world without leaving the city**. The real strength of Chinatown is on the culinary side of the coin, with delectable, exotic and well-priced eats to be had at spots like **Joe's Shanghai**, **Nha Trang** and **Doyers Vietnamese Restaurant**. In terms of the night, **there's an air of mystery which permeates the secretive dens of sin**, and you don't need to be driving a tricked out Civic to feel part of the fun. Catch us sporting bootleg Rouis Buitton bags, eating at **Pho Bang** and **Good World Bar**, then belting out karaoke duets at **Winnie's** with our new Falung Gong buddies. All in all, you can't help but have a truly happy ending.

RESTAURANTS Chinatown

Big Wong 67 Mott St. (Bayard & Canal Sts.) (212) 964-0540 Cantonese. With a name straight out of gay Asian porn, this no-frills joint is a favorite with soup-slurping seniors and hungry neighborhood shift workers on a tight budget. The grilled meats can be a bit greasy, and the noodles are on the slippery side, but don't be shy around the dumplings. They're tasty enough to take your mind off the institutional décor and shrieking wait staff. $10

Bingo Seafood 104 Mott St. (Canal & Hester Sts.) (212) 941-6729 Cantonese. Find Nemo – or just about any other fish that fits your fancy – in the dining room's enormous tank, and order him prepared in any number of tasty manners. As the name implies, seafood is the star attraction here: Stick to such ocean-fresh specialties as scallops swimming in divine black peppercorn sauce. $16

Bo Ky 80 Bayard St. (Mott & Mulberry Sts.) (212) 406-2292 Asian. Sample a savory medley of Vietnamese and Thai flavors, or stick with that old standby Cantonese noodle soup. You'll dig the hearty broths with seasoned shrimp, but table-campers beware: the polyglot staff will hustle you out the door faster than you can say "Zero population growth." $10

Brown 61 Ludlow St. (Grand St.) (212) 254-9825 Café. At a slight remove from the mainstream Chinatown hubbub, this comfy sandwich shop is a serene oasis of tree-trunk seating and quiet ambience. Grab a mag and let the time pass as you snack on stuffed sandwiches on fresh bread. And that cute girl behind the espresso bar serves up a mean dose of the bean. $12

Canton 45 Division St. (Bowery & Market St.) (212) 226-4441 Cantonese. Put down the printed menu and hush up a sec: Your waiter has the scoop on the kitchen's freshest and most exotic creations like stuffed clams or crispy chicken with scallions. Owner Eileen Leong is class itself, often working the subtly decorated dining room to greet her guests. The place has inspired fanatical regulars for three generations. $30

Chinatown Ice Cream Factory 65 Bayard St. (Elizabeth & Mott Sts.) (212) 608-4170 Ice Cream. Arriverdci, Ciao Bella. We're hooked on the Factory's generous scoops of cherry pistachio, coconut fudge and strawberry colada ice cream. Fat-phobes flip for longan, lychee and blueberry sorbet. The friendly counter kids will even whomp up milk shakes and egg creams. Wander in with spare change, leave with a smile. $3

Dim Sum Go Go 5 E. Broadway (Catherine St.) (212) 732-0797 Chinese. Save your singles – despite the name, it's a low-key, jiggle-free spot. The action here is all on the menu, with unique items like mini-burgers with succulent dumpling beef and sturdy standbys like chicken casserole with taro sausage. Try the Shepherd's Purse, a chicken-veggie special in an egg-white pouch. $18

Doyers Vietnamese Restaurant 11 Doyers St. (Bowery & Pell St.) (212) 513-1527 Vietnamese. How can you go wrong with five kinds of frog's legs? The less bold might opt for a pleasant curry salmon, caramel fish or satay squid. Favorites like lemonade beef under pineapple sauce are a tasting tour of the chef's tropical homeland. -$14 **BlackBook**

Evergreen Shanghai 63 Mott St. (Canal & Bayard Sts.) (212) 571-3339 Chinese. Instant gratification takes too long, but Evergreen's chicken roasted in lotus root is worth the wait. Couldn't call ahead the 12 hours the kitchen requires to do the dish up right? Hot soup dumplings are a slurpy marvel of kitchen chemistry. $20

Good World Bar & Grill 3 Orchard St. (Division & Canal Sts.) (212) 925-9975 Swedish. Strong-arm it through the fashionable evening bar crowd to a pleasant back patio for the best – probably only – Swedish food you've ever tasted. Yes, they do eat more than mini-meatballs. The menu changes when the chef gets bored. $25 **BlackBook**

Goody's 1 E. Broadway (Oliver St. & Chatham Sq.) (212) 577-2920 Chinese. A bare-bones cafeteria spit-shined with groovy touches like bamboo-painted mirrors and 70s rock, Goody's got soup dumplings to rival Joe's, and a memorably good orange fish. Earn the owner's respect and affection by ordering the cabbage with cream sauce. Yes, really. $15

House of Vegetarian 68 Mott St. (Canal & Bayard Sts.) (212) 226-6572 Chinese Vegetarian. The Germans like to shape their marzipan into flowers, bunnies and other whimsical forms. And certain Asian cultures sculpt and season versatile vegetarian building blocks like tofu and seitan into ersatz meat dishes. The fake pork, impostor duck and deceitful chicken will fool all but the most discerning carnivore. $15

Joe's Shanghai 9 Pell St. (Bowery & Mott Sts.) (212) 233-8888 Chinese. You're right to be suspicious of cult restaurants. They almost never live up to the hype. Joe's, however, is another story: Tissue-thin wontons hold flavorful pork and crab balls flooded with rich broth. This must be the Joe's of the "eat at" aphorism. $15

Les Enfants Terribles 37 Canal St. (Ludlow St.) (212) 777-7518 French & African. Palm fronds and gilded ceilings are a glimpse of old Imperials days, while cute, cool waitresses place you firmly downtown. The nigh-unpronounceable menu is a colonial mishmash of tropical and Continental flavors that's well worth the hike. $35

Lin's Dumpling House 25 Pell St. (Doyers St.) (212) 577-2777 Chinese. Weren't you saying, just the other night, that you can't find decent spicy pig ears in this town? If not, then order the exquisitely tender salt-baked soft-shell crabs or pan-fried little soup dumplings. The big dining room has a hustly vibe that's less hectic than other Chinatown spots. $15

New Green Bo 66 Bayard St. (Mott & Elizabeth Sts.) (212) 625-2359 Chinese. You're in your element here: simple decor, a genial crowd and a menu full of dishes you actually recognize. The pork with salty vegetables soup is reliable comfort food, but insiders order off the menu and get the chow fun with shredded pork and preserved cabbage. And, oh, those scallion pancakes... $20

Nha Trang 87 Baxter St. (Canal & Bayard Sts.) (212) 233-5948 Vietnamese. Ambulance chasers pour in from the nearby civil courts for grilled seafood in tangy barbecue sauce or hearty beef casserole. Grab a hot-and-sour soup and eavesdrop on writs and motions a-borning. Great service—if you can't decide, let them do it for you. $16

Peking Duck House 28 Mott St. (Park & Pell Sts.) (212) 227-1810 Chinese. Duck is such an indulgence on every level: Not only is it expensive, it's very, very bad for you. If you're going to do it at all, do it right – they do a fair fowl here, with crispy skin and tangy, mouth-watering flesh. Subdued decor and solicitous service make for a romantic night out that's well worth the splurge. $34 a duck.

Pho Bang 157 Mott St. (Broome & Grand Sts.) (212) 966-3797 Vietnamese. Pho, a Vietnamese beef noodle soup, gets a myriad of makeovers here, from hot and sour to sweet and mild. Buck up the broth with sides of grilled beef wrapped in lettuce or exquisitely greaseless spring rolls. Forgive the ho-hum ambience and careless service for the sake of good, ample eats at a decent price. $12

Sweet n' Tart Café 76 Mott St. (Canal & Bayard Sts.) (212) 334-8088 Chinese. Probably the neighborhood's most daunting culinary dare, Sweet 'n' Tart's duck's blood with ginger and scallion isn't nearly as scary as it sounds. Oh, all right, have the pan-fried noodles or the ginger-chicken drumsticks. They're equally good. But you're a wimp. $10

Yeah Shanghai Deluxe 65 Bayard St. (Elizabeth & Mott Sts.) (212) 566-4884 Chinese. Shanghai a couple cabs' worth of your best friends and head for this big, busy dining room, where delectable dim sums and luscious lo meins make for great sharing dishes. Large parties love the banquet menu, priced for tables of 10 or more. But oddities like pig colon casserole make more intimate dining just as memorable. $18

NIGHTLIFE Chinatown

169 Bar 169 E. Broadway (Rutgers St.) (212) 473-8866 Getting better with age. Laid-back, cheap and spacious, this arty little bar boasts a smoker-friendly garden out back. Crowds pack the joint late in the week for live music, spoken-word shows and cool retro DJs, while Monday and Tuesday nights are more manageable.

Winnie's 104 Bayard St. (Baxter & Mulberry Sts.) (212) 732-2384 With a vibe like those basement parties you used to have the minute your parents went away for the weekend, family-run Winnie's cobbles raffish charm out of its dingy, cramped quarters. Cheap Hawaiian Punch shots enhance the high school feel, while high rollers and a crooner named Kazumi lend an air of sophistication. **BlackBook**

"I'm astounded by people who want to 'know' the universe

when it's hard to find your way around Chinatown." —Woody Allen

---

SOHO

(map p. 192)

Where the streets all have names, and celebrities feel comfortable throwing phones at civilians' heads. **Disneyland for the Chanel set**. And the greatest concentration of cast-iron buildings in the world. In the 60s and 70s, artists needing cheap, open spaces, stepped in and turned an essentially derelict neighborhood into a vibrant art community, a pattern copied shortly thereafter by Tribeca. Make no mistake, though, the artists are long gone. **The only "happening" you're likely to experience these days is a Missy Elliott sighting at the Adidas store**, or Kate Moss buying panties at Agent Provocateur. Or aforementioned Aussie jerk making ass of himself at the Mercer Hotel. Walk through the Prada store on Broadway just to peep the haus Rem built. Move west on Prince and check your email at the Apple store. We still love standbys like **Lucky Strike**, **Café Noir**, and **Raoul's**. Or faceplanting in a bowl of guacamole at **Dos Caminos**, then rooting for our favorite futbol team at **Novecento**, toasting the sunset on the roof deck at **60 Thom**, before hitting **Blue Ribbon** late night feeling high on life.

RESTAURANTS SoHo

Antique Garage 41 Mercer St. (Broome & Grand Sts.) (212) 219-1019 Mediterranean. The road show parks it in former auto shop. Sparkly chandeliers and mismatched chairs of yore. Tasty mezzes. Shrimp and octopi aplenty. Look out for garlic overload. But, more importantly, how much can we get for granny's grand-father clock? $25

Aquagrill 210 Spring St. (6th Ave.) (212) 274-0505 Seafood. Supremely fresh fish prepared with little to no fuss. Sample Neptune's finest booty at the raw bar. Sunny days sit on the ample patio overlooking that section of 6th that every loud zooming truck in Manhattan likes to pass. Crowd is thirtyish, well-scrubbed and professional. $40

Balthazar 80 Spring St. (Broadway & Crosby St.) (212) 965-1414 French Bistro. McNally original. Invigorating breakfast starts many a SoHo player's day. Look for blonde, bespectacled bartender and his diabolical Ramos Gin Fizz. Grab some chocolate bread for late night binge. $50

Bistro Les Amis 180 Spring St. (Thompson St.) (212) 226-8645 French Bistro. Solid for great bread, decent steak frites, thrifty wine list and patio seats with top views of busy SoHo corner. Quaint, lively, Paris pix on walls. Forgo quick-fix of slice across the street and enter slow zone. $25

Blue Ribbon 97 Sullivan St. (Prince & Spring Sts.) (212) 274-0404 American. A godsend. Where else you gonna get duck clubs at fo' in the mornin'? Late night feast royale. No rezzies. Raw bar, matzoh ball soup, supreme steak tartare, shrimp provençal. Ask if they have sea urchins. Top it off with chocolate bruno. $40

Blue Ribbon Sushi 119 Sullivan St. (Prince & Spring Sts.) (212) 343-0404 Japanese. Nocturnal, superb, raw-dogs... and then when you're done with young Keiko, move on to the fatty tuna and spider rolls in an alcoholic daze. Tip top. High-impact Zen dining. Ideal spot to take your Fendi-rocking Japanese girlfriendo. $55 **BlackBook**

Café Noir 32 Grand St. (Thompson St.) (212) 431-7910 Mediterranean. Bring a "friend" to the bathroom and recreate a scene from Unfaithful. Strong drinks, Sangria, fried brie cheese with fried grapes, best tapas, steak frites, and paella! Sidewalk cafe when warm. Off the beaten track. Low key and inside. $30

Canal House at the SoHo Grand Hotel 310 W. Broadway, 2nd fl. (Canal & Grand Sts.) (212) 965-3588 American. Assorted SoHo street traffic pokes head upstairs and gets lured in by the delicious, nostalgic smell. And check out the size of those lamps. High-end comfort eats like gourmet mac n' cheese. $45

Cendrillon 45 Mercer St. (Broome & Grand Sts.) (212) 343-2583 Filipino. Super-charged Filipino home cookin'. Eccentric, dimly-lit joint for unique entrees like black rice paella, trout stuffed with mushrooms and other fusion-y variations on more traditional dishes. $27

Cubana Café 110 Thompson St. (Prince and Spring Sts.) (212) 966-5366 Cuban. Step below street level into low-key fun. Hanger steak quesadillas with mole and anejo cheese. Reputable rice and beans and café con leche. Beer and wine at the cozy bar. $15

Dos Caminos SoHo 475 W. Broadway (Houston St.) (212) 277-4300 Mexican. Pretty people in caged patio gorge on spicy guac. Who wants lobster tacos? Steve Hanson's tequila-fueled carnival moves downtown and hot white chicks seem to love it. $35

Downtown Cipriani 376 W. Broadway (Spring & Broome Sts.) (212) 343-0999 Italian. Double park your Bentley and dine with freshly-polished trophy companion (Is that Beyonce one table down?) Pretty ridiculous scene here. Boldface brashness. Eat rigatoni, sip specialty bellini while your supermodel date eschews her salad. +$55

Fanelli Café 94 Prince St. (Mercer St.) (212) 226-9412 American. The lighted sign is like beacon of friendship in the night. A taste of old SoHo. Hard to believe it survived flurry of redevelopment, until you taste the burger. Sloshed regulars at the bar. Menu does quiche, catfish, and pizzas with equal aplomb. $15

Felix 340 W. Broadway (Grand St.) (212) 431-0021 French Bistro. Sound system may be blown out but still a great corner location. Just up street from Deitch Projects. Pulls fair share of talent, does a hectic brunch for tourists, euros and locals. Lots of energy, not the place for an intimate dinner. Futbol games. $40

Fiamma 206 Spring St. (6th Ave. & Sullivan St.) (212) 653-0100 Italian. Power crowd, suits, downtown players making a good impression on their uptown guests. Fusion from Ruby Foo pro Steve Hansen via Italy via glass elevator. We'll get off at the tortelli floor after checking out the asparagus tips. $55

Giorgione 307 Spring St. (Hudson & Greenwich Sts.) (212) 352-2269 Nothern Italian from Dean & Deluca owner. Hot staff, fine ingredients, lots of SoHo regulars keep it busy all week long. Clam linguini and top pizzas. Long, gorgeous, dazzling space culminates in beautiful posterior. $40

Hampton Chutney Co. 68 Prince St. (Crosby & Lafayette Sts.) (212) 226-9996 Sandwiches. Bombay, Amanganssett, SoHo - a logical progression! Dosas and calm chanting music for frazzled shopping nerves. Contemplate armed struggle for a seat. Moms taking their daughters on shopping trips and local workers in a rush getting wraps to go. $12

Honmura An 170 Mercer St. (Houston & Prince Sts.) (212) 334-5253 Japanese. Dark-lit, dark-walled, Zen vantage point to watch cobblestoned street below. Upstairs ideal for soba buckwheat noodles and scrumptious jumbo shrimp. Not thrilled with the miniscule portions. Cubic, sake fuels forgiveness. $25

Ivo & Lulu 558 Broome St. (Varick St.) (212) 226-4399 French & Jamaican. Serene setting, minute open kitchen, lots of delicious little organic bites like jerk duck confit and avocado mousse. Mark & Blue transfer the mini A phenomenon downtown, replicate the magic in random spot by Holland Tunnel. -$25 **BlackBook**

Kelley & Ping 127 Greene St. (Houston & Prince Sts.) (212) 228-1212 Asian Noodle Shop. Pad Thai cafeteria with funky tables. Eat at the Asian tea bar if you like. Pick favorite dumpling, thai wrap, or noodle bowl. Area workers known to hit up daily. $18

Kin Khao 171 Spring St. (Thompson St. & W. Broadway) (212) 966-3939 Thai. Dark, hip, Asian-inspired look. Kelly & Ping peeps sibling has been doing the Thai thing rather well for quite some time. Go for the whole fried fish or Bangkok tapas at the bar. Slight hint of attitude for spice. $30

Kittichai 60 Thompson St. (Broome & Spring St.) (212) 219-2000 Thai. Star chef from Bangkok kicks Thom to the curb, hires Rockwell to paper the place with orchids and gets busy with the monkfish. Look for good-luck goldfish. Bold spice and ethereal essence presented family style. $60

L'Orange Bleue 430 Broome St. (Crosby St.) (212) 226-4999 French & Moroccan. Afro-Euros dancing on the bar, bystanders swept up in the moment, belly dancers work room. Colors clash on corner and flavors work on plate. Tagines and warm chocolate cake. Goes off on Bastille day. $45

Lahore 132 Crosby St. (Houston & Prince Sts.) (212) 965-1777 Pakistani Take-Out. Samosa shack straight outta Delhi. Cabbie to-go spot for lentils and diesel fuel. Spicy, quick and super cheap. They've opened a larger, cleaner one for The Man next to Punjabi further east on Houston but we like the dirty original the best. -$6

Lucky Strike 59 Grand St. (W. Broadway & Wooster St.) (212) 941-0479 French Bistro. Perennial for steak frites, goat cheese salad and multiple French martinis. Darling waitresses, energetic bar, accomplished DJs, mirrored dining room. Classic for after-the-party eats. $25

Melampo 105 Sullivan St. (Prince & Spring Sts.) No phone. Sandwiches. Alessandro passed the torch to new blood. We miss the old guy, but fortunately still has superior Italian sandwiches. Get the Roxie or the Fellini, choose your bread, and split a big bottle of peach tea. +$10

The Mercer Kitchen 99 Prince St. (Mercer St.) (212) 966-5454 American & French. Sit under the sidewalk and enter a culinary triumph in every sense. Modern industrial setting lit perfectly. Smidgen pretentious, but staff works hard. Raw tuna and wasabi pizza, yellowtail carpaccio, pumpkin ravioli. Excellent brunch serves best $12 pancakes ever. $60

Novecento 343 W. Broadway (Broome & Grand Sts) (212) 925-1700 Argentine. South American families, Italian sculptors from the area, the odd polo player, and preppy Argentine I-bankers drinking exquisite Malbecs and eating one of the better milanesas around. Hectic when they show soccer games upstairs. Lovely staff with good taste. $40

Pao 322 Spring St. (Greenwich St.) (212) 334-5464 Portuguese. Stone soup, good seafood. Mellow corner spot close to the water. Has potential to be fun, but it's often empty. Outside seating on warm nights. Delicate, tasty, bacalhao and a port to conclude. The sidewalk down here turns into a block party when weather's nice. $35

Peppe Rosso 149 Sullivan St. (Houston & Prince Sts.) (212) 677-4555 Italian. Super cheap, no-diet soda, five two-top tables, and delicious. Meeting next door makes for primo people watching as the AA crew smoke cigs and works shit out. Get the Caesar, then any pastas like penne with ricotta or papardelle. $10

Provence 38 MacDougal St. (Prince St.) (212) 475-7500 French Bistro. Opened on Bastille Day 1986; must be some proud Gauls. Cassoule d'escargots provençal and bouillabaisse in the covered garden. Goat cheese salads and sinful desserts. Amber glow in room. Sunflowers, lavender, Ricard, Edith Piaf and romance on a sleepy block. Timeless. $45

Raoul's 180 Prince St. (Sullivan & Thompson Sts.) (212) 966-3518 French. Old Soho bistro charms in dilapidated digs as glitzier spots fall by the wayside. Classic for perfect steak au poivre, excellent risotto with scallops munched by low-key celebs and regular folk alike. Unpretentious, always on point. Busy bar scene adds to the allure. $50

Salt 58 MacDougal St. (Prince & Houston Sts.) (212) 674-4968 American. Choose a protein and two sides for a main course. Toss it over your shoulder, but if you pass it, remember table first, never hand to hand. Long, white, communal tables, open kitchen, peeling white paint, exposed wood beams and the universal condiment. $40

Savoy 70 Prince St. (Crosby St.) (212) 219-8570 Mediterranean. Salt-crusted baked duck is sublime, striped bass and hanger steak also worthy selects. Fresh produce and homemade desserts. Quaint corner place looks like a country house on the cusp of SoHo. $45

Snack 105 Thompson St. (Prince & Spring Sts.) (212) 925-1040 Greek. Big lunch place, few tables, better as a take-out option. Get the incredible shrimp santorini, tomato broth with feta. Quick dip for super salads or sandwiches eaten in situ or nearby park on summer days. $12

Woo Lae Oak 148 Mercer St. (Houston & Prince Sts.) (212) 925-8200 Korean. A little Seoul in little SoHo. Lovely look. Get the pork, try not to burn it. Grilled shitake mushrooms and other veggies for those so inclined. Best neighborhood BBQ, made at your table. $50

NIGHTLIFE SoHo

A 60 60 Thompson St. (Broome & Spring Sts.) No phone. You need a special card for entry unless you have a room key. Extreme rooftop cocktailing with superb view of downtown. Mixed bag of not-so-slick hotel guests and incredibly attractive, hip others. Plastic cups are a bummer.

Circa Tabac 32 Watts St. (W. Broadway & 6th Ave.) (212) 941-1781 Comfortable chairs, heavy velvet vibe, champagne cocktails, and carbon monoxide. Dark Deco lounge declares immunity from smoking ban. 150-brand smoke list including a $25 pack of Treasurers for those who also enjoy shooting themselves with gold bullets.

Don Hill's 511 Greenwich St. (Spring St.) (212) 334-1390 Dirty dance-pit sweat-box for rock-n-roll. Super long bar, mobbed bartenders, barely legal crowd of hotties and the occasional slumming celeb. BeavHer gone but the place still rocks.

Ear Inn 326 Spring St. (Greenwich & Washington Sts.) (212) 226-9060 Neon sign is not a typo. Film crews and UPS workers agree on super-old, dark tavern. Perfect pints and lots of regulars. Classic NY on the waterfront feel. Drink outside on a lazy afternoon. Also ideal to start the evening. **BlackBook**

Emerald Pub 308 Spring St. (Hudson & Greenwich Sts.) (212) 226-8512 Looks like a typical 2nd Ave. pub, but with more sparkle. Draws an interesting mix of local workers, artists, and college kids who've strayed into SoHo. Good for throwing Led Zeppelin or U2 on the jukebox and buying a round for the lassies.

Grand Lounge 310 W. Broadway (Canal & Grand Sts.) (212) 965-3000 Open lobby lounge heads into smaller bar. DJs that can read and write take over decks on a guest basis. Mostly various breeds of electronica. Whoever's staying in the hotel swings through at some point in the night. Pricey house cocktails.

Green Room 286 Spring St. (Hudson & Varick Sts.) (212) 929-8560 if at first you don't succeed, try and try again. This space has been many things, most notably Jet Lounge. This time it also goes for an exclusive air, we shall wait and see what happens.

Kana 324 Spring St. (Greenwich & Washington Sts.) (212) 343-8180 Small, Spanish tavern with views of the Hudson River. Tables pushed aside to ramp up groove. Pumped-up crowd dancing to latin beats spills out onto the sidewalk and mingles with the Ear Inn lager louts. Cheap, huge portions of food available.

Merc Bar 151 Mercer St. (Prince & Houston Sts.) (212) 966-2727 Canoe, canoe? Low leather chairs, forgiving lights, stiff drinks. Good for a discreet rendezvous. Rich cats blowing bank. Copycat syndrome looms large. One of this block's pioneers.

Milady's 162 Prince St. (Thompson St.) (212) 226-9069 One of the few dives you'll find in SoHo and you may find Colin Farrell there' too. Looks like a typical, solid pub. Good for baseball, billiards and beer. Decent grub but pretty horrendous jukebox.

The Room 144 Sullivan St. (Houston & Prince Sts.) (212) 477-2102 Patriarch of the Room family is truly great spot for beer and wine. Heavy iron furniture, candles and close quarters. Goth décor and little more. Simple, but it works. Hot bartendresses pouring Belgian beers for attractive young set.

S.O.B.'s 204 Varick St. (W. Houston St.) (212) 243-4940 Sounds of Brazil, classy, live music spot, latin beats and jazz. Upholds a strict standard in both tunes and performance, though it does get really crowded. Amazing place to catch up-and-comers on the make or legends on their break.

SoHo:323 323 W. Broadway (Canal & Grand Sts.) (212) 334-2232 Hasn't quite earned the velvet ropes it prominently displays. Good locale across from SoHo Grand. Seems to be awaiting a calvary of revelers who may or may not show up. Maybe holding out for quality promoters and DJs. The space is cool, though.

Sway 305 Spring St. (Greenwich & Hudson Sts.) (212) 620-5220 Named after track 2 on Sticky Fingers. Moroccan-theme, long, narrow, killer booths and supersized Buds. Used to be the best place to do drugs with a celebrity at 7am, but Nur's since moved on to Hiro. Morrissey angst on Sundays.

Thom's Bar 60 Thompson St. (Broome & Spring Sts.) (212) 219-2000 Perfect acoustics let you hear the music and what that LA import in town for one night only is chatting about. Back patio for discreet smokes. Class act in the hotel, not as exclusive as the upstairs, but on point in all other respects.

Upstairs at Cipriani 376 W. Broadway (Spring & Broome Sts.) (212) 343-0999 The most exclusive attic party ever. Past socialites and up the stairs of Cippy's into a secret jet-set society. Harvey Weinstein watching Carmen Kass belt out karaoke at Seb's sunday night party. Pull up in Ferrari and spin off into orbit. **BlackBook**

Oct. 16th /06 - Bar 89
- Awesome cocktails!
Check out the bathroom...

"New York City is a great monument to the power of money and greed... a race for rent."

—*Frank Lloyd Wright*

NOLITA & LITTLE ITALY

(map p. 193)

Once a robust Italian enclave, much of this area's heritage has been gnawed off by the encroachment of gentrifying fashionistas and the constant expansion of Chinatown. Gone are the days of the Godfather. The dons have been pushed out into the outer boroughs, their shady social clubs converted to trendy boutiques, their homes inhabited by the Lenny Kravitzes of the world, but you'll still catch a matronly nona peering from her window as the fashion set dawdles below her sill. Yet, there remains a distinct old world charm to be appreciated here. Nolita, the northernmost section of the hood, is at its best on warm days during the afternoons and early evenings, when spots like **Gitane**, **Café Habana**, **Bread** and **Rice** become defacto day clubs for the city's just-waking nightlife elite. Yes, things have indeed changed, but step inside **Mare Chiaro** for an afternoon beer and you'll catch a glimpse of how they used to be in the old days. Catch us at **Café Colonial** for breakfast, sipping cucumber margaritas at **Café El Portal** for lunch, hitting **Café Habana** for coffee, before a glitzy tequila-hazed dinner being seen by all in the amazing downstairs cavern of **La Esquina**.

RESTAURANTS Nolita & Little Italy

Bread 20 Spring St. (Elizabeth & Mott Sts.) (212) 334-1015 Sandwiches. One of Nolita's many day clubs, where the nightlife scene congregates in the afternoon to pose for each other in bright sunlight. Perfect for a glass of wine and some Italian apps. Namesake food is fresh and amazing. Slick. $25

Café Colonial 73 E. Houston St. (Elizabeth St.) (212) 274-0044 Brazilian on the hood's northernmost fringe. Great for breakfast, good for lunch. Airy, bright, quaint with rickety tables and maps on the walls. Breakfast best enjoyed in the late afternoon after checking out that new little boutique on Elizabeth. -$20

Café El Portal 174 Elizabeth St. (Spring & Kenmare Sts.) (212) 226-4642 Mexican. Inviting downstairs nook is quiet in the day, busy-busy by night. Sweet sangria, incredible shrimp tacos and coffee by the jar for mere pesos. Go in the day to see the familia chatting and making delectable tortillas. Tasty, authentic, tiny, fresh. $15 **BlackBook**

Café Gitane 242 Mott St. (Prince St.) (212) 334-9552 Mediterranean. Europhiles wet dream. Parisian cafe is at its prime in the afternoon, so catch a table if you can. Excellent coffee and tea, great salads and eggs. This is where the fashion industry goes during the week to unwind and bitch about work. $25

Café Habana 17 Prince St. (Elizabeth St.) (212) 625-2001 Latin American. All about perfectly roasted corn and models, for whom that constitutes an entire meal. Cuban-inspired cuisine includes delicious pork tacos, goat cheese empanadas and mole enchiladas. Laura tries to accommodate impatient masses outside.-$25

Ferrara Pasticceria 195-201 Grand St. (Mulberry & Mott Sts.) (212) 226-6150 Bakery. Classic, vast café with perfect cappuccino and lovely cookies. Staff sports tuxes impressing the hoardes of Jersey tourists lining up for that sweet cannoli cream. Don't miss summertime gelato. Touristy, but perfect. $5

Ghenet 284 Mulberry St. (Prince & Houston Sts.) (212) 343-1888 Ethiopian. It's getting hot Injera. Exotic eats and international, sexy vibe. Playing with your food encouraged - just sop it up with your fingers and a piece of spongy pancake they way they teach it in Addis Ababa. Wash it down with some Tej. $20

Kitchen Club 30 Prince St. (Mott St.) (212) 274-0025 Continental & Japanese. Dutch Marja Sampson's stylish corner spot creates the most interesting food in the area. European classics with Japanese accents (kinda like Nolita itself), artfully and lovingly presented. Cod and sautéed chanterelles, followed with a supai sake at adjoining Chibi. $35

La Esquina 106 Kenmare St. (Cleveland Pl. & Lafayette St.) (646) 613-7100 Mexican. Authentic (not Tex-Mex) accomplishment from uber-scenesters Serge and Kordell. Upstairs low-key take out, cozy dining on the side, and through the kitchen and down the stairs for one of the city's best hideaways. Gorgeous place and people. **BlackBook**

Lombardi's 32 Spring St. (Mulberry St.) (212) 941-7994 Pizza. Recently expanded to accommodate the giant lines. Red and white checkered tablecloths to bang your fist in mid "best pizza in city" debate. You say it's the water, eh? I venture that it's all about the cheese. Repeat ad nauseam. $25

Lovely Day 196 Elizabeth St. (Prince & Spring Sts.) (212) 925-3310 Thai. When you see the prices, you'll know the world's alright. Colorful hole-in-the wall noodle shop serves up steaming bowls of noodles and tasty thai like chicken satay, pad thai, a delicious lightly fried tuna roll and creative desserts. +$15

Matsu 200 Mott St. (Houston & Prince Sts.) (212) 343-8017 Japanese. Pristine sushi spot much frequented by area boutique staff for fresh rolls and sashimi and non-Nolita prices. Summer sidewalk tables allow choice view of Nicole Kidman and her PA as she ransacks Calypso (true). $35

Nave 301 Elizabeth St. (Houston St.) No phone. American. Hotspot…in 1993. Still desperately trying to be cool. Astonishingly delusional: hosts a memorably bad poetry night. After drinking one too many EvilGirlfriend-tinis and munching on deez nuts, you'll hire that 20-year old hostess to run your business. Go back to the Hamptons, rich boy!

Nolita House 47 E. Houston St. (Mott & Mulberry Sts.) (212) 625-1712 American. Cozy digs for comfort food above Houston, thankfully low key. New joint makes up for questionable name with excellent cheese plates paired with solid vino selections. Nothing spectacular, but fits nicely into the 'hood. $20

Nyonya 194 Grand St. (Mott & Mulberry Sts.) (212) 334-3669 Malaysian. Big round table in the back is ideal for birthday parties. Brick and bamboo décor, varied menu of delicious, and strange Malaysian cuisine. Cool staff don't mind refilling your multiple orders of Singha while juggling plates of roti canai and mango chicken. $20

Plate 264 Elizabeth St. (Houston St.) (212) 219-9212 Latin & Asian. Former M & R digs jazzed up with modern flourish. Chef Ricardo Hernandez works the fusion into everything, including a Cuban sandwich with ginger-tamarind mustard. Small plates to accompany Thai-tini cocktail, which has ice cubs made from Thai iced tea. $30

Public 210 Elizabeth St. (Spring & Prince Sts.) Eclectic. Stunning, modern, embracing restaurant puts a smile on your face and a hurt on your wallet. Staff is hot and fun, as is the clientele. Brunch can be a wait but worth it for the coconut pancake alone. Interesting Aussie cuisine like kangaroo with coriander falafel, and clever design throughout, especially the card catalogue thing. +$50 **BlackBook**

Rice 227 Mott St. (Prince & Spring Sts.) (212) 226-5775 Asian. Perpetual favorite with downtown slicksters, health food nuts, artists, boutique staff, skaters, your grandma, everyone. Hearty, creative, cheap and delicious Asian comfort grub, all revolve around namesake grain. Opt for the chicken curry with sliced bananas and yogurt on Thai black rice. $15

NIGHTLIFE Nolita & Little Italy

Botanica 47 E. Houston St. (Mott & Mulberry Sts.) (212) 343-7251 Old Knitting Factory is the new drinking factory, and at these rates, you can put them back by the dozen. Unpretentious crowd appreciates the divey ambiance that's rare hereabouts. Loungey back room.

Chibi's Sake Bar 238 Mott St. (Prince & Spring Sts.) (212) 274-0054 Any kind of sake your heart desires plus nibbles from adjoining Kitchen Club. Elegant and upscale, compacted and presented with a warm and inviting touch. Chill with name-sake pug, a frequent visitor. Teeny but not sceney.

Double Happiness 173 Mott St. (Broome & Grand St.) (212) 941-1282 Memorable 25th Hour scene filmed here. Once a mob run restaurant/members-only club, embraces its roots as a historical haunt on the border of Chinatown and Little Italy. has vectored in and out of trendiness, and settled nicely. Nice cocktails, especially the frosty cosmo. **BlackBook**

Kos 264 Bowery St. (Prince & Houston Sts.) (212) 343-9722 Narrow, tiny boite came out with a bang, but has fizzled of late. Cramped quarters with celeb involvement from our fave cross over brothers, Lenny Kravitz and Denzel. Too bad Lenny's "cousin" sort of blew it for the rest of the team.

Mare Chiaro 176 1/2 Mulberry St. (Broome & Grand Sts.) (212) 226-9345 Thick with atmosphere of a different, older New York. Good fella bartenders serve cool afternoon beers with class and charm to a mix of firemen, neighborhood youngstas and the few remaining long-term residents. The owner will tidy your mess if you're sloppy. **BlackBook**

Pravda 281 Lafayette St. (Houston & Prince Sts.) (212) 226-4696 Early 90s hotspot still has some allure, what with the broken mirrors and commie chic. Ideal for multiple martinis in an overlooked location. Hot eastern Euro crowd hits the upstairs lounge.

Sweet and Vicious 5 Spring St. (Bowery & Elizabeth St.) (212) 334-7915 Huge, long wooden space is wildly popular with uptown marauders rocking white caps. Best avoided on weekends, unless East Village Radio is throwing a party (tune in for times). Great back garden is good for off-hour beer.

Vig Bar 12 Spring St. (Elizabeth St.) (212) 625-0011 Ideal location and a generally smooth and swanky vibe, draws various Nolita celebs for late late night lounging and cocktail tipping. Frequently overlooked back room is ideal for personal parties: Call Russell for info.

Xicala 151B Elizabeth St. (Broome St.) (212) 219 0650 Tiny, secluded and cute. Instant hit one big place, the class act behind El Portal decided on two diminutive ones. Look for the red lights, then nosh on tapas and swirl a Rioja around in your glass as you weigh your evening's options.

LOWER EAST SIDE

(map p. 194)

Upper East Siders, Strong Islanders and Dirty Jerz all up in this piece on weekends, but we like it anyway cause we keep reminding ourselves that New York is all about progress and change. (Try telling that to the Puerto Ricans and old Jewish ladies getting pushed aside to make way for another 15-story hotel here.) Nevertheless, though it gets packed with invaders Thursday through Saturday, the LES still has game, history and grit. Thus we take our John Deere hat off to the venerable hood (trucker hats are officially cool again, btw, don't tell nobody). You can still kick it with characters like Henry the PhD-having Pimp, obsessive-compulsive Mr. Clean, and any number of entertainingly strung out junkies sleeping and standing up at the same time – no wonder you kids love it! That and the good eating: the great Jewish delis, the fun, cheap Latino joints, those yuppified culinary delights on Clinton street like **71 Clinton**, **Alias**, and whatever else Wylie Dufresne has cooking at the moment. McNally still does his Pastis-type thing at **Schiller's**. We'll be checking out a flick at the Sunshine, before catching a drink and a band at **Rothko**. Evenings find us eating perfect steaks at **Azul** with that dude from "Entourage," hitting **Barrio Chino** for late night tequila shots, then taking that hip tourist to a glass-encased room in the towering Hotel on Rivington and making sweet, sweet love while overlooking the glittering urban sprawl below.

RESTAURANTS Lower East Side

Aka Café 49 Clinton St. (Rivington & Stanton Sts.) (212) 979-6096 Eclectic. Easy to love, laid back kooky joint with an ultra-friendly staff, always calms the nerves. The Lower East Side needs more low-key, welcoming spots like this. Hard to dislike a menu full of satisfying staples like corn chowder, empanadas, and a smartly updated Sloppy Joe. $20

Alias 76 Clinton St. (Rivington St.) (212) 505-5011 Breast the carny-bodega threshold and you're in an elegant upscale find, middle child of a restaurant family that includes nabe faves Aka and 71 Clinton. Seasonal ingredients make for an ever-changing menu, but flatbreads and roast pork are reliable features. $35

Apizz 217 Eldridge St. (Stanton & Rivington Sts.) (212) 253-9199 Southern Italian. The subdued, well-appointed interior suits the surroundings, just off the hustle-bustle of busier LES streets. Peasant's Frank DeCarlo fires you up with creatively constructed pizzas while the P.J.'s rage outside. A nice LES dichotomy. $25

Azul Bistro 152 Stanton St. (Suffolk St.) (646) 602-2004 Argentine. Stefano, Mariana, Chucho, Laura, Maxi, that Spanish girl: we love you like a fat kid loves perfect steaks followed by dulce de leche-filled pancakes. Sidewalk seats and a glass of Malbec can't be beat. $30 **BlackBook**

Bereket 187 E. Houston St. (Orchard St.) (212) 475-7700 Turkish. Young turks get their schwarma on here, where the 4 AM falafel scene is a nightlife ritual. Stick around long enough and you'll see your favorite hipster bartenders ending the shift with a late-night nosh. $6

Chubo 6 Clinton St. (Houston & Stanton Sts.) (212) 674-6300 Global. This international bistro sports a distinctly Asian accent, with lots of eastern veggie dishes. It's a festive little place with exposed brick and low lighting. At just under 30 bucks, the prix-fixe menu is a swell deal. Single-ingredient menu on Wednesday from creative Claude is a fun idea. $35

Clinton Street Baking Company 4 Clinton St. (Houston & Stanton Sts.) (646) 602-6263 American. Where do downtown fashion vampires eat, when they dare venture out by daylight? The lunch and brunch here are the area's best, with beautifully light French toast and buttermilk biscuits you'd like to pretend your mom used to make. $17

Congee Village 100 Allen St. (Delancey & Broome Sts.) (212) 941-1818 Cantonese. You half expect Indiana Jones to come charging through the immense dining room chased by 100 Thugee assassins. But cheap, plentiful Chinese and Indonesian mainstays can stand up to the distractions. $17

Dish 165 Allen St. (Rivington & Stanton Sts.) (212) 253-8840 American. The setting is arty, but not starkly so – you can actually sit comfortably and enjoy a big entrée, two sides and a drink for under 20 bucks. Upstairs used to be a whorehouse. Now they give cooking classes. Kids these days! $20

Doughnut Plant 379 Grand St. (Norfolk St.) (212) 505-3700 You've had a good run, Krispy Kreme, but know when you're beat. There's just no topping the gigantic, fluffy, all-natural confections that seem to float out of this tiny shop's busy ovens. If you must get fat, this would be the place to do it. -$5

Economy Candy 100 Rivington St. (Essex & Ludlow Sts.) (212) 254-1531 You know that big hotel across the way? They buy their nitey-nite sweets here. But you can get a Big League Chew, heavenly macaroons or thousands of other confections just by walking in. -$4

El Nuevo Amancer 117 Stanton St. (Essex St.) (212) 387-9115 Mexican & Dominican. This barrio boy from the PG (pre-gentrification) era is still, as the kids say, keeping it real. Chow down on arroz con pollo while digging the latest tune from Cheyenne. You'll want to wrap up at least half your enormous portion to save for later or give to a wino. $15

El Sombrero 108 Stanton St. (Ludlow St.) (212) 254-4188 Mexican. Known affectionately as The Hat. Prep for your bar crawl with a fatty, carby meal of rice, beans and tacos at this recently revamped Tex-Mex locale. It's fast, it's cheap, and you're out of control. And yes, they still serve the icy grain alcohol margaritas to go, just don't go tellin' everyone! $15

Epicerie and Café Charbon 168-170 Orchard St. (Stanton St.) (212) 420-7520 French. Rustic wood tables and tiled floors are authentically French, as is the chalkboard menu translated by friendly servers. Stick with simple dishes like mussels and a simple, creamy terrine of duck. $25

1492 Food 60 Clinton St. (Rivington & Stanton Sts.) (646) 654-1114 Spanish & Tapas. Low-key hip of a quiet Madrid side street. The menu takes its cue from the name, blending Old and New World cuisines: Hummus and matzo rub shoulders with hake and quail. The black paella is a voyage of discovery. $35

Freemans 8 Rivington St. (Bowery & Chrystie St.) (212) 420-0012 American. Super hip hunting lodge at the end of a dingy alley, authentic dead animals on the wall, wealthy downtown types and assorted scenesters sitting around worn wooden tables look extra cool in the perfect lights. Get the artichoke dip and the wild boar paté. $35

Fried Dumpling 99 Allen St. (Broome & Delancey Sts.) (212) 941-9975 Chinese. It's a steal: five biggies for only one buck, and lil' dim summers like scallion pancakes for 50 cents. Good at any hour. Unfortunately, staff are long sold out and safe in bed by the time our drunk zombie brains crave greasy midnight munchies -$5

Grilled Cheese NYC 168 Ludlow St. (Houston & Stanton Sts.) (212) 982-6600 Sandwiches. Presses all the right buttons, turning out best grilled cheese in the city. Lots of cheese choices, we like the mancheego cheese on sourdough. Cheap, reliable, quick and easy. Lovely lemonade, too. -$7

Il Laboratorio del Gelato 95 Orchard St. (Delancey & Broome Sts.) (212) 343-9922 Ice Cream supplier to the (culinary) stars. Many downtown restaurants have this stuff on their menu for good reason. Ever-changing flavors and some of the best iced coffee around, but it closes way early. -$5 '**inoteca** 98 Rivington St. (Ludlow St.) (212) 614-0473 Panini. Breezy, open corner. Oak-enhanced, always packed vino spot. Get the signature eggs early, the varied cheeses in the afternoon, follow with a glass of well-priced bubbly Prosecco and maybe stay for dinner. $25

Katz's Delicatessen 205 E. Houston St. (Ludlow St.) (212) 254-2246 Classic Jewish Deli. One of NY's best. Get the little red ticket and get in line for an impressive collection of meats and bulging guts. This is the real deal, and their locally-brewed beer ain't bad either. Send a salami to your boy in the Army. God Bless the LES. $20

Kuma Inn 113 Ludlow St. (Delancey & Rivington Sts.) (212) 353-8866 Asian tapas. Duck the dilapidated Bargain District streets but keep the 99-cent store budget. Tasty adobo washed down with overflowing sake or a San Miguel. Lost yuppies try and find it to no avail. -$15

Le Père Pinard 175 Ludlow St. (Houston & Stanton Sts.) (212) 777-4917 French Bistro. Downtown trendez-vous for city's Parisiennes. Champagne, steak au poivre a la Ludlow Street. Lots of wood, lots of energy, and a happening communal table out back. These frogs can really party. $35

Little Giant 85 Orchard St. (Broome St.) (212) 226-5047 American. Seasonal menu from eager newbies Julie and Iasha, who are as wholesome as their delicious farmer's market ingredients. Creative, hearty fare popular with approachable yuppies who switch their Ipod headphones when they venture below Delancey at night. $40

Oliva 161 E. Houston St. (Allen St.) (212) 228-4143 Spanish & Tapas. Basquing in the post-tortilla afterglow, or is that the best neighborhood sangria taking effect? Cozy corner, warm and toasty in the winter. Oliva how-to: Take the F train to Allen, point to anything on menu. Say hey to Bleecker Street Julio. $30

One91 191 Orchard St. (Houston & Stanton Sts.) (212) 982-4770 Mediterranean. Gil's new spot is on a touristy stretch of Orchard, but stands out with one of the best gardens around. Nice pastas and well done fish. Romantic date spot. $25

Petrosino 190 Norfolk St. (Houston St.) (212) 673-3773 Sicilian & Mediterranean. Incredible food from Patrick's kitchen, with skills honed in Florence's top-notch Cibreo. Antonio makes you feel at home, if your home were an impeccably and creatively attired, open, light, elegant space with a beautiful poured cement bar. $35 **BlackBook**

Rosario's Pizza 173 Orchard St. (Stanton St.) (212) 777-9813 Pizza. Amiable Sal is still a LES original. Catch Marco (art) getting his afternoon sustenance. Open really late, slices satisfy. Get the rollini and make sure they heat it up all the way. -$5

San Loco 111 Stanton St. (Essex St.) (212) 253-7580 Mexican. Three of these in the city, this one's the best. Awesome solution to late-night cravings: chipotle chicken and arguably the best guacamole downtown. Everything's fresh, some vegetarian options, great margs, notably good delivery service. $20

Schiller's Liquor Bar 131 Rivington St. (Norfolk St.) (212) 260-4555 Bistro. McNally's gorgeous, bustling bistro has exceptional energy, drinks and surprisingly abundant, tasty and solid eats. Wiener Schnitzel on your lucky days and a few bottles of cheap red wine. Pretty people. $25

71 Clinton Fresh Food 71 Clinton St. (Rivington & Stanton Sts.) (212) 614-6960 Continental & American. Make a rezzie now for 2006. Obsessive fan-base from all over flocks to joint that put Clinton St. on culinary map and kept it there. One of the city's most reputable yet casual tables. Ask the chef about his trip to Spain, while devouring his expertly crafted fare. $50

The Stanton Social 99 Stanton St. (Ludlow & Orchard Sts.) (212) 995-0099 Ecclectic mix of multicultural fare. Tries to be all things to all yuppies. Lofty space is energetic though and with its central location it's a magnet for Yorkville émigrés looking to experiment with "ethnic" food like upscale snapper tacos and kobe beef injections. $45

Suba 109 Ludlow St. (Delancey & Rivington Sts.) (212) 982-5714 Spanish. Owner Yann's a pretentious try-hard, but sort of pulls it off. A little two years ago (yeah we said it) but so's our three-year-old kid and we kept him, right? And there's salsa nights and a moat, unlike our useless brat. $45

Teany 90 Rivington St. (Orchard & Ludlow Sts.) (212) 475-9190 Vegan & Vegetarian Café. Organic, healthy eats, all manner of tea leaves for table brewing. Clean, shiny, white like its owner, M-M-Moby!! Full of attractive, health-conscious people who find spiritual validation in pricey infusions. Hey, is that stabbing organic? -$15

NIGHTLIFE Lower East Side

Arlene Grocery 95 Stanton St. (Orchard & Ludlow Sts.) (212) 358-1633 Stage for solid bands and a cozy bar off to the side. Still a fixture of the city music scene. Lots of singer-songwriters coming to grips with reality. Where else would Adrian Grenier's crappy band sell out?

Barrio Chino 253 Broome St. (Orchard & Ludlow Sts.) (212) 228-6710 The Sub-Delancey conquest blazed by Brown continues in a chill section of the LES. Comfy, serene, open front—drink one of the copious tequilas and breathe deeply. Tequila bars are all about wearing your very best Bad Idea jeans and seeing where the night goes. Serves some eats, too. **BlackBook**

BLVD 199 Bowery (Spring St.) (212) 982-7821 Club with fancy touches. Ghetto crowd some nights—check out the rim show on the street outside. Looks like a car show! Hit Crash Mansion downstairs for top live acts in a decked out space. Lots of release parties and magazine launches.

Bowery Ballroom 6 Delancey St. (Bowery & Chrystie St.) (212) 533-2111 Like Irving Plaza but less commercial, BB is one the last great music clubs left in New York. Exterior merges into the derelict Bowery with ease, yet is exquisite inside. If you're a bartender, the upstairs bar is a pretty cherry gig.

Chibitini 63 Clinton St. (Stanton & Rivington Sts.) (212) 674-7300 Seeing red all the time. A cute little crimson cube of a room, Marja Sampson's post-Chibi experiment occasionally hosts thoroughly educational sake tastings. Other nights, nosh on edamame and succulent salmon dumplings.

The Dark Room 165 Ludlow (Houston & Stanton Sts.) (212) 353-0536 Dark, sexy smooth and slightly gothic with Joy Division playing all the time: where the local bands head after the show. Past the wee hours, can be impossible to reach the bar, gets as packed and steamy as a sauna. PACKED.

Delancey 168 Delancey St. (Clinton St.) (212) 254-9920 The Williamsburg Bridge has been continually under repair for over 13 years, which is odd, considering it took only 7 years to build. See it from the roof garden here in all it's glory. Great deck for smoking, cold beers and bands on the come-up.

The East Side Company Bar 49 Essex St. (Grand & Hester Sts.) (212) 614-7408 This company includes Sasha of Milk & Honey, he of the meticulous and creative pour. Walk past the unmarked door into secluded comfort and delicious cocktails like the honey and bourbon Gold Rush. Raw bar, too.

Happy Ending 302 Broome St. (Eldridge & Forsyth Sts.) (212) 334-9676 Massage parlor-cum-bar-cum-literary hang-cum-on-your-blue dress. Grab a potent drink, slip into a downstairs booth and listen to the angst drip from the reader's mouth.

Living Room 154 Ludlow St. (Stanton & Rivington Sts.) (212) 533-7235 What the —? A downtown hangout where the regulars actually smile? Don't they know the rules? Grand but comfy, this folksy spot often welcomes Nora Jones and artists of her ilk. Check your 'tude, enliven your mood.

Lolita 266 Broome St. (Allen St.) (212) 966-7223 Anything sub-Delancey is 20% cooler in our book. Exposed brick, corner location, heavy pours, feels cozy. Less palpable attitude than most downtown spots. Thick accented Euro-trendies seek it out, loads of Brits (why?). Lots of readings and literary stuff goes on downstairs.

Lotus Club 35 Clinton St. (Stanton St.) (212) 253-1144 This is a local place, open late. George, the bartender, supplies the beers and rock music from behind the bar. LESbian parties and a general intellectual vibe makes your buzz seem almost, dare-we-say, sophisticated. Ok, maybe not. Think Tony Yayo but less tony.

Max Fish 178 Ludlow St. (Houston & Stanton Sts.) (212) 529-3959 Myspace.com, the musical. Block veteran with the killer jukebox and cheap drinks. Skater kids, artists, rock-types all swarm weekday nights and make a crazy scene on weekends. Regulars late night in back. Watch out for flying bottles… a really weird mix of people.

Mercury Lounge 217 E. Houston St. (Ludlow & Essex Sts.) (212) 260-4700 Read The Voice, check the scene, get amped on indie rock or whatever else is on the menu for the night. Good, small room with nice acoustics, where everyone from Jeff Buckley to the Yeah Yeah Yeahs played back in the day.

Milk and Honey 134 Eldridge St. (Delancey St.) No phone. Sasha's not-so-secret spot. (It's not a secret if more than two people know about it.) Is it worth the trouble? Read the rules. London branch is better. Don't ask the ladies for digits. Adhere to the strict no star-fucking policy.

Motor City Bar 127 Ludlow St. (Rivington & Delancey Sts.) (212) 358-1595 Rock & Roller on the auction block. If we had the cash we'd buy it so it doesn't become a fusion restaurant. Dive-theme, good rock DJs. Hard core following and a pleasing, dirty vibe.

151 151 Rivington St. (Essex & Norfolk Sts.) No phone. Joey raises the roof in the basement bar with Flintstones siding and mod details. Strong pours, hot crowd. Reliable and consistently cool, although nothing's happening before midnight. Fine with us…

Pianos 158 Ludlow St. (Stanton & Rivington Sts.) (212) 505-3733 It's got everything: bar, restaurant, lounge, stage, recording studio, sauna, gym, hair salon, helipad, Finns, Tam, Ron, your friend's "rock & roll" roommate, ironic comedy nights. Love it or hate it, you will be forced at hipster gunpoint to go sooner or later.

Rothko 116 Suffolk St. (Rivington St.) That rock chick walking east on Houston isn't going to the projects on Avenue D. She's on her way here (we hope). Live performance and bar. Output Records parties, heavy band-of-the-moment vibe and general winning attitude. Check out rothkonyc.com for line-up. **BlackBook**

Sin-é 150 Attorney St. (Houston & Stanton Sts.) (212) 388-0077 Non-descript, medium-sized music room from the Arlene people, so it gets the really, really good acts. Check the no-name LA techno kids before they break big. Party is the smoking scene outside between sets and at their nearby bar after the show.

6's & 8's 205 Chrystie (Stanton St.) (212) 505-6688 DJ spins Strokes, Blondie, Skynyrd, while you drink overpriced Pabst in the can. Would love to hate on this place if only it wasn't always such a mess of fun. Big banquettes. Packed with certified hotties, coked-up coolies, and holy-shit that's Gina Gershon!

Tonic 107 Norfolk St. (Rivington & Delancey Sts.) (212) 358-7503 Independent edifice for indie acts. Ask your neighborhood vinyl addict for the line-up. Kooky noise acts, bizarre spoken word in the downstairs dingy dungeon. Check tonicnyc.com. Yoko campaigned to save this place, possibly to compensate for breaking up The Beatles.

Welcome to the Johnsons 123 Rivington St. (Essex & Norfolk Sts.) (212) 420-9911 Where suburban chic meets urban angst over $2 beers, and PBR marketers research their target audience. Wear your Sunday worst and talk some smack over who won that last round of Galaga on the tabletop video game.

"Everyone ought to have a Lower East Side in their life." —Irving Berlin

EAST VILLAGE

(map p. 195)

The story of the East Village's social makeover from artistic anarchist junkiedom to holy-shit-there's-a-Whole-Foods is basically a closed chapter in New York history. The former punk flop district, for the most part, serves as a party district for collegiate and recently post-. Even with the new money, the restaurant scene is loaded with an array of unique budget eats. The bars include underground sake dens, swank lounges and some of the best $2 beer dives in the city. Though many in the neighborhood got a haircut and got a real job, there are still some ruffians about and the overall energy remains decidedly alt. Strollers are the new panic of Needle Park aka Tompkins Square, but at least the mommys and daddys pushing them are inked from wrist to shoulder. Brunch at **Prune** and dinner at **Jack's Oyster House** remain reliably adventurous trips through the land of awesomeness, but both require a Javert-like tenacity to get a table. Fortunately PBRs at the **Lounge** and Jenga outdoors at **Joey's** are pretty hassle-free. Find us closing down Lit with a bevy of derelict rocker chicks.

RESTAURANTS East Village

Alphabet Kitchen 171 Ave. A (10th & 11th Sts.) (212) 982-3838 Portuguese & Spanish. Paella in the garden? Or take your tapas on the slick bar where sangria flows like the waterfall? Nightly it's lit-low for first casual dates chosen by girl who spent semester in Seville. Chill in the late afternoon when the sun's sinking low. $35

Angelica Kitchen 300 E. 12th St. (1st & 2nd Aves.) (212) 228-2909. Vegan Organic. The anti-McDonald's. Nothing served here ever mooed or clucked at any point. Lots of green things, brown-ish things and things that are supposed to taste like other things. But do they know that carrot's scream silently when they are pulled out of the ground? $16

Banjara 97 1st Ave. (6th St.) (212) 477-5956 Indian. Basically, the best of Little India and it has a lounge too. Genial and dusky, slightly more expensive than its neighbors but the food is a little fresher, a little cleaner. Do the Dumpahkt dishes: vegetable, shrimp or chicken, or get the sharabi bababi. $20

Bao 111 111 Ave. C (7th & 8th Sts.) (212) 254-7773 Vietnamese. A feng shui stunner of sloping lines and little clutter. Red drapes and candles set the mood. Both fusion and traditional Vietnamese, washed back with house-made sakes between courses. Get the ribs - that's what all the chefs do. Give big what-up to Michael. $25

Blue 9 Burger 90 3rd Ave. (12th & 13th Sts.) (212) 979-0053 Burgers. Former In 'n' Out worker brings West Coast drive-thru king's secrets to l'il old NYC. Everything is made to order. Burger is hot off the grill, dripping with grease, oozing cheese and pretty fucking delicious. The double is a jaw-tester. Best consumed in under two minutes. $7

Café Mogador 101 St. Marks Pl. (Ave. A & 1st Ave.) (212) 677-2226 Moroccan. Sludgy Turkish coffee opens bleary eyes of the breakfast-at-noon crowd. Moroccan cereal warms the hearts of the neighborhood bartender cuties that frequent. Outdoor patio, pleasant service and phenomenal sparkling lemonade. $17

Caracas Arepa Bar 91 E. 7th St (212) 228-5062 Venezuelan. Not had an arepa? Basically tasty corn hockey pucks stuffed with cheese and other goodness. Where do you think Venezuelan girls get those slammin' bootangs? Bring that skinny blue-eyed devilette in need of hips to hold on to and she'll be tricked with curves in no time. -$15

Casimir 103 Ave B (6th & 7th Sts.) (212) 358-9683 French. Cute bistro with blazing, charmingly disaffected staff. Veteran spot popular with local restaurant owners. Good energy, incredible grass-fed steak frites even the Gauchos give props to. Excellent brunch in the smoke-friendly garden. Sexy place. $35

Chikalicious 203 E. 10th St. (1st & 2nd Aves.) (212) 995-9511 Dessert for dinner. Clean, sharp shop serves incredible concoctions like warm chocolate tart with pink peppercorn ice cream and brown sugar panna cotta with Meyer lemon sorbet. Amuse your inner fat kid and give f-you to dining convention. +$15

Crif Dogs 113 St. Marks Pl. (1st Ave. & Ave. A) (212) 614-2728 Hot Dogs. You gotta love any restaurant whose CPR sign begins with "Hey Assholes!" and ends with "Good luck!" Attitude-heavy dog shack satiates cravings of local lushes. Video and board games, a Sigmund Freud action figure and hot dogs wrapped in bacon -$7

Dok Suni's 119 1st Ave. (7th St. & St. Marks Pl.) (212) 477-9506 Korean. Tiny stop hops with the bebimbop. Like an ornate wooden music box minus the tunes. Top eats dished by cutie staff. Get the banchan and bulgogi, and finish with that delicious cinnamon-inflected tea; all praise is due Jenny and her moms. Cash only, no reservations. $25

Dumpling Man 100 St. Mark's Pl. (1st Ave.) Small shop (212) 505-2121 Chinese. Creative handcrafted dumplings. Chicken, pork, shrimp and tofu, stuffed with veggies served rolled up. Bright and modern in décor, it maintains traditional values in the taste department. Fluffy snow ice and homemade pumpkin flan for dessert. $12 ☆

The Elephant 58 E. 1st St. (1st & 2nd Aves.) (212) 505-7739 Thai with French accent. Mussels and superior salmon. Like the jungle but with a disco ball. Leopard print seats, tight tables and towering decibels. Best off eating at the bar where tender will help you navigate snakelike river of Asian beer. $25

Esperanto 145 Ave. C (9th St.) (212) 505-6559 Latin American. Solid new wave Latin (plantain-crusted goat cheese) on great corner. Warm-weather go-to and Alpha City fave. Menu has something for everyone...even whitey! Live music and great vibes; speaks the universal language. $25

Evviva 186 Ave. A (11th & 12th Sts.) (212) 674-6230 Italian. Stellar new date spot churns out powerful flavors. Featured ingredients change monthly, but the tasting menu hits all corners of the palate. Choice vinos from southern Italy. Look for sea urchin pasta (wow!), or the amazing fried gnocchi with sausage. +$30

Flor's Kitchen 149 1st Ave. (9th & 10th Sts.) (212) 387-8949 Venezuelan. Cute, cheap, tiny spot for arepas and other sudamericano treats. Latin food done authentically and right, best South American comfort in the city. Must get the cachapas con queso: corn pancakes with Venezuelan cheese. Always a wait, but almost always worth it. $16

Forbidden City 212 Ave. A (13th & 14th Sts.) (212) 598-0500 Asian. You cannot come here. Just kidding, you can, and when you do, get the Green Hornet. Lively oval bar makes fun in vast, low-slung blue-toned lounge. Tasty tapas and dim sum done with surprisingly limited amount of grease. Asian mix with Blade Runner twist. $20

Frank 88 2nd Ave. (5th & 6th Sts.) (212) 420-0202 Southern Italian. Delish dishes for few ducats make this one popular. Always crowded between 7-10pm, relaxes late night when it becomes a pretty cool wine bar. Divine garlic bread, rich gnocchi. Tender meatloaf and Moretti on tap! $23

Gnocco Caffe 337 E. 10th St. (Aves. A & B) (212) 677-1913 Italian. Flowery room. Back garden. Chefs right off the boat, deliver latest and greatest food from Modena. Namesake specialty, slew of carpacci, deep-fried lamb racks, young pork tenderloin. Velvety carbonara at brunch. $20

Haveli 100 2nd Ave. (5th & 6th Sts.) (212) 982-0533 Indian. One of the better Indians, just off the 6th St. strip. Potent mango 'n' brandy cocktails knock sox off. Gives curry row crowd the high hat. Attentive staff bends. Best dish is the chicken malai kebab. Lots of NYU kids with parents, Amato Opera attendees and Punjabi princesses. $22

Hearth 403 E. 12th St. (1st Ave) (646) 602-1300 Italian. Marco Canora's heart-warming cooking in cozy atmo. Snapper crudo and sardine apps, blue-foot chicken and zucchini raviolo mains, fried blueberry and peach ravioli for dessert. Chef's tasting menu is worth the $70. Diverse selection of after dinner teas. Avoid the back room. $35 ⋆

Hedeh 57 Great Jones St. (Bowery & Lafayette St.) (212) 473-8458 Japanese. Plain in décor but atmosphere is a flair-filled affair. The kind of sushi place one would like to drink a lotta beers at. Maybe it's the huge bar. Jovial staff wields serious precision with the knives. Upscale without being outrageous. $40 ⋆

I Coppi 432 E. 9th St. (Ave. A & 1st Ave.) (212) 254-2263 Italian with a Tuscan inflection. Great comfy little place, romantic and secluded back garden. More mature than Max or the other East Vil Italians. Get the boar tenderloin, or any one of the fresh, robust pastas. We also love the spaghetti and crisp brick-oven pizzas. $3

Il Bagatto 192 E. 2nd St. (Aves. A & B) (212) 228-0977 Italian. Crowded, X-Mas lights, rustic Tuscan feel. Innocenti ladies represent the big boot. Wild boar tenderloin, pear and gorgonzola pasta, minestrone and well-priced wine list all worth devouring. Wine tastings the first Monday of every month. $25

Jack's Luxury Oyster Bar 246 E. 5th St. (2nd & 3rd Aves.) (212) 673-0338 Another jewel from the couple behind Bako. Converted carriage house with zero elbow room. Fun with a mild white wine-induced roar. Lighten your wallet while letting loose on insane seafood prix-fixe. Focused (limited) raw bar superfresh daily. Deconstructed Rockafellas oh-so PoMo. +$40 **BlackBook**

Jeollado 116 E. 4th St. (1st & 2nd Aves.) (212) 260-7696 Japanese & Korean. Big, pink room with copious tables for late night cravings. Fairly large slabs come in multiples. Start with some sake or Sapporo, and definitely cop the namesake roll with salmon and avocado. Now has kooky karaoke back room that draws the random celeb. Neighborhood fave. $20

Jewel Bako 239 E. 5th St. (2nd & 3rd Aves.) (212) 979-1012 Japanese. Slick, bamboo-lined walls, stylish gem. Stunningly-fresh fish, perfectly sliced and diced. Nobu for those in-the-know. That fresh fatty tuna is flown in fresh from a Tokyo fish market: top that, Matsuhisa! Get the tasting menu (omokase) for orgiastic assault on senses. $40

Jewel Bako Robata 239 E. 5th St. (2nd and 3rd Aves.) (212) 979-1012. Jack and Grace Lamb continue their 5th St. empire with grill-oriented annex to their bustling sushi spot. Take a seat at the long bar and watch slabs of Kobe cooked to order. Some would call it a crime to put anything on such expensive meat, but you try passing up the wasabi butter. $45 ⋆

Jules Bistro 65 St. Mark's Pl. (1st & 2nd Aves.) (212) 477-5560 French Bistro. Yummy and cozy, on classic St. Mark's Place. Loyal fan base, loved by Gauls and others who appreciate the best paté in the land. Incredible filet mignon, go ahead and order that. Block perennial maintains cred of this fastly co-opted street. $27

Le Gamin 536 E. 5th St. (Aves. A & B) (212) 254-8409 French. There's a bunch of these and they're all good. When you see a Le Gamin, you cant go wrong. But this one's the chillest. Rustic nook. Out of the way, off to the side. Giant cappuccinos get you wired in the a.m. / p.m. tea time calms your nerves. Good magazines. Say hey to Eddie, the Mayor of 5th St., outside (he's the one with the pearls). $7

Le Souk 47 Ave. B (3rd & 4th Sts.) (212) 777-5454 Moroccan. In the summer this place is great. Garden in the back, a tent, hookahs, hotties, belly-dancing. All the makings of a good time. Winter you lose the garden but the food is still on point. Good option for tasty tagines if Max next door is booked. Huge after hours scene in the next door lounge temporarily on hold. $25

Lil' Frankie's 19 1st Ave. (1st & 2nd Aves.) (212) 420-4900 Italian. Outside, the chalkboard sign promises 12" of hot Italian goodness. Of course they are talking about the salami pizza. Frank's offspring is equally tasty and easier to cop a seat. Lil' Frankie's salad rocks as does multitude of stellar pizzas. Sit in the back room if you can. $20

Luca Lounge 220 Ave. B (13th & 14th Sts.) (212) 674-9400 Italian. Rustic bar in front, plush couches in the middle, nice garden out back for veggie lasagna and designer pizettes. Great olives, solid wine list and nice owners. More low-key and relaxing than it's Tribeca sister, hidden dining room on the side is a perfect date spot. $30

Mama's Food Shop 200 E. 3rd St. (Aves. A & B) (212) 777-4425 American. Don't lie, you know your own mama—fine woman though she may be—can't cook like this. Go hungry cause it stuffs you, but you might have to wait a while for a seat. Take-out across the way. Meatloaf, grits, fried chicken, fish, mashed potatoes Mmmm. $15

Mara's Homemade 338 E. 6th St. (1st & 2nd Ave.) (212) 598-1110 Cajun Comfort. Down-home goodness served with sweetness. Chicken fried steak, crawfish boils, meatloaf, mash. Some takes on Creole dishes not quite on par with Big Easy. Can be uneven, but when it's on it's on. Live Dixieland jazz on weekends. $30

Mermaid Inn 96 2nd Ave. (5th & 6th Sts.) (212) 674-5870 Seafood. Nautical-themed raw bar serving clams and oysters. Not exactly undiscovered, there's always a wait. If you don't want to, pull up a stool at the bar and beat the crowds piling in for the Red Cat owners' life aquatic. Skate wing. $35

Milon 93 1st Ave. (5th & 6th Sts.) (212) 228-4896 Indian. Blaring Bengali beats, subcontinental hip-hop. More hanging chili pepper lights than scientists thought possible. Really cheap food, spicy vindaloos, flaky samosas. Only drawback is that it's BYOB, but luckily for us, discounts on beer at the store below. $10

Miracle Grill 112 1st Ave. (6th & 7th Sts.) (212) 254-2353 Southwestern. Fantastic garden is the main attraction. Catfish tacos for brunch and then indulgent desserts. Get the pork chops adorned with orange-ancho chile recado. It's all about the garden here. Are those real New York birds chirping? How quaint. $30

Miss Williamsburg Porta Via 228 E. 10th St. (1st & 2nd Ave.) (212) 228-5355 Italian. Off-shoot of Miss Williamsburg Diner. BK import brings reputation of fierce lasagna made with rich béchamel. It's pretty damn good. The REAL secret ingredient? Love. We shit you not. BYOB and hopefully you like your neighbor's lap cuz guess where you're sitting. $20

Montien 90 3rd Ave. (12th St.) (212) 475-6814 Thai. Really popular with the NYU kids, who may be too young/naive to realize how good the food is. Spicy, just how we like it. Low-key atmo, vivid flavors: we like the Thai sausage and tam salad. Groups: get the talay. Fried banana for dessert. $20

The Mud Spot 307 W. 9th St. (1st & 2nd Aves.) (212) 228-9174 Café. Local success story sees little orange java truck that could gains stationary quarters and becomes the Gray Dog of the East Village. Breakfast burritos, vegan paninis and stunningly fresh joe. Belly bombing French toast at weekend brunch. A real cult following. $10 ★

Prune 54 E. 1st St. (1st & 2nd Aves.) (212) 677-6221 American Eclectic. Small, quaint, open, inviting, restaurant row vet. Gabrielle Hamilton's food is a little bit crazy, but she just might be onto something. Serves the best, liveliest brunch around, and always makes for interesting dinner, if you're lucky enough to snag a table (might try on a weeknight). At brunch get the pancake (singular!), and at night get the roasted pork. $45 **BlackBook**

Nesto Lann 251 E. 12th St. (1st & 2nd Aves.) (212) 375-8483 French Bistro. Sexy French waitresses, late nights, no longer the smoky enclave it was pre-ban. Ex-pats who miss Parisian smoking laws and dig their pints of Stella. Huge, steaming bowl of mussels in creamy white-wine broth is perfect on a chilly night. $20

Second Avenue Deli 156 2nd Ave. (10th St.) (212) 677-0606 Jewish Deli. Classic, kosher. Stacked sandwiches and possibly the best matzo balls in the city. Too bad Al Goldstein is no longer a greeter, but the aged staff still talks enough sass. They will push you to try the tongue, but don't bite. Corned beef and brisket on rye, pickle plates. $18

Secretes 513 E. 6th St. (Ave. A) (212) 228-2775 Fusion. Former Mercer Kitchen chef's small plates outpost. Experimental tapas draw inspiration from all corners of the globe and hit their mark for the most part though there are a few stumbles. Sautéed ostrich, seared duck, and "spaghetti" made from cucumbers. Portions are tiny, so if you want to leave satiated you gotta be ready to open the wallet. $35 ☆

SobaKoh 309 E. 5th St. (2nd Ave.) (212) 254-2244 Japanese. Dope new soba spot has oodles of noodles. Mostly Asian clientele slurps happily. Other small dishes include a tuna and avocado plate, albacore with spicy miso, grilled duck. But the focus here is the soba. Get the uni ikura cold soba. It's kinda pricey for what you get, though, and if you're shelling out the dough, you might just want to step it up to Hommura An. $40 ☆

The Sunburnt Cow 130 Ave. C (8th & 9th Sts.) (212) 529-0005 Australian. Bovine in need of Coppertone, stat! Faux-rustic, outdoorsy Outback feel. Grilled roo kababs left some poor mother with an empty pouch. Aussie burger has more fixins than Mason's got Dixon. Every bottle of down under vino available by the glass. $25

Supper 156 E. 2nd St. (Aves. A & B) (212) 477-7600 Northern Italian. Frank's, Lil Frankie's and then this place. Might just be the best of the bunch. You're safe with anything on the menu. Good patio, cool staff. Always a wait for killer pasta. A few doors down from Ginsberg's old apt. for you hip beatniks out there. $18

Teresa's 103 1st Ave. (6th & 7th Sts.) (212) 228-0604 Polish. Pierogis? Puhleeze! Half order of potato pancakes could feed a/the village. Kraut, keilbasa, kasha and Kishka- more Ks than a David Duke fundraiser. East Village standby known for its generous portions and sumptuous waitstaff. $15

26 Seats 168 Ave. B (10th & 11th Sts.) (212) 677-4787 French. Friendly staff tripping over you in really tight quarters as they bring you juicy rib-eyes and striped bass. Cozy, cool and delicious. Get the duck breast drizzled with cherry juice and mashed sweet potatoes. BYO chair and you can so mess with their heads. $26

Veselka 144 2nd Ave. (9th St.) (212) 228-9682 Ukrainian Diner. Open late, homey classic for bloc parties. Late-night coffee and Eastern Euro comfort food. Chix noodle soup is off the sickle. Get ice cream on that blueberry blintz, even tastier at 4am after the 9 beers you had down the block. Weirdos and the painfully normal all dig this one. Bright. $13

Xunta 174 1st Ave. (10th & 11th Sts.) (212) 614-0620 Spanish. Tapas with a little Galician flavor. Head downstairs and pull up a barrel. Homey and entertaining, with a mixed crowd and 51 tapas for 51 tastes. Functions as a bar just as well. Flamenco rings in the candle-lit air as Sebastian and Co. swill the sherry. $17

NIGHTLIFE East Village

Angel Share 8 Stuyvesant St. (9th St. & 3rd Ave.) (212) 777-5415 Intimate upstairs palace of bartending perfection. Does not accept large or loud groups. Pretty much like going to yoga, except balance is achieved in the lychee martinis and sumptuous snacks. Slightly precious, but one of the more elegant downtown spots to sip and chat.

Baraza 133 Ave. C (8th & 9th Sts.) (212) 529-0811 Hispanic causin' panic on Ave C. Packed most nights, latin beats, caipirinhas and sweat. Pick-up spot by the sheer proximity of the patrons, many of whom have a pickle in their pocket and are indeed happy to see you. One the East Village's best dance options.

Beauty Bar 231 E. 14th St. (btwn 2nd & 3rd Aves.) (212) 539-1389 Used to be a fairly low key drink spot, known for it's strong pours and ultra kitschy beauty salon bric-a-brac. With a renovation of the back room and some 80s-inclined DJs, it caught on with the Williamsburg types. Best dancing in the area.

Blue and Gold 79 E. 7th St. (1st & 2nd Aves.) (212) 473-8918 Famed dive for young toughs and barely legals. Beloved old 45 juke replaced with new model as have some of the decaying banquettes. Still a good call for beer drinking and pool shooting in a comfy, rec-room style hole in the wall.

B-Side 204 Ave. B (12th & 13th Sts.) (212) 475-4600 You liked the cassingle, but did you flip the tape? What? No one uses tapes anymore? Punk and indie rock crowd with a sheen. Slightly busted atmo. Be the wizard on the Who pinball machine or hustle suckas on the felt.

Cherry Tavern 441 E. 6th St. (1st Ave. & Ave. A) (212) 777-1448 Rolls DJ tequila & Tecate combo special. Dark, dank and cramped. Young alcoholics in training rub elbows and thighs with East Village models just beginning to bud. Eazy-E on juke tells your mama to get off of his tip. Can't she see he has no time to give her his dick? Probably a good thing considering how our fave Compton G went out.

Cock 29 2nd Ave. (1st & 2nd Sts.) No phone. The Cock is now in the Hole. Randy rooster moves back to its original space and legion of gay downtowners happily slums it up. Seedy, sweaty pick-up joint. Eye-watering curtain of smoke and trashy boy on boy bathroom antics. It's inevitability as an end-up makes it less of a guilty pleasure and more of a way of life.

d.b.a. 41 1st Ave. (2nd & 3rd Sts.) (212) 475-5097 Who knew there were so many bourbons in the world? Dive known for liquor selection & bathroom graffiti. Bartenders are straight up rude to all but the most hardcore regulars. One week shy of your 65th birthday? They're still gonna card you. Sign up for the summer booze cruise.

Decibel 240 E. 9th St. (2nd & 3rd Aves.) (212) 979-2733 Well-hidden underground sake lair. Ring buzzer and enter into den renowned for impressive list of rice wines and Japanese beers. Super soba. Cool interior. Best for parties of four so you can take over a booth rather than be stuck at the tiny table. Often a wait, but definitely worth it. **BlackBook**

East Fourth Street Bar 70-80 E. 4th St. (Bowery & 2nd Ave.) (212) 253-2237 Young theater crowd gathers to drink pints and play Buck Hunter II way too seriously. Classic bar food menu satisfies all cravings. Monday nights this place gets rowdy with aspiring Juliets, budding playwrights, and gnomelike techies.

Hanger Bar & Boutique 217 E. 3rd St. (Aves. B & C) (212) 228-1030 Dress shop, hat shop, drink stop. Cutesy boutique turns cocktail lounge after hours. It's daytime retail role limits the amount of outrageous behavior and/or drink spillage. Vibe is like kicking it with the employees after-hours. Check the rotating drink specials. ☆

Hi-Fi 169 Ave. A (10th & 11th Sts.) (212) 420-8392 Raucous addition to the hood. Big space, cool b'tenders, futuristic jukebox. Early-twenties crowd represents modern breed of East Villager rock kid: Yeah he's got the scummy T-shirt, but flesh is too rosy to have any kind of real vitamin deficiency.

Holiday Cocktail Lounge 75 St. Marks Pl. (1st & 2nd Aves.) (212) 777-9637 East Village institution. Not the kind of place to bring a date. Light-deprived dive with shockingly cheap imported beers and mixed drinks. Stefan, the octogenarian bartender, continues to defy all scientific explanation. Get him singing and out comes the Jäger bottle. Crazy cast of characters.

Joey's 186 Ave. B (11th & 12th Sts.) (212) 353-9090 A most excellent establishment. One giant family of hot young art whores, rhythm guitarists and supermodels. Deceptively trendy, or rather, where the trendy go for unpretentious chilling.

Unwind over board games in their back garden while checking out the latest in treated denim. **BlackBook**

Karma 51 1st Ave. (3rd & 4th Sts.) (212) 677-3160 Non-descript, save the redness. Yes, you really can smoke here. Yes, you really can smoke here. Yes, you really can smoke here. Yes, you really can smoke... here. Must have lots of pristine, expendable karma to bypass the mayor.

KGB 85 E. 4th St. (2nd Ave. & Bowery) (212) 505-3360 Secret literary plottings on second floor. Readings by Jerry Stahl, Barry Gifford, Jonathan Letham and the like. Go early and grab seat at the bar. Nice to see the commie bastards share our love for the King of Beers.

Korova Milk Bar 200 Ave. A (12th & 13th Sts.) (212) 254-8838 Rock n' roll nights, spacious. It would be cooler if you could drink from the plastic tits like in the movie, but maybe we're just dreamers. Drink a Lolita instead: 15-year-old scotch and a crushed cherry.

Lakeside Lounge 162 Ave. B (10th & 11th Sts.) (212) 529-8463 Well-worn bar, unpolished, gruff. Younger blue-eyed-soul crowd, excellent blues-driven jukebox. Makes for long nights of drinking Wild Turkey straight up and listening to newest 2-piece garage band.

Lit 93 2nd Ave. (5th & 6th Sts.) (212) 777-7987 Erik Foss's bar continues as prime rock destination du jour. Cool kids. Tight squeeze due to popularity. Claustrophobia or coziness downstairs, depending on your taste. Lots of nooks for hookin' up and private bathrooms for whatever it is that goes on in there. **BlackBook**

Louis 649 E. 9th St. (Aves. B & C) (212) 673-1190 Great, super mellow, little place to have a few drinks, listen to some jazz. Named for Mr. Armstrong. Most intellectual bar in the vicinity. Custom woodwork by the owner. Best when live piano player rolls jelly like Morton.

Lounge 83 1st Ave. (5th St.) (212) 388-0059 Basement bar of Three of Cups, never changes except of thick curtain of smoke now vanished (for the most part). Love this place. Candles and blacklights, badass bartenders, decrepit couches, punk attitude, cheap PBRs from the tub.

Lucky Cheng's 24 1st Ave. (1st & 2nd Sts.) (212) 473-0516 Holy shit! Definitely makes for a weird/memorable night out. This is the place to hear a drag queen sing "Supercalifragilisticexpialidocious" as "Supercalifragilistic-double-headed-dildo." Bring the in-laws. Trannies, drags, girls and boys who like trannies..

Manitoba's 99 Ave. B (6th & 7th Sts.) (212) 982-2511 Make a stop at Handsome Dick Manitoba's saloon. Not much for looks, but for badass crowd, cans of PBR and that good punk rawk it's perfect for a night of destruction, guaranteed. East Village institution.

McSorley's 15 E. 7th St. (2nd & 3rd Aves.) (212) 473-9148 Ancient tavern. House beer comes in light or dark, two mugs at a time. Cool because it's classic, not because of the crowd. Tanked fratboys in several exciting varieties of white hat. Girls, this place wouldn't even let you in well into the 1970s.

Mona's 224 Ave. B. (13th & 14th Sts.) (212) 353-3780 Solid, narrow no-nonsense little local bar with great Guinness and a pool table in back. Live Irish music one night, punk on the juke the next. Crowd runs from the trendy girls in designer jeans to older fellas nursing Jameson's at the bar.

Niagara 112 Ave. A (7th St.) (212) 420-9517 Always busy, decent crowd. Mod Squad certain nights. Young Hollywood types sometimes drop by when in town so they can tell their plastic friends in LA about hanging out in the gritty, hip East Village. Crowd is definitely looking to flirt.

Nublu 62 Ave. C (4th & 5th Sts.) Bar/lounge and record label all in one from multi-tasking owner Ilhan Ershahin. Clever, mellow space and lush back garden are setting for chill weeknight parties, with an emphasis on electronic and world music. Brazilian Girls got their start here.

Nuyorican Poets Café 236 E. 3rd St. (Aves. B & C) (212) 505-8183 Legendary poetry venue with a worldwide influence on spoken word over the past 25 years—Miguel Piñero, Danny Hoch, Carl Hancock Rux. Friday night slam gets packed so show up early.

Porch Bar & Café 115 Ave. C (7th & 8th Sts.) (212) 982-4034 Cool spot. If you can't hunt with the big dogs, get back on the porch. The one lit with the torches. The ones lit like your cigarette. The one you're allowed to smoke there. Front room is comfy, clean and certainly cool. Request recessed booth inside during winter for 8 person orgy.

Pyramid Club 101 Ave. A (6th & 7th Sts.) (212) 228-4888 Club has been on the block for over 15 years. Perennial drum n' bass night Konkrete Jungle, open-mic poetry Wednesdays. Weekends are mixed gay/ straight with an additional college student thrown in. Still has the flavor of old-school Ave. A, thank God.

Rue B 188 Ave. B (11th & 12th Sts.) (212) 358-1700 Gem of a jazz bar. Sophisticated and intimate. A warm contrast to rest of the bars on Ave. B, a little more mature. Fresh sandwiches, Belgian beers and live jazz with no cover. Obviously Fri/Sat can get nuts, but mostly for chilling.

St Dymphna's 118 St. Mark's Pl. (1st Ave. & Ave. A) (212) 254-6636 Irish pub staffed by hot Portuguese girls. Crowd is mix of young artists, models and creative types from the neighborhood kicking it low-key. Nice outdoor space, solid Irish breakfasts and burgers.

Sutra 16 First Ave. (1st Ave.) (212) 677-9477 Former home of Bar XVI, now a sexy and cozy scene with South Asian accents. Red velvet, candles, and sloping stone bar. Sometimes hosts the occasional live music or performance act. Otherwise it's DJs playing fairly generic beats. Padded back billiard room is ideal for taking over with a small party. ☆

Zum Schneider 107 Ave. C (7th St.) (212) 598-1098 German. New-school Teutonic. High ceilings, energetic, young. Works better as a bar, but the schnitzel, sausages, kraut and others are fantastic drinking foods. Some of the best beers on tap for quality stein hoists at one of the large picnic tables.

"New York is a city of geometric heights, a petrified desert of grids and lattices,

an inferno of greenish abstraction under a flat sky, a real Metropolis

from which man is absent by his very accumulation." —Roland Barthes

GREENWICH VILLAGE

(map p. 197)

The times they have a changed. **The heart and soul of American bohemia has metastasized into a gold coast of Manhattan real estate**. NYU continues to buy and build. The long, gray ponytails get slowly replaced by long, blonde ones that came to the Big Apple with "Sex & the City" dreams. If the Village could stand up to Robert Moses, it will surely stand up to anything. Recent plans to fence in the beloved, derelict melting pot that is **Washington Square** were scrapped thanks to a noisy chorus of "no!" by residents. Loaded with record shops, chess shops, excellent cafés like the **Dante** and the **Reggio**, and more folk-y open mics than one would ever want to visit in a lifetime, the hood carries the torch of artsy nonconformity. To eat here is to sample some of New York's best Italian (**Babbo**), Japanese (**Tomoe**), and Middle Eastern (**Mamoun's**) cuisine. Hot night clubs like **Butter** and **Joe's Pub** bring the noise nightly. Catch us breaking bottles at **Black & White** at wee hours on weeknights.

RESTAURANTS Greenwich Village

Arturo's 106 W. Houston St. (Thompson St.) (212) 677-3820 Pizzeria. Unbelievable, coal-fired pies with tangy sauce and blackened crust. One of the city's top purveyors of pizza. No slices, but makes great takeout. Jazz trios and casual, knickknack-laden décor. Also serves reputable pastas and salads, but how can one pass up pepperoni this good? -$25

BB 120 W. 3rd St. (6th Ave. & MacDougal St.) (212) 473-7500 Cheesesteaks. There's only one thing on the menu, but it's pretty damn good: an upscale cheesesteak, dressed with grilled onions and a snappy tomato-based relish. Purists may fume at lack of authenticity (no Whiz, no hoagie roll), but are likely to shut their traps at first bite. $5

B Bar & Grill 40 E. 4th St. (Bowery & Lafayette St.) (212) 475-2220 American. The hottest spot in town in the mid-90s, now a beloved standby. Former filling station transformed by Eric Goode into airy, multi-roomed hangout with nice outdoor garden. Good burgers, pizzas, etc. Best for low-key weekend afternoon cocktailing. $32

Babbo 110 Waverly Pl. (6th Ave. & MacDougal St.) (212) 777-0303 Italian. Mario Batali's pinnacle of Italian dining. Star-studded non-stuffy room. Mint "love letters," beef cheek ravioli, grilled branzino, and other meticulously prepared dishes. Killer Italian wines. Tuscan doughnuts for dessert. And it all tastes that much better when you're sandwiched between a former mayor and Gwenyth Paltrow. $50

Bar Pitti 268 6th Ave. (Houston & Bleecker St.) (212) 982-3300 Northern Italian. This place rules! Fresh food and low-key glam with chalkboard of nightly specials scrawled in Italiano. Quintessential sidewalk patio is quite the scene. Veal Milanese and pasta fagioli. Think vino and sunglasses, but remember your cash cuz they don't take cards. +$28 **BlackBook**

Blue Hill 75 Washington Pl. (6th Ave. & MacDougal St.) (212) 539-1776 American. Located in old speakeasy. Hear the foodies battle cry as they take the hill. Seasonal produce from the Hudson Valley. Foie gras with rhubarb and black pepper, poached duck and roast pork among many spectacular achievements. Unparalleled commitment to freshness and ingenuity in a wonderfully unpretentious atmo. Find your thrill. $50

Bond St. 6 Bond St. (Broadway & Lafayette St.) (212) 777-2500 Japanese. Former Nobu London chef jumped ship to claim her Iron Chef belt. Decadent and creative takes on raw fish. Look for the kobe beef carpaccio and blue crab cocktail. Amazing flavors abound. Sake menu reads like a subtle, expensive epic. Svelte, black-clad crowd. $60 **BlackBook**

Caffé Dante 79 MacDougal St. (Bleecker & Houston Sts.) (212) 982-5275 Café. Rules the block with Reggio, the other original gangsta of MacDougal. Aged photos of Firenze on the walls provide picturesque espresso. The iron fist of the smoking ban hits one the hardest in places like this. The cannoli and sorbetto are must-haves. -$10

Café Reggio 119 MacDougal St. (Bleecker & W. 3rd St.) (212)475-9557 Italian Café. Everything you could want in an authentic Village coffee house. As seen in Godfather II. Serves possibly the greatest cappuccino known to man, cranks up the opera and still attracts a loyal local following despite its touristy location. Cheap food menu befits tortoise-vs-hare mentality of servers. $8

Cru 24 5th Ave. (9th St.) (212) 529-1700 Creative American. Shea Gallante is the chef, and he's our hero. Bright and beautiful cuisine covers our fair land from sea to shining sea: Columbia river sturgeon, Long Island striped bass, Maine soft shell lobster. Truly intimidating 65,000 item wine list: if you've got an extra 13K, we recommend the 1899 Lafite Rothschild. +$55

Danal 90 E. 10th St. (3rd & 4th Aves.) (212) 982-6930 American & Mediterranean. Inspired country food, boffest brunch. How lovely in it's rusticity. Superior french toast avec sides like apple sausage assisting egg. Steamed cockles with almond broth and loaded salads appear on revolving menu. Weekends best advise to bring your waiting shoes. A reasonably priced trip into total Cuteland. $33

Da Silvano 260 6th Ave. (Bleecker & Houston Sts.) (212) 982-2343 Italian. Media-whore and celeb-spotters wet dream. The famous and infamous immersed in the good life. Sidewalk tables allow great view of passerby, but it's best to keep focus on other tables. Admire Anna Wintour's willpower, but dig heartily into the osso bucco. Daily specials served with a side of dish. $45

Five Points 31 Great Jones St. (Bowery & Lafayette St.) (212) 253-5700 American. Totally nice place that draws a mix of downtown hip creatives and uptown yuppies, all happily slurping oysters. It's all about happy hour, though, where said oysters are only a buck each (!), plus tasty cocktails. Great burger and onion rings, too. $25

Gotham Bar & Grill 12 E. 12th St. (5th Ave. & University Pl.) (212) 620-4020 American. Alfred, hand me my bat-fork! Chef Portale's destination is still a draw after more than 10 years. Knowledgeable, friendly servers ensure it all goes smoothly. Flock of town cars out front. Miso cod, sweet shrimp risotto, roast squab, succulent sides. $60

Gray's Papaya 402 6th Ave. (8th St.) (212) 260-3532 Hot Dogs. Two charred, zippy franks and a fruit drink for two bills and change. Even street vendors can't low-ball these guys. Get papaya drink, cuz enzymes ease digestion. Décor? Well, is the tableau of pro-environment stickers, panhandlers, and drunk Jersey girls wolfing down hot dogs under a harsh lighting scheme not intense enough for you? -$3

Great Jones Café 54 Great Jones St. (Bowery & Lafayette St.) (212) 674-9304 American & Cajun. Can't miss bright orange facade. Delivers shit-kickin' good times. A rare juke joint in the concrete jungle. Hollerin' blues and diabolical vodka lemon-ades. Legit gumbo and best blackened catfish. Sucks you in for hours. Elvis looks on through the window. $22

Il Buco 47 Bond St. (Bowery & Lafayette St.) (212) 533-1932 Italian. So romantic your date may end up in your lap. Antiques Roadshow meets secrets of the Old Country. Candles and kerosene, upscale olive oils, ever-changing menu of delec-tables. Pretty much perfect in every way. If it's a party for one, you could do much worse than at the bar with apps and a fierce red. $45

Il Cantinori 32 E. 10th St. (University & Broadway) (212) 673-6044 Italian. One of downtown's finest restaurants. Veal, pounded chicken, smoked salmon carpac-cio, spinach gnocci among other mouthwatering pastas. Very dimly-lit; open-faced serenity on lovely stretch of 10th St. Sit in the elevated patio and flaunt your good fortune while the envious, stoned NYU kids saunter past on the way to the dining hall. $55

Indochine 430 Lafayette St. (Astor Pl. & E. 4th St.) (212) 505-5111 Vietnamese & French. Colonial fusion set in a tropical and warm interior. One of the original too-cool-for-school spots on the block is still cool minus some pretension. Gigantic coconut prawns, crispy red snapper, sticky rice and more served by smokin' hot staff. $40

Kati Roll Company 99 MacDougal (Bleecker & West 3rd Sts.) (212) 420-6517 Indian. Sublime Indian street food. Chicken tikka wrapped in paratha (think taco with subcontinental spices). Ideal for drunken pit stop, though onions and spices may impair future kissing prospects. Hit in the morning when the unda rolls with egg and beef vanquish all hangovers. $8 ☆

Knickerbocker Bar & Grill 33 University Pl. (9th St.) (212) 228-8490 Steakhouse. Village classic for ginormous T-bones, strips, and filets. Revamped menu has been updated for the times: penne with kobe beef Bolognese, ahi tartare with Granny Smith apples. Room oozes character, especially when the excellent live jazz kicks in. Impressive wine and liquor list. $45

Lupa 170 Thompson St. (W. Houston & Bleecker Sts.) (212) 982-5089 Italian. Inviting, warm, energetic and generally packed. Mario Batali eats at prices below Babbo. Hard to say what's best since it all rocks. Ricotta gnocchi, proscuito plates, crispy raisin duck, wood-oven red peppers. Reservations still essential, unless you hit it late. $30

Mamoun's Falafel 119 MacDougal St. (3rd St. & Minetta Ln.) (212) 674-8685 Falafel. Though located basically in a walk-in closet on a block that is teeming with food options, Mamoun's resides in a class by itself. The $2 falafels have saved more NYU kids than suicide prevention pamphlets. The freshly carved shwarma cannot be bested. $5

Minetta Tavern 113 MacDougal St. (Minetta Ln.) (212) 475-3850 Italian. It was the school before the old school. Historic Village eatery is an oasis of pleasantry on a block full of hooligans. Hearty food, stiff drinks and charismatic owner Taka's superb command of the ship. Check out the mural of the neighborhood's past in the back. Don't skip the rabe. $35

Otto 1 5th Ave. (8th St.) (212) 995-9559 Italian. The least expensive, but no less shining jewel in Batali's Village trifecta. Fresh, delectable pizzas and anitpasti. Prosciuto, pancetta, octopus, calamari. Tricolore salad. Warm-hued, energetic dining area is good for groups. Small bar scene gets going. We give most propers to the olive oil gelato with sea salt. $35

Strip House 13 E. 12th St. (5th Ave. & University Pl.) (212) 328-0000 Steakhouse. Black and white framed photographs on the walls, otherwise very red. Steaks are outrageously good. and the scene has slightly more flair than Gotham across the way. Really stylish. This place and Dylan Prime make us see the char-broiled light. $60

Tomoe Sushi 172 Thompson St. (Bleecker & Houston Sts.) (212) 777-9346 Japanese. Line out front rivals Space Mountain as folk of all types jockey for entry to raw fish paradise. Way cheaper than a night at Nobu, some could say an equal experience food-wise. Décor is fairly non-existent. Best spider rolls, money toro. $30

GREENWICH Greenwich Village

Bar 13 35 E. 13th St. (Broadway & University Pl.) (212) 979-6677 Spacious cool upstairs spot, tucked away. Can be rollicking for the area, heavy on student bodies, so make sure you have ID to get signed in to the dorms later on with your new under-age buddies. Mud Squad still takes over Sunday nights for long-running Shout.

Black & White 86 E. 10th St. (3rd & 4th Ave.) (212) 253-0246 Restaurant becomes cramped, sexy, sweaty hotspot after ten. Neutral meeting ground for local and tour-ing rockers. See Kings of Leon kick it with the Strokes' manager over whiskey shots. Tattooed groupies scout for the next Interpol. Long bathroom lines. **BlackBook**

Bowlmor Lanes 110 University Pl. (12th & 13th Sts.) (212) 255-8188 The Classic for pin-striking, one of only three in Manhattan, definitely the coolest. Loud beats, trippy glow-in-the-dark night, lots of suds and the pleasure of seeing your urban companions morph into Roseanne extras and your Midwestern pals release their inner Lebowski.

Butter 415 Lafayette St. (Astor Pl. & E. 4th St.) (212) 253-2828 International. Young Hollywood flocks to Richie Akiva's wood-covered homage to deforestation. Mondays are strictly for the créme de la trend. Models, promoters and assorted trustafarians try to secure their foothold on the scene. Multiple Olsen sightings. **BlackBook**

Cedar Tavern 82 University Pl. (11th & 12th Sts.) (212) 929-9089 Classic. Seen the movie Pollock? Then you know how homeboy overdid it with the funny juice at this gorgeous 145-year mahogany bar. Crowd doesn't come as cool as old ghost Kerouac, but wooden booths in back and quiet upstairs make for serious, scene-free drinking.Good burgers, too.

Dove Parlor 228 Thompson St. (Bleecker & W. 3rd Sts.) (212) 254-1435 Classy, Big Easy-style parlor with red velvet wallpaper, fireplace and ceiling mold. Sidecars, Negronis and other classics co-exist with modern drinks made with soy milk. All are served with a smile and on doilies. Cool regulars and a sophisticated and sexy alternative to the usual blotto Bleecker hijinx. ★

Joe's Pub 425 Lafayette St. (Astor Pl. & E. 4th St.) (212) 539-8770 Speakeasy still magnificent for fan-based artists you either love or don't know. Pricey drinks. Goldfish at the bar. World music, cabaret acts, and soul legends you'll never get a chance to see in so intimate a venue. Late night always a funk-hip-hop-Caribbean dance party.

Sullivan Room 218 Sullivan St. (Bleecker & W. 3rd Sts.) (212) 505-1703 DJ-driven dance room. Technofreaks and baseheads descend on the late-late shift to bounce it and shake it in cramped basement quarters. Gets big names like Ritchie Hawtin. Hard to find as it is, so don't go early.

Table 50 643 Broadway (Bleecker St.) (212) 253-2160 Subterranean swank, brick archways, low lights, overall a pretty hot scene. Catch Q-Tip spinning his own hits as dance floor gets abstract with nice mix of white and black. Bar pick-ups can be whisked away to canoodle dens off to the side.

V Bar 225 Sullivan St. (Bleecker & W. 3rd Sts.) (212) 253-5740 Café a and wine bar, stocked with NYU grad kids, chess, and a little bit of a superiority complex: "Let the plebes have their 'mixed drinks,' we prefer the tang of crisp whites by the glass." Though khakis and horn-rims may be better than khakis and ball cap. ★

Von 3 Bleecker St. (Bowery and Elizabeth St.) (212) 473-3039 Former wine bar, now trades in hard liquor. Cozy and candlelit with lots of wood and brick. The once laid-back weekends have become a bit meat market-y with hoards of singles vying for the few coveted tables. Crowd is generally pretty cool, but the secret is out.

"An' after a rockin' reelin' rollin' ride I landed up on the downtown side of Greenwich Village."

—Bob Dylan

WEST VILLAGE *(map p. 196)*

With its beautiful, leafy blocks, quaint brick row houses and a meandering layout that confuses even permanent residents, the West Village has retained the charm of old Europe, **and spawned enough bistros to please even the most discerning Francophile**. By far the most tranquil spot for a romantic walk, adding to the ageless atmosphere is the neighborhood's illustrious literary and bohemian history. According to some, the West Village's largest population is its ghost population, with **famous figures like Aaron Burr, John Adams and Thomas Paine haunting hallowed halls**. These days, the cobblestone streets have seen the onslaught of designer boutiques, especially along Bleecker St., where Marc Jacobs, Lulu Guinness and Ralph Lauren twinkle ominously amongst the Federal style townhouses. But the W. Vill has managed to conserve a good deal of its glory. Head to 200 year-old **Chumley's**, a former speakeasy at 86 Bedford, famous for coining the term "86 it"; it still gets the sawdust floor churning every night. Or pop into the dilapadated **Corner Bistro** for one of NYC's best burgers. Though we lament the loss of Ma & Pop joints of yore, we welcome gastronomic virtuosos like **Wallse**, **Mas** and **Perry St.**: the latest addition to Jean Georges' empire. This hood is the ultimate destination for a serious foodie experience. The W. Vill isn't all so imposing, though, party people kick off their heels at **Little Branch**, rip off their bras at **Tortilla Flats** and see into the future at **Employee's Only**.

RESTAURANTS West Village

A Salt & Battery 112 Greenwich Ave. (12th & 13th Sts.) (212) 691-2713 Fish n' Chips. Looks like a no-frills Dover seaside fast food joint, staffed with lovely ex-pats. Perfect fish n' chips wrapped in London newspaper spotted with grease. Pop a pepcid then order a chip buttie, basically bread, fries and butter. Also serves Britney Spears. Brilliant, innit? $15

A.O.C. 314 Bleecker St. (Grove St.) (212) 675-9463 French. Escape boisterous Bleecker St. at this sweet corner spot with cozy bistro looks. One of the cutest gardens in the W.V., perfect for an intimate Sunday brunch. Dinner rocks rustic French fare like Grandma's stew, steak frites, thrown back with a delicious Beaujolais from the extensive wine list. $30

A.O.C. Bedford 14 Bedford St. (Downing & Houston Sts.) (212) 414-4764 Mediterranean. Star in your own gothic tale. Morose, mysterious candlelit place with deep, luxurious banquettes and antique touches. Ideal late night date spot in the dead of winter. We love the crispy duck with vanilla potato puree. Bring your own candelabra. $30

Agave 140 Seventh Ave. (10th & Charles Sts.) (212) 989-2100 Southwestern. Get tanked on thirty-five kinds of tequila, wander into the mountains to hallucinate yourself eating lobster and mango quesadillas. Mahi Mahi tacos swim past your eyes in a colorful dining room of adobe walls, mahogany floors and trellised ceilings, reminiscent of your Taos ski lodge. $30

Aki 181 W. 4th St. (6th & 7th Aves.) (212) 989-5440 Japanese. Tucked inside a quaint townhouse, creative Japanese with flair. Minimal digs with exposed brick walls; the highlight here is the food. The name implies autumn, but seasonal menu takes on a unique Jamaican bent: try the Banana Boat roll or the Jamaica roll with Jerk Chicken. $20

Alfama 551 Hudson St. (Perry St.) (212) 645-2500 Portuguese. Whitewashed front gives way to a mellow interior, accented with photographic panels depicting scenes of Alfama, Lisbon's historic port neighborhood. Drink your weight in Vinho Verde and try chorizo stuffed squid and fragrant seafood stew, served by the barefoot girl next door. Wednesdays have live fado jams. +$30

Annisa 13 Barrow St. (W. 4th St. & 7th Ave. So.) (212) 741-6699 Pan Asian. Innovative cuisine on a quaint, old-fashioned block. Cozy and elegant with creamy walls and flickering candles. Chef A. Lo is the J. Lo of haute cuisine, an ambitious seasonal menu with awesome rack of lamb and succulent striped bass. Share the chocolate fondue for dessert. $50

August 359 Bleecker St. (Charles & W. 10th St.) (212) 929-4774 Eclectic European. Replenish after a long, hard day of shopping on Bleecker and work up an appetite waiting ages for a table. Locals love this claustrophobic, cave-like spot on the main drag. The skate with brown butter is utter perfection. Hold hands in the romantic garden and sigh. +$30

Bivio 637 Hudson Street (Horatio St.) (212) 206-0601 Italian. Brother of Bottino lures the Gagosian crowd with similarly stylish digs, Italian eats. Reliably obnoxious staff serves fabulous food to beautiful people who wait eons to be seated. Candles to illuminate the Pappardelle with lobster, a fave amongst regulars. $45

Blue Ribbon Bakery 33 Downing St. (Bedford St.) (212) 337-0404 American. Baskets of homemade bread are beautiful and bountiful here. Oh sweet relief! Simple wooden interior with mirrored walls to watch yourself cheating on your diet with foie gras, escargots and mix n' match cheese platters. Deserving of the accolades, this place rocks our world. +$40

Café Loup 105 W. 13th St. (6th & 7th Aves.) (212) 255-4746 French. Understated interior for wooing sophisticates. Effortless charm attracts literati and thank god, very few glitterati. Meticulous menu, presentation, service. The tuna carpaccio is like butter but nothing's better than the burger, saddled with roquefort. Romance, carnivore-style. $30

Café Topsy 575 Hudson St. (W. 11th & Bank Sts.) (646) 638-2900 British. Take a butch's over here: stodgy food for podgy dudes in a simple wooden way. Makes the best out of the universally acknowledged worst cuisine. We dare you to try the Topsy Coddler, made of bacon, sausage, potatoes and sauerkraut. Knock it back with a warm pint. $20

Casa 72 Bedford St. (Commerce St.) (212) 366-9410 Brazilian. Cozy white wood interior with eclectic chandeliers. A wall of windows reflects glowing candles and your amazed face as you dine on some of the best melhor feijoada in the city. Carioca represents something more than churrascaria, as evidenced by the attractive Brazilian sipping delicious caipirinhas. Worth the wait. $25

Chez Michallet 90 Bedford St. (Barrow St.) (212) 242-8309 French. Charm your date at the cutest corner spot on the sweetest block in the tres romantique Ouest Village. Ooh la la, the passersby stare enviously at your delectable pork loin or tender monkfish. The well-worn tables and peeling wallpaper hearken back to the French country vacation you never took. $40

Chick Inn 420 Hudson St. (Leroy St.) (212) 675-0810 American. Country inspired wooden space with rooster motif, sans the squeaky screen door. Pulled chicken with tangy BBQ sauce and meatloaf that certainly ain't your mama's, it's actually edible. Sidle up to the soda counter and order an egg cream for the road. Y'all come back now, ya hear? $20

Chocolate Bar 48 8th Ave. (Horatio & Jane Sts.) (212) 366-1541 Dessert. Baby blue façade, green tiled mod interior: the backdrop to your choc-orgasm. Find your sweet spot with four types of liquid chocolate shots. Torres truffles and treats like the PB&C: peanut butter and caramel bar. Indulge in a Punk Rock Box and help save CBGB's! $10

Cornelia Street Café 29 Cornelia St. (Bleecker & W. 4th Sts.) (212) 989-9319 American. Historic downstairs hosts histrionic poetry readings and a Science series that draws more Nobel laureates than you can shake a particle at. Upstairs is a quaint and brick with creative café fare. We love the sesame salmon and the juicy burger. Intelligent eating. +$30

Corner Bistro 331 W. 4th St. (Jane St.) (212) 242-9502 Very American. The grease spot. Ancient, crooked bar manned by ancient crooked bartender. Wildly popular amongst preppies, good luck getting through the door after 5pm. Famous for the incomparable Bistro Burger, one of NYC's carnivorous wonders. $2 McSorley's to wash it down. $7

Deborah 43 Carmine St. (Bleecker & Bedford Sts.) (212) 242-2606 American. Not in the sushi mood? Two words: Cheese Fries. Modern American comfort food defined, in an appropriately homey setting. Narrow, minimal space with close tables for sharing the cutest mini meatloaf or the dangerously good mac n' cheese. Debbie does delicious. +$25

Diablo Royale 189 W. 10th St. (Bleecker & W. 4th Sts.) (212) 620-0223 Mexican. Chanterelle's Keith runs for the border, brings us satanic mex served by a crew in 666 t-shirts. Festive interior for wild romps in margaritaville- flavors like blood orange. It's all about the tacos here- try carnitas or tilapia. Add some amazing guac and you're good to go. $25 ☆

Do Hwa 55 Carmine St. (Bedford St. & 7th Ave. So.) (212) 414-1224 Korean. Dark, atmospheric Zen-inspired space with slick black wood and big white screens. Tarantino-invested, so bring your own skull-crushing flail. Do request one of the DIY BBQ tables for a laborious, but rewarding experience. Delicious kimchee and glass noodles for vegetarian wimps. $25

Extra Virgin 259 W. 4th St. (Perry & Charles Sts.) (212) 691-9359 Mediterranean. Moody, dark brick space with smoky mirrors. Claustrophobic made cozy by the cute factor of the diners. Try the five-onion soup and blow your date away, literally. Nightly specials for two, we love the Branzino, infused with the subtle extra virgin flava. Long wait. +$30

Fish 280 Bleecker St. (Jones St.) (212) 727-2879 Seafood. Nautical-themed spot, doubles as a retail market. Taylor owns the local fishing company as well, giving him top billing for the some of freshest sea-dwellers in NYC. Sea bass, tuna prepared in a refreshingly straightforward manner, robust and delicious. Raw bar to boot. Note the happy smiles exiting the establishment. $30

Flaco's Taco & Tequila Co. 470 Sixth Ave. (11th & 12th Sts.) (212) 243-0228 Mexican. Small spot it's bright, blurry and boisterous. Satisfy your grease fix with tacos heaped with awesome guac and crispy flautas. Like Tijuana, though you might actually remember it tomorrow. 50 tequilas available if you need to address that particular jones. $15

Galanga 149 West 4th Street (6th Ave.) (212) 228-4267 Thai one on. Small, modern, cozy, with authentic, flavorful Thai. Mom can teach you a thing or two, her green curry packs a punch, while the crispy duck salad is a delicate delight. Already has a devoted following, expect a wait. $25

Gonzo 140 W. 13th St. (Sixth & Seventh Aves.) (212) 645-4606 Italian. What is better than Muppets in Space, you ask? Out-of-this-world Northern Italian. Osso Buco melts in your mouth. Grilled pizzas send us into orbit. Upscale crowd with sophisticated palates. Check the ornate painting ceiling in noisy dining room packed with loyal devotees of chef Vincent Scotto. $30

Good 89 Greenwich Ave. (W. 12th & Bank Sts.) (212) 691-8080 American. Creative. Great, actually. Simple décor with creative comfort food like pulled pork with sage grits or molasses tuna. Brunch draws a serious crowd, with kick ass baked goods and strange egg concoctions. Chef Steven Picker hand rolls your orange sour cream doughnuts, so bow to your master. $25

Gusto Ristorante e Bar Americano 60 Greenwich Ave. (Perry St.) (212) 924-8000 Italian. Where Sophia Loren would probably sip her wine. Elegant interior, warmly lit with retro-Italian feel, already has a devoted fan base. Chef Jodi Williams destroys the competition with tender homemade pastas, succulent seared scallops, and one seriously bad-ass baccalau. Order a Campari cocktail while you wait endlessly for your table. $35 ☆

Home 20 Cornelia St. (Bleecker & W. 4th Sts.) (212) 243-9579 American. Understated wood space and cute garden. Locals love the comforting cornmeal-crusted fried oysters, blue cheese fondue with apples for dipping. Home plate specials like fried chicken, turkey meatloaf. Make sure to get a side of onion rings, these guys are proud of their homemade ketchup. $28

Hue 91 Charles St. (Bleecker St.) (212) 691-4170 Vietnamese. Entrancing spot glows with atmospheric waterfalls and colorful recessed lighting. A luscious chocolate wood bar to savor crazy cocktails. Modern Vietnamese to please your palate. Pucker up for the ginger-kissed cod. Chao tom to die for. Downstairs, lounge on swanky beds. $35

'ino 21 Bedford St. (Houston & Downing Sts.) (212) 989-5769 Italian. Sister to the LES' 'inoteca. Quaint and crafty little spot seats 25, so get there early. Exposed brick, buttery walls are a comfy backdrop for Italian market dining. Impeccable antipasti, endless bruscetta choices and an incredible paninis like artichoke, fennel & fontina. $15

Inside 9 Jones St. (Bleecker & W. 4th Sts.) (212) 229-9999 American. Feel like a bowling ball approaching its lane as you peer down the super long and shiny space. Relaxing atmo to enjoy new American dishes like buckwheat fried oysters or baby lamb chops. Super inventive bar menu with unexpectedly good nibbles. $25

Jefferson 121 W. 10th St. (6th & Greenwich Aves.) (212) 255-3333 Asian. Sleek, minimal décor with a hip clientele. White oak floors and recessed light boxes, pan-asian/fusion fare infused with inventive flavors. Order the grilled toro with foie gras as a prelude to the awesome red snapper with caramelized persimmon. +$40

John's Pizza 278 Bleecker St. (6th & 7th Aves.) (212) 243-1680 Pizza. There is a long line for a reason, buddy. This pizza is a top contender for the best in the city- and it ain't hype. Thin crispy crusts baked to perfection in a wood-burning oven, old-fashioned booths where we huddle like wolves over the perfect pie. $15

Le Gigot 18 Cornelia St. (Bleecker & W. 4th Sts.) (212) 627-3737 French. On the sweetest block, Francophiles converge and sit shoulder to shoulder in this tiny spot. Understated, romantic décor gets high marks for wooing. Namesake gigot d'agneau aux flageolets is awesome, as is steak frites and cornish game hen. $30

Little Havana 30 Cornelia St (Bleecker & W. 4th Sts.) (212) 255-2212 Cuban. Bring your little chiquita to this diminutive Cuban place. For what it lacks in décor, it makes up for with flavor. The spicy chorizo kicks ass and the salmon with plantains is unbelievable. Officially our favorite Cubano sandwich. $20

Magnolia Bakery 401 Bleecker (W. 11th St.) (212) 462-2570 Bakery. Much beloved corner bakery is a Betty Crocker dream world with sunshine walls you hard-ly notice as you lunge for those addictive cupcakes with green icing. We've seen actual fights over the last slice of German chocolate cake. Inspires rabid devotion, long lines of hungry ladies. -$10

Maremma 228 W. 10th St. (Bleecker & Hudson Sts.) (212) 645-0200 Italian. Cesare Casella, of Beppe fame, directs an Italian Spaghetti Western in the Village. Wacky space, wacky eats like "earn-your-spurs" short ribs, "wild-bill-cody" pappardelle with chocolate wild boar sauce and a succulent "cowboy steak". Pony up, young men. $35 ☆

Mary's Fish Camp 64 Charles St. (W. 4th St.) (610) 400-2188 Seafood. A sea-side shack in the W.Vill. Oysters, steamers, cockles- if it comes in a shell, Mary Redding will crack it. The lobster rolls are luscious and the Mako Shark BLT is sur-prisingly good. Small, cute, tucked amidst the brownstones, fits no more than twen-ty campers at a time. $30

Mas 39 Downing Street (Bedford St.) (212) 255-1790 French. Elegant, airy space with soft, sensual glow. Chef Galen Zamarra whips up masterpieces like scallop crusted halibut and short ribs with butternut risotto. You and your lucky date are entranced and romanced with an extensive French wine list to accompany your superb meal. Phenomenal desserts good like a post-coital smoke. +$40

Mexicana Mama 525 Hudson St. (Charles & W. 10th Sts.) (212) 924-4119 Mexican. Wait a lifetime for a table in this hallway-sized space with big, spicy flavor. Chef Julieta Ballesteros serves creative twists on authentic Mexican cuiz. Robust, fresh flavors, we especially like the chorizo and cheese and amazing pollo con mole. Fruity margaritas to quench the fire. $20

Mi Cocina 57 Jane St. (Hudson St.) (212) 627-8273 Mexican. Upscale Mex in a cute space the size of a jalapeño. Some of the tastiest Mexican in the city with maize walls, colorful folksy décor. Grandma is definitely going to heaven for her enchiladas de mole poblano recipe. Try the DIY taco platter, then get sauced on sauza. $40

Miracle Grill 415 Bleecker St. (Bank & W. 11th Sts.) (212) 924-1900 Southwestern. The simplistic space is not as big as its E.Vill. sister, but the food is equally as delicious. A miracle if you get a table on a weekend. Seasonal menu usually includes lots of spicy kicks like portobello fajitas, and blue corn fried chicken tacos. Big Brunch scene, too. $25

Moustache 90 Bedford St. (Barrow & Grove Sts.) (212) 229-2220 Middle Eastern. Tiny storefront space gets enormous praise. We'll brave the long lines to savor the zippy zattar bread and garlicky babaganouj. Try the delicious falafel or merguez sandwich. Upper lip hair doesn't usually trigger one's appetite… make an exception. $22

One if by Land, Two if by Sea 17 Barrow St. (7th Ave. So. & W. 4th St.) (212) 228-0822 American. Listen my children, and you shall hear… Aaron Burr's haunted carriage house is true romance: flowers, firelight, and a piano that plays the soundtrack to your dream date. Order the rack of lamb, then try the molten chocolate fondant- the only thing hotter is the fire in your date's eyes. $65

Paris Commune 99 Bank St. (Greenwich St.) (212) 929-0509 French. Recently relocated, the Commune may have lost intimacy and intrigue, but still retains its delicious flavors. Big space with a packed bar, long waits for tables. Start with the blue cheesecake with poached pears. Le Burger is le best pour le carnivore. For dessert, the famous warm gingerbread. $30

Partage 92 7th Ave So. (Bleecker & Grove Sts.) (212) 242-2207 French. Paradou's sister has a cozy farmhouse feel with firelight, candlelight, rustic chandeliers. A romantic retreat for crepes both savory and sweet, we suggest the smoked salmon. Seafood Provencal is light and flavorful, moules are a delicate treat. $30 ☆

Pearl Oyster Bar 18 Cornelia St. (Bleecker & W. 4th Sts.) (212) 691-8211 Seafood. Come out of your shell in this renowned raw bar with a small-town Norman Rockwell feel. Something for everyone: oysters, lobster rolls, mussels are all delicious. Hugely popular, prepare yourself for a ridiculous wait, only to get packed in like a sardine. $40

Perry St. 176 Perry St. (West St.) (212) 679-0204 Don't hate the sedate Jean-Georges at large in Richard Meier's controversial glass tower. Minimal décor of gray, beige, white- sleek and clean. Decidedly less adventurous dishes, still yummy. Rabbit medallions, red tuna in a rice cracker crust, steamed black bass. As cool, calm and imposing as the building itself. $50 ☆

Petite Abeille 466 Hudson St. (Barrow & Grove Sts.) (212) 741-6479 Belgian. Miniscule space with homespun charm, buzzing with Belgian food addicts. Wear your lifejacket for a kilo of moules mariniere while downing endless Stellas. Cute and cramped with blue checkered tablecloths: the best seats on the sidewalk to watch passing cuties. $25

Philip Marie 569 Hudson St. (W. 11th St.) (212) 242-6200 American. Who Cozy, eighteenth-century farmhouse allure with seafood to die for. Sweet décor is sets the stage for your "singing scallops" or "dancing shrimp". Clambake on Tuesdays. The stuffed pork chop is delish, but who the hell is Philip Marie? $30

Po 31 Cornelia St. (Bleecker & W. 4th Sts.) (212) 645-2189 Italian. You can't be po' if you want to dine at this classy joint. Small space with pristine tin ceilings and elegant décor. Foodie's paradise for homemade pastas, especially the tender gnocchi. Try the lamb sirloin with cumin yogurt sauce or the porcini-crusted cod. Desserts to die for. $45.

Salon 505 West St. (Jane St.) (212) 929-4303 American. Art Nouveau paradise inside the Riverview Hotel, decked with sensuous nude paintings. Parquet floors, purple velvet booths and a leaf-motif dining room. Chef Michael Davis, formerly of Daniel and Bouley, creates eclectic dishes like duck schnitzel, skate wing stuffed with oxtail. Try the white star cocktail with lillet and champagne. $50 ☆

Sant Ambroeus 259 W. 4th St. (Charles & Perry Sts.) (212) 604-9254 Italian. Popular, upscale restaurant, café, pasticceria all at once. Sit behind a wall of windows, admire the quaint village view. Sweeter than its sisters in the Hamptons and Upper East Side. Unbelievably tender risottos with unexpectedly potent flavors. Great paninis, too. $45

Sapore 55 Greenwich Ave. (Perry St.) (212) 229-0551 Italian. Cozy corner spot with excellent people-watching. True to W. Village form: quick, hot, cheap and delicious, like the clientele. Pick from dozens of delicious pastas, we like the spaghetti and turkey meatballs. Traditional sausage and peppers is smashing. Devoted regulars come by the droves. $17

Shopsin's General Store 54 Carmine St. (Bedford St) (212) 924-5160 American. Inventive hours at this eclectic mom & pop. Exhaustive, bizarre menu with over 200 soups and awesome entree concoctions like the "cashew spinach brown rice mushroom burrito". Don't even think about substituting ingredients, your deadpan waitress will mercilessly oust you. Their house, their rules. -$22

Snack Taverna 63 Bedford St. (Morton St. & Seventh Ave.) (212) 929-3499 Greek. Chic Greek from the neighborhood that brought you Greek love. Intimate corner spot with picturesque windowrama, exposed brick, elegant interior. This food rocks our world, especially the grilled fishies, braised lamb and marvelous moussaka. The wine soaked figs are little balls of love. $30

The Spotted Pig 314 West 11th St. (Greenwich St.) (212) 620-0393 American. Crowded corner spot with a long wait. Batali's olde new English pub, got an investment boost from Hova himself. Lovely fish mains, but that artery-clogging burger is darn delicious, with shoestring potatoes more like crunchy dental floss. Old-world vibe, littered with bric-a-brac to charm your sophisto-date. +$35 **BlackBook**

Sumile 154 West 13th Street (6th & 7th Aves) (212) 989-7699 Big buzz over Chef Josh DeChellis' upscale Japanese. Narrow, modern spot with a warm stylish glow. Tiny portions, big flavor, creative clout. Sip a signature ginger martini and start with the grilled octopus and pickled watermelon. Try the poached duck in sake consommé or attack the Atlantic wolf fish. $40

Sushi Samba 7 87 7th Ave. So. (Bleecker St.) (212) 691-7885 Japanese. Nothing subtle about it. Kaleidoscopic neon color scheme delights the senses of the senseless singles that pack the bar. LatAm/Japanese fusion makes for a foodie fantasia of grilled meats and amazing sushi. Crazy ceviches and inventive rolls. Dazzling drinks list. $45

Tanti Baci 163 W.10th St. (Waverly Pl. & 7th Ave.) (212) 647-9651 Italian. Hidden, romantic spot below an anonymous staircase is a secret agent rendezvous for delicious homemade pasta and nightly fish specials. Mind-numbingly good tiramisu inspires you to spill your secrets by candlelight. Attentive service can recognize if you're "having a moment". $25

Tartine 253 W. 11th St. (W. 4th St.) (212) 229-2611 French. Cute and tiny corner spot is a long-standing favorite for long hours standing outside for a table. But we love the BYOB policy. Croque Monsieurs rock, but this place is best for brunch. Brioche french toast and delectable pastries are the perfect hangover cure on Sunday mornings. $30

Tea & Sympathy 108-111 Greenwich Ave. (12th & 13th Sts.) (212) 807-8329 British. Fancy a cuppa? Perfectly lovely afternoon tea for two, cucumber sandwiches, scones with clotted cream, bangers and mash. Custards, puddings and all things bad for your health. How very civilized. A Celebrity fave that's packed on the weekends, prepare to wait. $15

Voyage 117 Perry St. (Greenwich St.) (212) 255-9191. Global. Elegant space where mild-mannered reporters get their rocks off. Vintage suitcases and B&W photos of ships. Sophisticated dining room with walls upholstered in silk. Seasonal menu with creative flair. Oxtail croquettes are delightfully different. We recommend the cod with a rose lentil crust. $40

Wallsé 344 W. 11th St. (Washington St.) (212) 352-2300 Austrian. Rock me Amadeus, Austrian fare that makes us long for Vienna. Minimalist setting hung with selections from Schnabel's collection. Unbelievable food like juicy wiener schnitzel and the fabulous crispy cod strudel. For dessert, ask for the "unusual black forest". $45 **BlackBook**

Westville 210 W. 10th St. (Bleecker & W. 4th Sts.) (212) 741-7971 American. Breezy, white beach shack aesthetic at this Heavyweight contender for West Vill. burger supremacy. Medium rare with cheddar is always a solid choice or try the turkey burger for a change of pace. 3 kinds of hot dogs, tasty assortment of homemade cookies and pies. $20

Ye Waverly Inn 16 Bank St. (Waverly Pl.) (212) 929-4377 American. Keats and Yeats are on your side in this 19th-century spot for ye oldies but goodies. Edna St. Vincent Millay hung out here, but now this townhouse is better known for its outstanding beet salad and pork chop with apple whiskey sauce. Sorry, Edna. $35

Yumcha 29 Bedford St. (Downing St.) (212) 524-6800 Creative Chinese. Looking to overcome a rocky start... Beautiful people descend upon the ultra-clean, super-modern, ultimately cold interior to sip green tea martinis in style. You're looking haute. Creative dishes like ginger-lacquered veal cheeks or tea-smoked chicken are dressed to impress. $45 ★

NIGHTLIFE West Village

Arthur's Tavern 57 Grove St. (7th Ave. So. & Bleecker St.) (212) 675-6879 Fat cats and hip dolls hit this historic, wooden saloon to taste the spit and spirit of jazz clubs past. Notable live trios overpower miniscule stage. Reminds us of Village of yore.

Automatic Slims 733 Washington St. (Bank St.) (212) 645-8660 Once dazzling, now dingy black 'n' white floor. Blank white walls hold shadows freaky people dancing to Blondie, blues, and rock 'n' roll on tabletops made out of old 45's. Cheap beers and cheaper pick-up lines. Always packed on weekends.

Blind Tiger Ale House 518 Hudson St. (W. 10th St.) (212) 675-3848 Stately wooden bar in a cozy spot, perfect for rising up to the challenge of our rivals. 26 micro brews on tap, you'll be blindly tanked in no time. Don't miss "You cut the cheese" Wednesdays, where beers are paired with free artisinal cheeses.

Chow Bar 230 W. 4th St. (10th St.) (212) 633-2212 Noisy, crowded corner spot. Décor that is decidedly "Chinese", as exemplified by the presence of bamboo. Fun and creative house cocktails for the professional types who pour in at happy hour and the party people who rage through the night.

Chumley's 86 Bedford St. (Barrow & Grove Sts.) (212) 675-4449 Sonny boy, when I was your age, we drank homebrewed beer poured over a metal trough this big... former speakeasy with sawdust coated floors, healthy pours. Young professionals spill out the side door into the courtyard for belligerent bantering.

Employees Only 510 Hudson St. (Christopher St.) (212) 242-3021 Bizarro world at this 1920's style bar with rich mahogany interior. A strange gypsy psychic greets you at the door; the bartenders sport handlebar moustaches in an exaggerated old-world style. Eclectic concoctions. We love the lavender scented gin, and the Pimms just pops. ★ **BlackBook**

Hudson Bar and Books 636 Hudson St. (Horatio & Jane Sts.) (212) 229-2642 A loophole in the law gives us this smoker's lounge with high end drinking for the literary minded. The bookshelves gather dust while cancerous clientele mingle. Your hostess looks like a Yale graduate impersonating Jackie O. Delightful classic cocktails like sidecars, mint juleps.

Julius 159 W. 10th St. (Waverly Pl.) (212) 929-9672 Wacky hustler bar on a breezy corner, has been around forever, pre-Stonewall. Sawdust on the floor to muffle the sounds of boots and spurs for Urban Cowboys. Hustlers here are as old as the day is long. If you wake up in the West Village with sawdust between your teeth, you probably passed out at Julius' again.

Kava Lounge 605 Hudson St. (W. 12th St.) (212) 989-7504 Yoga for alcoholics in these laid-back digs. Subdued couples drink cocktails laced with kava, the all-natural Maori valium. According to the staff, it tastes like "dirty dishwater with a hint of clove". Mmmm. Drink enough and work up the nerve for whale-riding.

Lips 2 Bank St. (Greenwich Ave. & Waverly Pl.) (212) 675-7710 Intimate cabaret with nightly performances by Cher! Oh my god! Appeals to bachelorettes on the loose, Long Islanders looking for a laugh, chicks with dicks and girls getting their drunken kicks. Lip service always available here.

Little Branch 20-22 7th Ave. So. (Leroy St.) (212) 929-4360 Apparently, Little Branch is Native American speak for "get loaded". The western cousin of Sasha Petraske's Milk & Honey, is an underground lounge stocked with the usual fabulous suspects. Retro cocktails served with cool swizzle sticks to tall drinks of water. Noisy, fun, but ultimately more chill than it's LES counterpart. ✮

Monster Bar 80 Grove St. (W. 4th St.) (212) 924-3557 Large, festive corner location in beautiful landmark building. Sugar Daddy central for the gay scene. An institution. Biweekly drag shows, legal dancing. Young boys come to this grandpa of the W. Village to hook grandpas who remember when it actually was a village.

Movida 28 7th Ave So. South (Bedford & Leroy Sts.) (212) 206-9600 Johnny T. of "Motherfucker" fame, brings us a humungous multi-level pleasuredome. DJ booth shaped like a bullet hole, dancy rock n' roll for self-important guys and the women who love them. Mirrors, chandeliers, marble, space-age VIP room for sipping Cristal. Be afraid. ✮

The Otheroom 143 Perry St. (Greenwich & Washington Sts.) (212) 645-9758 You know, that other room over there, as opposed to Room and Anotheroom. Chill neighborhood hang is a best bet- steel bar, exposed brick walls, rough-hewn minimal feel. Small, packed with hipsters. Beer and wine only, but no complaints. **BlackBook**

Shag 11 Abingdon Sq. (Bleecker & W. 12th Sts.) (212) 242-0220 60's mod hangout that's shagadelic in every horrible way. White shag carpeting covers the walls while gluttons for punishment down drinks that mix coke and milk. Lounge on white and orange space-age Barbarella furniture and order bar food like "evil eggs" and "shag-a-licious lamb balls"… or better yet, don't.

Stonewall 53 Christopher St. (7th Ave. So.) (212) 463-0950 Colorful and historic, read it on the walls, home of the Stonewall riots is finally out and about. Recently redone, still a W. Village classic. Boys who like boys who like girls who like boys get their drink on here. Gay pride paradise.

Tortilla Flats 767 Washington St. (W. 12th St.) (212) 243-1053 Margarita madness, or just plain madness? Girls gone wild turn muy moronic. Ahh, the real Cancun right here in Manhattan, sans the tans. Piñata madness. Festive lights and decorations in a cramped, overcrowded space that smells faintly of armpit.

Village Vanguard 187 7th Ave. So. (11th St. & Waverly Pl.) (212) 255-4037 One of the few legendary Jazz spots left in the W. Village. Serious cats willing to pay hefty prices. Crimson lounge with unrivaled jazz. Take your dad. A show you'll probably tell your kids about.

West 425 West St. (11th St.) (212) 242-4375 Way out. West of nothing cause it's this and the water and that's where it ends. Sophisticated and polished black interior with stainless steel accents. Leather banquette to be cool and collected. Chill music and chilly pours. Nightly cocktail specials, impressive draft list.

White Horse Tavern 567 Hudson St. (11th St.) (212) 243-9260 Under Milk wood as recited under wood bar. Everyone and their pledge brother know that Dylan Thomas bit the dust here, but couldn't name one of his poems to save their life. Avoid the weekends when frat boys take over and puke on themselves.

"In New York City, everyone is an exile, none more so than the Americans."

—*Charlotte Perkins Gilman*

MEATPACKING DISTRICT
(map p. 198)

These days most of the flank steak in the Meat Packing District comes packaged in $800 pants, but by the early light you'll still see butchers in their bloodied body smocks. Or they're just assisting Damien Hirst with his next installation? Regardless, **we propose a long overdue name change** to something a bit more accurate. **How about, the Model-Packing District**? After all, **Double Seven**, **PM**, **AER** and other exclusive venues here seem to draw waifish lovelies to their velvety insides as if every day were Fashion Week. **Or maybe the Money-Packing district**? With the exception of a few upscale dives like **Hog Pit** and **Hogs & Heifers**, you'd better be willing to drop serious dough if you desire to feel even the slightest buzz. **We voted for the Tranny-Packing District**, but were quickly overruled by the area's defacto mayor, the honorable Diane Von Furstenburg, who lords over her fiefdom with a well-manicured iron fist. Whatever you want to call it, this neighborhood is now undoubtedly pound-for-pound the most stylish and exclusive in all New York. Catch us **breaking celebrity fast at Pastis**, dining with our sizeable entourage in one of **Ono's** tatami rooms, heading up to **Plunge** to breathe in the views (and a smoke), before retiring to the exclusive, refined opulence of **Double Seven** for a perfectly made Pimm's Cup.

RESTAURANTS Meatpacking District

Florent 69 Gansevoort St. (Greenwich & Washington Sts.) (212) 989-5779 Diner & Bistro. Slick diner buzzing with life. Come early and stay late for juicy burgers, big salads, steaks and mussels accompanied by some of the best fries in the city. An all-day, all-night, prime weekend scene long before this area blew up. -$25 **BlackBook**

Macelleria 48 Gansevoort St. (Greenwich & Washington Sts.) (212) 741-2555 Italian. Enormous space with old world touch, serves one of our favorites: house-made macaroni with soft, delicious oxtail ragu. Name literally means meat market, and the generous cuts of steak pay proper homage to the area's history. +$40

Markt 401 W. 14th St. (9th Ave.) (212) 727-3314 Belgian Brasserie. Conspicuous corner spot. Rich, dark wood interior, friendly crowd hoisting Chimay, and an enormous pail of steamed mussels in Hoegaarden broth are perfect for a cold night. Lots of Belgian bistros these days, this one's still tops. Outside seats for prime people watching. +$35

Old Homestead 56 9th Ave. (14th & 15th Sts.) (212) 242-9040 Steakhouse. Area landmark since 1868, self-proclaimed King of Beef. No argument here. Enormous cuts, like the daunting ribeye, are measured in pounds not ounces. Lots of tasty sides, too, like the bleu cheese salad and garlicky mashed potatoes. $60

Ono 18 9th Ave. (13th St.) (212) 660-6766 Japanese. Gansevoort hotel hotspot from Chodorow. Tented cabanas in the sprawling patio worthy of an all inclusive resort, and Japanese grillables in the more demure interior restaurant space. Tatami rooms for your crew.

Paradou 8 Little W. 12th St. (9th Ave. & Washington St) (212) 463-8345 French. Provençal-inspired bistro à vin, with an intimate dining room and one of the cozier back gardens around. Radishes with butter and salt are a nice freebie at the bar, followed by delicious crepes and tartines. $30

Pastis 9 9th Ave. (Little W. 12th St.) (212) 929-4844 French. The drug models love. McNally's landmark bistro that sent his stock skyward. Simple, tiled interior is simply gorgeous. Permanently crowded and lively. Great eggs for brunch, savory onion soup and pommes frites, with Gitanes Blondes for dessert. A must. -$35 **BlackBook**

Pizza Bar 48-50 9th Ave. (14th & 15th Sts.) (212) 924-0941 Pizza. If next door Pop Burger served pizza. Same owners, same scene, though this one has the kooky psychedelic ceiling to trip out on while munching on crispy, creative pies. Snazzy lounge in back. $15

Pop Burger 58 9th Ave. (14th & 15th Sts.) (212) 414-8686 American. Late night fast-food counter pushes killer burgers, dogs, onion rings and fries in slick, designy digs featuring famed crayola Basquiat lithos. To stay? Canoodle on low-slung banquettes in the swank lounge and pool hall in back. $20

Son Cubano 405 W. 14th St. (9th Ave. & Washington Sts.) (212) 366-1640 Cuban. Big Cuban sandwiches and tasty tapas in a buena comida social club from F. Castro (Frank, not Fidel). Festive and colorful, a mixed crowd of yups, scenesters and refugees make for good fun. $35

Spice Market 403 W. 13th St. (9th Ave.) (212) 675-2322 Thai. Jean Georges is everywhere, don't even try and evade this guy. Lavish, sceney spot of Taj Mahal-like proportions. Small portions of so-called Asian street food are hit or miss - chicken samosas and mussels steamed in lemongrass are good bets. $50

Vela 39 W. 21st St. (5th & 6th Aves.) (212) 675-8007 Fusion. Super sceney fusion joint in unique locale, mixes Orient flavs with Brazil. Cleverly conceived dishes like yellowtail sashimi with mango salsa abound, along with more traditional sushi and rolls. Peep the waterfall and order a Soltini while you wait, girls. $45

NIGHTLIFE Meatpacking District

Aer 409 W. 13th St. (9th Ave.) (212) 989-0100 Vast, strange fantasyland club popular with pretty people. Girls love it like they give out shoes and purses. Expensive drinks, danceable beats, and trippy décor like glowing floors to distract you while you get loaded.

APT 419 W. 13th St. (9th Ave. & Washington St.) (212) 414-4245 A dizzying range of DJ talent on display in a variety of smart spaces, Only drawback is it's sheer popularity: be prepared to jostle for dance space. DJ Cucumber Slice, or whatever Bobbito's calling himself these days, is the lick. **BlackBook**

Cielo 18 Little W. 12th St. (9th Ave. & Washington St.) (212) 645-5700 You still there? Former Ibiza DJ Nicolas Matar's foray into NYC nightlife has dimmed. Hyper-futuristic airport lounge was once the hotness – now rumor is they're trying to sell the joint.

The Double Seven 418 W. 14th St. (9th & 10th Aves.) (212) 981-9099 Exclusive lounge from Lotus peeps. Lotus distilled, one might say. Beautiful dark wood, conversation-friendly and party worthy. Monica runs a smooth, flawless operation with perfect drinks from Milk & Honey dude. Serious star wattage and drink prices. The top girls love it. **BlackBook**

Lotus 409 W. 14th St. (9th & 10th Aves.) (212) 243-4420 Classic hotspot. Just when you count 'em out, they smack you on the head with a dope party. Lotus is still Lotus and David, Mark et al cannot be kept down, though they now party at their new joint across the street.

One 1 Little West 12th St. (Gansevoort St.) (212) 255-9717 Warm, sexy, womblike space draws them in like moths to the flame. Girls: order the Naughty Schoolgirl and proceed to tease your date. Stella, that would be McCartney, not Artois, and Nicole, Kidman, not Ritchie, retreat to the downstairs salon for some privacy.

Plunge 18 9th Ave. (13th St.) (877) 426-7386 High life atop the Gansevoort. Incredible Western views alone worth the ride up. Crowd isn't the coolest assortment of human beings ever assembled, but you should be looking at the Hudson, not each other. And you can smoke.

PM 50 Gansevoort St. (Greenwich & Washington Sts.) (212) 255-6676 Still seems intimate, despite squeezing in a fistful of beautiful peeps. Awesome, festive wall mural dominates this Haitian-themed voodoo lounge, from Unyk and Kiki. Party with ID honcho Paolo Zampolli and his squadron of skinny chicks.

Soho House 29-35 9th Ave. (13th & 14th Sts.) (212) 627-9800 Luxe members-only club, dotted with celebs. Opulent environs include 40-foot Chesterfield sofa and infamous roofdeck pool. You'll either be hanging with Franz Ferdinand or a gaggle of snaggle toothed British bankers. Guess which happens more often than not?

Level V 55 W. 21st St. (5th & 6th Aves.) (212) 675-8007 Triangular, Flatiron-esque digs for cachaca and sake fueled revelry. Cozy nook beneath Vela can get super hot in summer, so wear little clothing like everyone else. Soooo much cooler than Level IV, no competition.

"Sometimes I get bored riding down the beautiful streets of LA. I know it sounds crazy,

but I just want to go to New York and see people suffer." —Donna Summer

CHELSEA

(map p. 199)

What do **Jeff Koons**, **Boy George** and **Jessica Simpson** have in common? **You can find them or their plebeian clones on any given night in Chelsea: NY's art capital, gay capital and the city's undisputed club capital**. The art scene is at its prime on Thursday afternoons, with legions of art stars and their followers spilling out of openings and into hangs like **Bottino** and **Bette**. The gay contingency is particularly omnipresent in this part of town, with the ubiquitous Chelsea boys packing haunts like **XL**, **G Lounge** and **View Bar**. But it's the straighter clubs that have gained the most ground of late, with one stop club shopping on 27th street, at places like **Home**, **Groovedeck**, **BED** and **Crobar**, all thisclose to each other. Catch us drinking smuggled Bud lights in the Chelsea Art Museum with Baird Jones , moving the party on to **Marquee** with the celeb du jour, getting horizontal at **BED**, ascending to catch the stunning views of **Groovedeck**, then, once completely wasted, standing in the amazingly long line at **Bungalow 8** with a few stacked coeds from **Scores West**.

RESTAURANTS Chelsea

Amuse 108 W. 18th St. (6th & 7th Aves.) (212) 929-9755 Eclectic. Modern, golden-lit rooms for various levels of immersion into inventive eats. Has the soba on lock, porcini in check and the arancini by the risotto balls. Slightly sceney. Courses available in small, medium and large. Top brunch. +$35

Biltmore Room 290 8th Ave. (24th & 25th Sts.) (212) 807-0111 Gorgeous dining space from a founder of fusion. Robins revives 90's Asian-American glory. Outfitted in vintage Biltmore Hotel, down to the marble walls. Bustling bar scene while you wait, courtesy of Billy Shine. Get the foie gras with mango sauce appetizer, followed by top notch rack of lamb. $35 **BlackBook**

Bette 461 W. 23rd St. (9th & 10th Aves.) (212) 366-0404 American. Club queen Amy Sacco brings all her Bungalow 8 buddies out for dinner in decidedly more demure setting. Neighbors still hate on her cause of construction fiasco, but rich, elegant wood tones should calm them down. Art superstars. $50

Bottino 246 10th Ave. (24th & 25th Sts.) (212) 206-6766 Italian. Ground zero for art world superstars and their sycophantic entourages. Impossibly hot but perchance a smidgen run down after all these years. Push past air-kissing crowd in the front bar for some antipasto in garden. Impeccable pastas and great service. $40

Bright Food Shop 218 8th Ave. (21st St.) (212) 243-4433 Southeast Asian & Tex-Mex. Odd mix, but then again, this is Chelsea. Chicken-satay tacos and moo-shoo mex confounds but delights. Super-fresh huevos rancheros. Next-door Kitchen Market has fantastic take-out treats like Negra Modelo gingerbread. $20

Cafeteria 119 7th Ave. (17th St.) (212) 414-1717 American. Food is so not the point here, though it's incredibly tasty at 4 am. Shiny white plastic and concrete are perfect backdrop for after hours pick up post-Hiro debauchery. Just don't fall asleep with your head in a plate of fried chicken and waffles, lest you miss the scene. Open 24 hours. $30

Cuba Libre 165 8th Ave. (18th & 19th Sts.) (212) 206-0038 Latin American. Roxanne, you do, in fact, have to put on the red light. Havana heights. Long and lean space, super-friendly and attentive staff. Lobster boniato mash and a seafood salad with sour orange mojito sauce. Dulce de leche desserts top it all off. $30

The Dish 201 8th Ave. (20th & 21st Sts.) (212) 352-9800 American. Glorified diner with suburban looks. Popular with Chelsea boys and chatty female friends. Big reuben sandwiches, hearty and juicy burgers, and crispy grilled cheeses and as an added bonus: appropriately titled cocktails like the Jealous Biotch. $20

El Cocotero 228 W. 18th St. (7th & 8th Aves.) (212) 206-8930 Venezuelan. Tropical themed newcomer boasts those delectable arepas and a similarly wonderful staff. One of few Venezuelan spots in the city, try the grilled meats. Everything's fresh. Get the Say hi to Linda and Hugo Chavez on the way in. $25

Elmo 156 7th Ave. (19th & 20th Sts.) (212) 337-8000 Continental. Hotter than it's talking namesake at Christmas. You'll be tickled by the relatively low-key food (meat-loaf) in a trendy, Wallpaper-esque space with dope lighting. Striped banquettes and a Ross Bleckner, for those who care. Lethal cocktails, as well. $35

F & B 269 W. 23rd St. (7th & 8th Aves.) (646) 486-4441 Take-Out Hot Dogs. Brings together popular American street food and unlikely toppings. Corn and salsa. Sauerkraut and bacon. The first but less favored now that we have Crif Dogs. Ikea'd out in Scandinavian décor. $10

Food Bar 149 8th Ave. (17th & 18th Sts.) (212) 243-2020 American. Pretty Euro-boys with guidebook in hand, rush off their flights at JFK muttering "Food Bar, Food Bar" (true). Dark 'n sexy bi-level room. Drinks fit for a king, uh, queen. Global menu but we like the cobb salad and great sandwiches. $30

Havana Chelsea Restaurant 190 8th Ave. (19th & 20th Sts.) (212) 243-9421 Cuban. Dirt cheap digs. Make a mean Cuban sandwich. Greasy croquettas go down easy with a cold batido. Better not to stay and sit at a wobbly table with who knows what lurking beneath. Get it to go with rice pudding: then die dreaming. $15

La Bottega 363 W. 16th St. (8th & 9th Aves.) (212) 243-8400 Italian. The Maritime´s glammed up version of a brasserie flipping Italian eats. Sceney, lovely with rows of bottles lining the walls for a shimmering effect. Beautiful people watching as you munch on your crispy pizzeta. $45 **BlackBook**

La Luncheonette 130 10th Ave. (18th St.) (212) 675-0342 French. Behind nondescript concrete exterior lies a surprisingly upscale menu likely to burn a hole in your pocket. Traditional skate, escargots and a truly excellent cassoulet, which warms your gut come wintertime. $40

Le Singe Vert 160 7th Ave. (19th & 20th Sts.) (212) 366-4100 French. Paris embraces its outer boroughs and kicks some Senegalese flava into that French ass. Sibling of Jules and Café Noir. All-night original, in a city full of McBistros. Can't go wrong with the steak frites. $45

Le Zie 172 7th Ave. (20th & 21st Sts.) (212) 206-8686 Italian. A Venetian retreat. Glowing large dining room and rippled ceiling some may call tacky. Homemade pastas, salt-crusted snapper, and stand out antipasto. The spaghetti and meatballs. gets big propers from local papers, deservedly so. $35

Matsuri at the Maritime Hotel 369 W. 16th St. (9th Ave.) (212) 243-6400 Japanese. Modelicious, white-tiled, large bar, round lamps. Fresh and delicious sushi and sashimi. Chef Ono's stylin' locale for duck soup and sesame panna cotta. Huge model dinners. $45

O Mai 158 9th Ave. (19th & 20th Sts.) (212) 633-0550 Vietnamese. Oh my, this place is tiny! Exposed brick. Old photos of Vietnam on the walls. Green papaya salad, shrimp dumplings, red snapper with chili and lime sauce, caramelized shrimp and pork ribs. Sweet and sour right down to the drinks. +$25

Riazor 245 W. 16th St. (7th & 8th Aves.) (212) 727-2132 Spanish & Tapas. Rio Mar peeps move slightly north and keep the same menu, prices and general vibe. A bit more spiff, but the sangria-fueled revelers keep the party happy and the amiable staff keeps the tapas flowing. Predictably delicious paella. $30

Rickshaw Dumpling Bar 61 W. 23rd St., (6th Ave.) (212) 924-9220 Asian. Foodie lunch spot across the street from the institute for culinary education. Aspiring chefs in smooth surroundings chomping down on different versions of the dumpling, and washing it down with watermelonade, courtesy of Annisa's fab Anita Lo. Tasty and quick. $10

Rocking Horse Café 182 8th Ave. (19th & 20th Sts.) (212) 463-9511 Mexican. Looks more Oslo/Tokyo than Mazatlan. Creatively fused menu befits the concept. Bocadillos, are better than the platos fuertes; duck epazote confit and crispy calamari citrus salad. You'll be speaking French, dreaming in Spanish and partying like you're from Reykjavik. $30

Sueños 311 W. 17th St. (8th & 9th Ave) (212) 243-1333 Mexican. Downstairs paradise with a desert rock garden, cactus trees, splashy paintings and a young man making corn tortillas fresh off the press. Has definitely garnered loads of positive press. Divine watermelon margaritas, lobster fritters, flaky pork empanadas and a Tequila-hazed bliss. $35

The Viceroy 160 8th Ave. (18th St.) (212) 633-8484 American & French. Chelsea boy epicenter for flaunting fruits of David Barton workouts. Only place to brunch after burning your budget at the Barney's Co-op. Portions are immense. Creamed spinach and lobster pot pie. $25

Tia Pol 205 10th Ave. (22nd St.) (212) 675-8805 Tapas. Creative variations on Spanish finger foods from Alexandra Raij. Slender, cozy, perpetually packed and lively. Tough to get a table – don't make your night's plans hinge on it. Great sangria pitchers and spicy chorizo and chocolate. Good spot. $25

NIGHTLIFE Chelsea

Barracuda 275 W. 22nd St. (7th & 8th Aves.) (212) 645-8613 Unassuming door front leads into den of Chelsea boys on the prowl. Circular orange lit lounge in back is one big grope-fest. Gay bar with supposedly little attitude. Is there such a thing? If so, this may be the place.

BED 530 W. 27th St. (10th & 11th Aves.) (212) 594-4109 Miami's horizontal hotn i ii heads north, thanks to Lotus owners collaboration Niivim for some fun nights, especially after hitting the sixth floor party at Groovedeck. Lots of playboys in billowy white shirts surrounded by blazing Miami-type talent.

Bongo 299 10th Ave. (27th & 28th Sts.) (212) 947-3654 Fifties-style artsy hangout for Chelsea residents, gallery hoppers and design buffs. Retro Brady living room look and fancy cocktails served right. Small and anonymous. Meet for a drink before Thursday night gallery hopping.

Brite Bar 297 10th Ave. (27th St.) (212) 279-9706 Bright because of all the windows up front. Big, too. A clear sign this is not shading itself as a secret paradise for man-love, but rather a nod to the yuppies that also live in Chelsea. Leather stools and exposed brick.

Bungalow 8 515 W. 27th St. (10th & 11th Aves.) Chelsea diva Amy Sacco's Disneyland for adults. Private right down to the unlisted number, still draws the big name celebs and their entourages. Hard core door. Still, if you're the billionaire scion of a wealthy Italian family, here's a tranquil repose to bring your ten favorite 17-year-old Czech models.

Cain 544 W. 27th St., (10th & 11th Aves.) (212) 947-8000 Super hot, African-themed hunting lodge. Hunters seek celeb game like Lindsay Lohan, who in turn seeks out prey that's chopped up with a black AmEx. In summer they've got a Hamptons satellite – that sort of crowd. Softcore porn lighting makes everyone want to fuck.

crobar 530 W. 28th St. (10th & 11th Aves.) (212) 629-9000 Biggest club in the city. Get lost from your party amid a throbbing sea of B&T, scenesters, gays, homies, basically every NY demographic. Relaxed door, relaxed security inside. Long live crobar. Tim Bauman is the chillest GM in the world.

The Frying Pan Pier 63 (23rd St. & West Side Hwy.) (212) 989-6363 A true dive bar: it used to rest at the bottom of Chesapeake Bay until it was salvaged. Now home to one of the scarier/weirder nights out in NY: you could get lost trying to find the bathroom in the rusty hull. Hosts Turntables on The Hudson.

G Lounge 225 W. 19th St. (7th & 8th Aves.) (212) 929-1085 Painlessly graduated from trendoid yacht to reliable, comfortable cruise ship. Juice bar, coffee bar, and bar bar draws the Banana Republic crowd plus dancers from next-door DTW. You'd better be gay if you want to hang here.

Glo 431 W. 16th St. (9th & 10th Aves.) (212) 229-9119 Huge, former Powder space, slick, modern, easier door than many of the surrounding venues. Big name DJs, fun if you want to dance rather than profile. Clean, white design, clever white pebble bar. It does, in fact, glow.

Groovedeck 530 W. 27th St., 7th Fl. (10th & 11th Aves.) (212) 594-4109 Stunning roooftoop views of New York and its gorgeous peoples. Feels like Miami without the gusanos. If the weather changes you can hit Home, BED or Spirit, conveniently located in the same shopping mall.

Half King 505 W. 23rd St. (10th Ave.) (212) 462-4300 Sebastian Junger's easy going writer's haunt. Occasional readings. No scene, pretense, design or décor. Friendly wooden bar for drinking with old friends and pounding a pint or four.

Hiro 366 W. 17th St. (9th Ave.) (212) 727-0212 Architecturally blessed, vast rock-inflected venue for the glam set in the Maritime Hotel. Nur is really kicking ass and taking names, like it's old school Wax up in there. Hit the upstairs for a loungey feel. Cool spot. **BlackBook**

Home 532 W. 27th St. (10th & 11th Aves.) (212) 273-3700 In the middle of the madness, new joint from veteran Spa team is all about bottles, celebs and pretty peoples. Say hey to Megan. Old Spirit anti-drug bathrooms need to go, though.

Marquee 289 10th Ave. (26th & 27th Sts) (646) 473-0202 Jason & Noah's joint is all about celeb power, Page Six sightings, and of course a tight door. Inside it's relatively vast, but crammed with talent. Head up to the red room to kick it with the players.

Naima 513 W. 27th St. (10th & 11th Aves.) (212) 967-4392 New, slick loungey eatery on, you guessed it, the club mecca that is 27th. Good place to kill time after work while waiting for the raucous places get going. Wine and pastas by way of Capri for men in Capri pants.

Opus 22 559 W. 22nd St. (11th Ave.) (212) 929-7515 Nice, open, breezy drinking spot way out west. Good luck sitting down Thursday nights. Former Open locale maintains same basic look, tones down the art-world craziness a tad. Tops in summer, mellow. DJ friendly.

The Park 118 10th Ave. (17th & 18th Sts.) (212) 352-3313 Legendary night guru Eric Goode's joint. Yuval and Nur revitalize the upstairs roof deck with a little Japanese flav. Hot tub still for champagne, strippers and Jacuzzi Joe. Most scandalous private bathroom in the city off to the side. Bow down.

Passerby 436 W. 15th St. (9th & 10th Aves.) (212) 206-7321 Artist Gavin Brown's off-to-the-side bar. Good DJs on the regular, funky light-up floor, private, spacious bathrooms are communal yet discreet. Go late for the most hopping scene on the deadest block. Toby at the bar is pure genius. **BlackBook**

Quo 511 W. 28th St. (10th & 11th Aves.) (212) 268-5105 Miami meets NY meets The Jetsons, with a little tacky feel that seems to suit the crowd just fine. It's an odd mix of hip and Long Island, perhaps attributable to the owners-manager dynamic. VIP room hooked up artist by Damon Johnson.

The Roxy 515 W. 18th St. (10th & 11th Aves.) (212) 645-5156 Classic, massive mostly gay mecca way out west, infamous Wednesday nights for roller disco. See dudes in neon spandex sashaying past giddy bachelorettes to that one ABBA track. Gf's draging their bf's there for their sister's b-day.

Scores West 533-35 W. 28th Street (10th & 11th Aves.) (212) 868-4900 Uptown's upscale tittie club in the middle of the club district. Sprawling and crawling with above average talent prowling the floor for suckers willing to get loaded and wake up with a 128k tab. But Candi sure can make it clap.

Serena 222 W. 23rd St. (7th & 8th Aves.) (212) 255-4646 Basement level Moroccan lounge from entertaining guru and socialite Serena Bass and son Sam. Multi-roomed exotic flair a serious 180-degree turn from the digs of the upstairs Chelsea Hotel.

Spirit 530 W. 27th St. (10th & 11th Aves.) (212) 268-9477 New agey spot has trimmed down in size to a smaller space, still has the hard-core clean, no drug, approach. Big DJs and popular for events. The underwear nights are pretty fun, too.

View Bar 232 8th Ave. (21st & 22nd Sts.) (212) 929-2243 Glitzy, hopping homo haunt, complete with requisite boys in towels getting the crowd worked up certain nights. Others it's a tad tamer, but the drinks/crowd remain equally stiff.

xl 357 W. 16th St. (8th & 9th Aves.) (212) 995-1400 Hyper-trendy, hyper-gay. Communal urinal a design disaster the gay contingent just loves; see the goods before you put down a one drink payment. Girls, get the straight bartenders to buy you drinks. Gay Family Feud.

"Not only is New York City the nation's melting pot, it is also the casserole,

the chafing dish and the charcoal grill." —John V Lindsay, former Mayor of NYC

FLATIRON & UNION SQUARE & GRAMERCY PARK (map p. 200)

Hey, you know what's missing from that world-renowned architectural gem the Flatiron building? A giant H&M ad covering it up. Thankfully that brilliant idea was fleeting, as are many of the people and places in this area, which is a bustling transitional hub for post work lubrication. Hectic Union Square is like a younger, cooler version of Times Square, with skaters, goth kids, activists, students and assorted others vying for space in the verdant oasis. Park Ave South is all about plastic PR chicks dropping plastic while networking and schmoozing their media connects. The streets of Gramercy, meanwhile, are pleasantly refined - like a bubble of serenity. More stately dining destinations dot majestic Irving Place. Find us impressing our in-laws at the perennial classic **Union Square Café**, lunching at model-laden **Coffee Shop** with our favorite club promoters from **Rock Candy** and **Gypsy Tea**, before hitting the unannounced Interpol show at **Irving Plaza** and ending the night with Pablo Banks and the boys at next door **Bar 119**.

RESTAURANTS Flatiron, Union Square & Gramercy

Bao Noodles 391 2nd Ave. (22nd & 23rd Sts.) (212) 725-6182 Vietnamese with French inflection. SVA kids blend in with the New Balance young pro set. Long, narrow space with disheveled yellow walls. Delicious noodles for cheap budgets, one of the better deals around here. Michael wants to take you to Vietnam. -$20

Blue Water Grill 31 Union Sq. W. (16th St.) (212) 675-9500 American. Seafood in every form from Steve Hanson. Constantly packed. The inside's boisterous and expansive, outdoor tables worth the wait though. Perfect for people scoping. Order one of over 20 kinds of oyster dishes. Lesser-known jazz room downstairs. Locals & Tourists. $45

Candela 116 E. 16th St. (Irving Pl. & Park Ave. So.) (212) 254-1600 Eclectic. You guessed it bitches: candles and more candles. Dark, romantic – even fugly people look crushable. Asian BBQ pork chops, seared yellow fin, sushi and superb pasta in a sure-fire date spot. $30

Caviar and Bananas 12 E. 22nd St.(Broadway) (212) 353-0500 Pseudo-Brazilian. Yo Chodorow, did you really kick out Rocco and his moms just to flip fake-ass caviar and crappy faux Brazilian food here? The place is lively, and though the caviar is fake, there are bananas in some patron's pants. $50

Chat n' Chew 10 E. 16th St. (5th Ave. & Union Sq. W.) (212) 243-1616 American. Comfort food heaven on a quiet side street. Perfect brunch, lunch or dinner like creamy baked mac and cheese, sweet sodas (free refills! Yay!) and shakes. Contrived clutter. $15

Choshi Sushi 77 Irving Pl. (19th St.) (212) 420-1419 Japanese. Long lines and brisk service greet you, as do bang-up Dragon rolls. Everything's fresh, snappy service, warm edamame with sea salt are an appropriate starter. Stick with the traditional treats—tempura, eel rolls, noodles and the like— and you'll be rewarded with a traditional experience. $25

City Bakery 3 W. 18th St. (5th & 6th Aves.) (212) 366-1414 American. Save yourself the hassle of going to the Union Square Market on the weekend and let them do it for you. Fresh bread, fruits and veggies. Good hot chocolate and chocolate chip cookies. $12

Coffee Shop 29 Union Sq. W. (16th St.) (212) 243-7969 American. One of the true day clubs, full of promoters during the day networking via text messages while they read about their parties in Page Six. Skinny girls wait on you when the modeling money runs out. Good burgers, fries, and yes, coffee. $20

Craft 43 E. 19th St. (Broadway & Park Ave. So.) (212) 780-0880 American. Sleek lines, designer lighting, warm atmosphere. Choose your own adventure from Tom Colicchio, featured in a memorable Sex and the City episode. Big date spot, loved by nearby shop staff. Step next door to Craft Bar for impromptu panini at lesser rates. +$55

Duke's 99 E. 19th St. (Park Ave. So. & Irving Pl.) (212) 260-2922 Southern. Chicken fried steak crispy and perfect, and ribs like they're right off the cow. Comforting. Wash it down with a cold, refreshing PBR, in lieu of water. A plate here could feed an Eastern European family. $20

Eleven Madison Park 11 Madison Ave. (24th St.) (212) 889-0905 Eclectic. Danny Meyer's joint has a fab wine list and finer park views. Constantly shifting $60 prix fixe featuring pan-seared fluke and braised pork loin. Or just skip the restaurant and go straight for the hotdog cart outside. $50

Fleur de Sel 5 E. 20th St. (Broadway & 5th Ave.) (212) 460-9100 French. The salt'g flavor, named aptly because of the specialty sea salt used to make it all the more savory. Sultry spot for terrine of fois gras, veal confit and spare ribs. Decidedly underrated, totally delicious. +$50

Friend of a Farmer 77 Irving Pl. (18th & 19th Sts.) (212) 477-2188 American. Shake the city out of you at this farmland style joint. Enormous egg picks at brunch, crab cakes, daily fresh fish, and chicken and artichoke sandwiches. Mellow vibe, if anything bring a book, not the laptop. $20

Gramercy Tavern 42 E. 20th St. (Broadway & Park Ave. So.) (212) 477-0777 American. Danny Meyer's pride and joy is classy but just enough so. The delicate, fantastic food such as a perfectly roasted lamb with fava beans. Sophisticated American rustic digs, perfect service make it an example of New York dinning excellence. $60

Kitchen 22 36 E. 22nd St. (Broadway & Park Ave. So.) (212) 228-4399 American. Twenty-five dollar prix fix dinner gets you three courses of inventive quality from Charlie Palmer disciple Scott, one of the best deals in the area. Packed, sleek décor. $25

L'Express 249 Park Ave. So. (20th St.) (212) 254-5858 French Bistro. Packed 24 hours a day. Models from nearby agencies watch other models watch civilians eat actual food. Hit the low-lit Lyonaise room and try the steak au poivre or chicken paillard served with amazing pommes frites. $20

Mayrose 920 Broadway (21st St.) (212) 533-3663 Diner. Industrial, Traditional comfort in this well located industrial looking hang. Make a pit stop in between shops or before hitting the movie down the street. If time allows, we recommend the Thanksgiving dinner with extra gravy any time of year. $18

Mesa Grill 102 5th Ave. (15th & 16th Sts.) (212) 807-7400 Southwestern. Suffers a little from the tired southwest theme craze… shame, the food is tasty: blue-corn crusted snapper and mango-basted short ribs washed down with cactus pear margaritas. Was once a scene-making groundbreaker, still best brunch in the neighborhood +$40

Ora 9 E 19th St (Broadway & Park Ave. So.) (212) 777-2201 Creative Mediterranean. Fun place, fun sidewalk drinks on a tranquil street. Bountiful plates of Medi fare like merguez sausage and cous cous in a glitzy yet casual setting. Downstairs for some hooka hits with gracious host Sahle. $35

Patria 250 Park Ave. So. (20th St.) (212) 777-6211 Latin American. Crowded, spacious, buzzing corner bistro serves Latin American specialties, at prix fix. We especially love the incredible red snapper, but check the specials. Chef Rodriguez has moved uptown to OLA but left the flavors downtown, right here. $60

Periyali 35 W. 20th St. (5th & 6th Aves.) (212) 463-7890 Greek. Il Cantinori and Aureole's sib, great grilled fishes and all your Greek faves. All in all a bit pricey, but the massive skylights, grilled branzino, creative Panhellenic fare and garlicky tzatziki does impress. $45

Pipa 38 E. 19th St. (Broadway & Park Ave. So.) (212) 677-2233 Spanish for US Weekly crowd that gets gossipy and giddy after one glass of on-point sangria. Tasty tapas in an ornate, golden-lit setting that makes you want to stay forever. Abuzz with chatter.

Pure Food and Wine 54 Irving Pl. (17th & 18th Sts.) (212) 477-1010 Raw Food. Nothing cooked above 118 degrees. Hmmm. Sounds suspicious… but what's on your plate is subtle, interesting and totally delicious. Beet "gnocchi" sure has got an interesting texture, tasty, too. Wine list is less befuddling. Good takeout option, too. $22

Republic 37 Union Sq. W. (16th & 17th Sts.) (212) 627-7172 Asian. Minimal Asian eatery with communal tables -you know the type. Loud, simple, fast, cheap and tasty like the spicy chicken with noodles in coconut broth. Don't skimp on the coconut-crusted shrimp, washed down with any number of tasty cocktails and sake.-$12

Shake Shack in Madison Square Park (23rd St. & Madison Ave.) Burgers. Truly delectable burgers in the oft-forgotten oasis that is MSP. Wash them down with heavenly shakes and laugh at the suckers hitting Mickey D's and Wendy's across dirty 23rd street. $12

Sushi Samba 245 Park Ave. So. (19th & 20th Sts.) (212) 475-9377 Japanese/Brazilian/Peruvian. Fashionable sushi joint with touches of Peru and Brazil. Draws swanks from uptown downtown. Real sushi chef cooks in the center isle while hot waitresses bring things with names like sambatinis. $45 **BlackBook**

Tamarind 41-43 E. 22nd St. (Broadway & Park Ave. So.) (212) 674-7400 Indian. One of the classier Indians in the city. Antique Asian mixed with colorful modern décor. Extensive menu of vegetarian dishes, rice, lamb and goat; tandoori salmon and mulligatawny soup. Relaxing tea room next door. $50

Tocqueville 15 E. 15th St. (5th Ave. & Union Sq. W.) (212) 647-1515 American & French. Classy French salon with a rare 60-second minute steak. Consistently interesting specials, quiet, refined atmo, a bit stuffy, but not without its charms. $45

Union Pacific 111 E. 22nd St. (Lexington Ave. & Park Ave. So.) (212) 995-8500 American Creative. Power lunches or trendy evening cocktails and expensive engagements. Eastern twists on solid fish staples, an all-around interesting and varied menu. Chef training ground. Changing daily and weekly prix fix menus make repeat visits necessary. +50

Union Square Café 21 E. 16th St. (5th Ave. & Union Sq. W.) (212) 243-4020 American. A NY classic, absolutely essential for foodies with amazing culinary delights, deserves any and all accolades. Mixes comfort and creative with equal aplomb, great place to take the folks when in town. Consistently varied and interesting menu.+$60 **BlackBook**

Veritas 43 E. 20th St. (Broadway & Park Ave. So.) (212) 353-3700 American. A virtually endless wine list. Swanky modern space. Seafood and steak reign supreme, but the vino is the trump card. Your prix-fix dinner should include the braised short ribs. $65

'wichcraft 49 E. 19th St. (Broadway & Park Ave. So.) (212) 780-0577 American. If you can't cop a table next door, cop a cold veal sandwich in a slightly less designy, but equally fun atmosphere. Love the warm pressed duck sandwich. The breakfast sandwiches are amazing so get there before 11. $20

Zen Palate 34 Union Sq. E. (16th St.) (212) 614-9291 Vegetarian & Asian. Leave the appetite at home, fresh veggies and tofu rule at this always-busy, Buddhist-inspired spot. Everything with the word "delight" in it actually is. Delicious teas, don't skimp on the yam fries. Ideal for Union Square scene checking or take-out. $25

NIGHTLIFE Flatiron, Union Square, Gramercy Park

Avalon 662 6th Ave.(20th St.) (212) 807-7780 The old Limelight church has basically become an event space. Concerts once in a while. Ghosts of party monster Michael Alig make for conversation if nothing else. One time we saw DMC chillin' here with his friends, and he was totally cool.

Bar Demi 125 1/2 E. 17th St. (3rd Ave. & Irving Pl.) (212) 260-0900 Leave the entourage at home at this très petit five-tabled romantic vino room built for two. Have an expertly picked red in the tasting-room-atmosphere. Nothing to do with Ms. Kutchor.

Belmont Lounge 117 E. 15th St. (Irving Pl. & Park Ave. So.) (212) 533-0009 Post-Irving crowd settles into deep-seated couch lounge for spacey beats and kicked-back good times. Cute fashiony girls flirt with wannabe rich kid rockers while NYU kids watch.

Craftbar 47 E. 19th St. (Broadway & Park Ave. So.) (212) 780-0880 From Craft's Tom Colichio, similar attention to details. A dynasty in the making? Vino paradise and haute drinking foods including a dreamy pecorino fondue. Big after work scene for well-dressed professionals.

Cutting Room 19 W. 24th St. (Broadway & 6th Ave.) (212) 691-1900. Bar. Chris Noth's sprawling performance joint. Crowd's not so great, but the shows are pretty decent. Jazz and cabaret shows, salsa troupes, and generally good line-ups. Mr. Big himself frequently in attendance.

Discotheque 17 W. 19th St. (5th & 6th Aves.) (212) 352-9999 Sometimes show-cases hot DJs since it has a damn good system. Go if there's a party, and say hi to our cousin from Queens. Otherwise if you still have the stamina go for Sunday morning after-hours.

Duvet 45 W. 21st St. (5th & 6th Aves.) (212) 989-2121 Fashionable, horizontal party palace. Pricey cocktails sipped atop luxurious linens, justified velvet ropes, a few key nights, including a popular gay party on Thursdays. Nice thread count.

Flatiron Lounge 37 W. 19th St. (5th & 6th Aves.) (212) 727-7741 Glorious hide-away from the typical Flatiron aesthetic. Brand new yet has an old-school feel. Walk down the hall into the deco decadence, drink a martini and start practicing your wink.

40/40 6 W. 25th (Broadway & 6th Aves.) (212) 989-0040 Jay-Z's hot spot—one of many of his ventures now that he's "retired". Like being in a Hip hop video minus the fish eye. All white, super sleek. Surprise b-day parties for LeBron James.

Gypsy Tea 33 W. 24th St. (5th & 6th Aves.) (212) 645-0003 Multi- leveled club with cool red vinyl room courtesy of night nabob Ronnie Madra. Things get kinda… dirty…downstairs. Lots of pretty young things dancing here and there. Decadent locale, fun after parties, and a fairly strict door.

Irving Plaza 17 Irving Pl. (15th & 16th Sts.) (212) 777-6817 Medium-spaced concert hall. Most bands only dream of making it here. Mogwai, Catpower, The Streets, Guided by Voices, etc. Lots of indie rock, but also some more fringe acts like Squarepusher or DJ Krush.

Luna Park 1 Union Sq. E. (Union Sq. Pk.) (212) 475-8464 Outdoor summertime spot for after-work, match.com crowd and NYU kids from the nearby dorms. Come early if you expect to sit. Otherwise, prepare to stand. Can't beat drinking in a park, even if it is legal.

Old Town Bar 45 E. 18th St. (Broadway & Park Ave. So.) (212) 529-6732 Welcoming spot, once a Stillman set, is gladly unchanged over the years. Dilapidated charm, enchanting, incredibly lofty ceilings. Much-needed beers acquired for a reasonable price.

119 Bar 119 E. 15th St. (Irving Pl. & Park Ave. So.) (212) 777-6158. Divy bar with a pool hall smack in the middle. The staff are ridiculously blasé. Probably cos' they served the Strokes once. A lot of the bands end up here after Irving so depending on who's in town there can be some serious drinking going on. **BlackBook**

Pete's Tavern 129 E.18th St. (Irving Pl.) (212) 473-7676 Landmark rustic pub's charm still intact. Old-school patrons and birds looking for lively talk make it worth a beer or three—includes a fairly impressive variety of brews. Energetic, historic. Great bar and summer sidewalk tables.

Rock Candy 35 E. 21st St. (Park Ave. So. & Broadway) (212) 254-5709 New hotspot from omnipresent Steve Lewi, celeb-studded, music ranges from hip hop to rock to '80s on any given night. Say hey to promoter Chris Anthony and his posse of underage models.

Snitch 59 W. 21st St. (6th Ave.) (212) (212) 727-7775 L.A. dive feel. Upscale rock and roll bar with some real grimy touches. Bucket of wings and beers while catching a Group Sounds midnight show on the little stage. An intimate venue for some great acts, and a dirty, glam aesthetic. **BlackBook**

"New York seems conducted by jazz, animated by it. It is essentially a city of rhythm."

—Anais Nin

MURRAY HILL & KIPS BAY

(map p. 202)

Perhaps best known as the grayish, anonymous blob on NYC taxi maps, **Murray Hill** might not be a Mecca of Manhattan nightlife. Still, we're always rooting for an underdog, and this playground Ivy-grad playground has more to offer than just the Midtown Tunnel entrance and plentiful dog parks. Kips Bay provides a quiet, albeit WASPy, solace from the chaos of Midtown, while **intrepid urban explorers will be rewarded with top-notch ethnic food and the potential for late-night debauchery**. We're not denying that it's often the home of charmless urban strivers and couples making their last Manhattan stand before suburbia, but this oft-maligned 'hood deserves a sympathy hug. While some may sneer and call it a sports bar wasteland, we're betting that the Hill soon sheds its lackluster veneer and comes into its own. If not, you can still count on a few local highlights to make your Hilltop experience worth it, from the resplendent **Asia de Cuba** and peaceful **Hangawi** to the creative and colorful Ixta. Find us attacking a porterhouse at classy **Wolfgang's Steakhouse** before taking in the sunset at **Rare View** and finishing the night pondering the surreal décor of the **Cabin Club**.

RESTAURANTS Murray Hill & Kips Bay

Artisanal 2 Park Ave. (32nd St.) (212) 725-8585 French Bistro. True craftsmanship lurks in the cheese cave below, with over 250 global varieties, including vacherin, reblochons, and other bitterly unpronounceable delicacies. Pair the fromage with an appropriate vintage and nibble on the excellent bistro fare, really just a distraction from the cheese at hand. +$50

Asia de Cuba at Morgans Hotel 237 Madison Ave. (37th & 38th Sts.) (212) 726-7755 Asian & Cuban. The original multi-culti mash-up experiment that illuminates the area, always loaded with beautiful people. Action unfolds on the Phillipe Starck-designed communal table, bursting with creative, artfully presented dishes like oxtail spring rolls and Thai beef salad. $50 **BlackBook**

Barbès 21 E. 36th St. (Madison & 5th Aves.) (212) 684-0215 Moroccan. Daytime brochettes and sandwiches for a hectic lunch, or fragrant tangines and cous cous for a low-key dinner. Exposed brick and North African flavor conjures the Parisian 'hood that's it's namesake, from Chazal and Ferrier's Omar Balouma. -$25

Black Duck at the Park South Hotel 122 E. 28th St. (Park Avenue South & Lexington Ave.) (212) 448-0888 Classy, slightly uppity tavern, no ugly ducklings, for creative seafood and a delicious namesake mojito. Menu highlights include the crispy duck breast, seasoned burger, and the espresso-rubbed filet mignon which left us jittery and sated. -$40

Blockheads 499 3rd Ave. (33rd & 34th Sts.) (212) 213-3332 Mexican. Only an idiot would fail to appreciate this spicy staple of the Murray Hillian diet, with huge burritos to munch beneath a cascading rainbow of margaritas. Sidewalk seating sweetens the deal, and $10 brunch (with all-you-can-drink champagne) closes it. +$15

Blue Smoke 116 E. 27th St. (Lexington Ave. & Park Ave. So.) (212) 447-7733 BBQ. Open-pit grilling ain't allowed in Manhattan, but Danny Meyer (of Gramercy Tavern and Union Square Café fame) avoids the problem with hi-tech scrubbers and 15-story smokestacks. Gorge on Memphis-style baby backs and hot links—a bourgeois barbeque, plus 30 types of bourbon. +$45

Cosette 163 E. 33rd St. (3rd & Lexington Aves.) (212) 889-5489 French. Monsieur Bernard keeps it cozy at this low-key and humble French inn. Try the tender lamb shakes and steak tartare, then linger with escargot and onion soup. Unbelievable moules et frites and a daunting gigantic cassoulet left us shouting oui. +$30.

Curry in a Hurry 119 Lexington Ave. (28th St.) (212) 683-0900 Indian. The Raj of Murray's curry row, beloved by Sikhs, Paks, cabbies and Hill residents. For about $7, assemble-your-own piles of spicy homemade curries on basmati rice and naan, with a side salad and soda pop. Jolly's dancing on the Bollywood boob tube upstairs. +$8

Da Ciro 229 Lexington Ave. (33rd & 34th Sts.) (212) 532-1636 Italian. Often overlooked Italian spot is the best in this area by far. Rustic, exposed brick trattoria serves up tender calamari and wonderfully eye-opening fresh pastas, Atkins be damned. Follow with cheese focaccia drizzled with truffle oil, Ciro Verdi signature. -$30

Dos Caminos 373 Park Ave. So. (26th & 27th Sts.) (212) 294-1000 Mexican. Posh Mexican joint sports wild colors, exotic fruit margaritas, and a mind-numbing array of tequilas. Start with freshly-mashed guac in a volcanic mortar bowl, followed by shrimp ceviche and chicken en mole poblano. South of the border brunch never fails to satisfy. -$40

Hangawi 12 E. 32nd St. (5th & Marison Ave.) (212) 213-0077 Korean. Zen retreat from the chih life of the mid-30s shakes up staid vegetarian cuisine with leek and kimchi pancakes, intense salads, and dozens of eclectic variations on modest tofu. Breath deep, leave your shoes at the door, and dive in. $-30 **BlackBook**

Icon at the W Court Hotel 130 E. 39th St. (Lexington Ave.) (212) 592-8888 American. Lurid, seductive décor may conjure images of Patrick Bateman, and we'll certainly go psychotic for the ahi tuna with citrus vinaigrette. Though the interior is in need of a gentle renovation, the outdoor garden still hums with W's lively crowd. -$45

i Trulli 122 E. 27th St. (Park Ave. So. & Lexington Ave.) (212) 481-7372 Italian. Straight outta Puglia, the culinary heel of Italy's boot. Warm, attractive décor revolves around the center glass-enclosed fireplace. Try the Sardinian dumplings with ground sausage and saffron, hand-rolled by the owner's Mama Mia, trulli a labor of love. $55

Ixta 48 E. 29th St. (Park Ave. So. & Madison Ave.) (212) 683-4833 Mexican creative. Illuminates an otherwise dreary block with colorful, leafy décor, fancy top shelf 'ritas and creative Mexican cuiz from Linda Japngie of Jimmy's. Fresh guacamole to start, then tortilla-crusted tuna with roasted banana and chipotle and crab stuffed shrimp. Sublimely finished with the blood orange sorbet. +$40

Josie's 565 3rd Ave. (37th St.) (212) 490-1558 Vegetarian & Organic. Fresh, clean, modern eats for health nuts and their patient friends. Water is filtered, napkins are unbleached and most of the menu is organically raised, unlike the well-heeled patrons. Lots of glowing girls fresh from NYSC, nibbling on oven-roasted free-range chicken, tofu duck and Japanese yams. $25

La Petite Auberge 116 Lexington Ave. (27th & 28th Sts.) (212) 689-5003 French. Surrounded on all sides by curry shops, tiny bistro is practically an institution with almost 30 years under it's loosened belt. Indulge your Francophile angst over roasted duck in orange sauce, filet mignon with béarnaise, or a simple cheese plate and pastry. $35

Les Halles 411 Park Ave. So. (28th & 29th Sts.) (212) 679-4111 French. Breezy feel transports you to Latin Quarter, except for all the suits stuffing the banquettes. And, no, Anthony Bourdain is not sautéing your steak in the kitchen, he's in Xanghou, eating bamboo shoots. Naked. The beef's here in all forms, cut before your eyes. +$45

Milant 158 E. 39th St. (Lexington & Third Ave.) (212) 682-0111 Gourmet Deli. Jared may stay away, but we'll gladly get fat at this meaty throwback to the heyday of delihood. Like a dream from a Ben Katchor cartoon, this spot will satisfy carnivores and vegetarians alike. Pate, brie, grilled eggplant, and homemade gazpacho for the summer. -$10

Noodles on 28 394 3rd Ave. (28th St.) (212) 679-2888 Chinese & Vietnamese. The Midtown delivery stalwart looks ghetto but still tastes great. Chinese dumplings in sesame sauce, Hong Kong steak, Vietnamese dim sum and everything else from the giant menu. Noodles for an extra buck. Reliable corner spot with nice faux-meat platters. $12

Penelope 159 Lexington Ave. (30th St.) (212) 481-3800 American & Bakery. Breezy corner country kitchen on Curry Hill, multitasks as café, bakery and bar. Friendly owner Jenny's top brunch serves up Nutella french toast and excellent eggs. All the bread, pastries and confections are baked on premises, and go down well with a glass of merlot. -$20

Pinch 416 Park Ave. S. (27th & 28th Sts.) (212) 686-5222 Pizza. You're not dreaming when counter man asks how much hot sausage you'd like at this chi-chi pizza boutique. Sublime thin-crust pizzeria lets you choose your own dimensions. Baked pastas and chicken cooked under a brick at this clean, cheery space where they'll remember your name. -$20 ✯

Pizza 33 489 3rd Ave. (33rd St.) (212) 545-9191 Quite a late night scene of drunken Hillians jostling for a piece of owner Rino LaCerra's stripped down pies. Quality ingredients like fresh mozzarella, marzano tomatoes and basil make the grease worth it. Light, crispy pizza margherita is a local legend waiting to be born. -$12

The Pump 113 E. 31st St. (Lexington & Park Aves.) (212) 213-5733 Organic. They're totally baked and never fried at this health food spot that proves seven grains are better than one. Get pumped for egg-white breakfast specials, innovative tofu, grilled chicken, whole wheat pizza, and other guilt-free ingredients prepared with much natural love. -$20

Rare in the Shelburne Hotel 303 Lexington Ave. (37th St.) (212) 481-1999 Burgers. Red meat for blue bloods. The best burger on the Hill, perhaps all of Manhattan. Pampered patties run the gamut, with a panoply of ingredients and toppings ranging from portabellas to foie gras and fried eggs. Pickles come courtesy of LES legend Guss. -$35

Rice 115 Lexington Avenue (30th St.) (212) 888-3400 NEW Sister to Nolita and Dumbo branches, aptly-named joint offers every kind of grain topped with your choice, so revel in basmati and Thai black. Indulge with edamame, kick up the curry, simmer with lemongrass, sip a shake courtesy of healthy heroes at Soy Luck Club. Simple brilliance. -$20. ✯

Scopa 79 Madison Ave. (28th & 29th Sts.) (212) 686-8787 American. Six enormous rooms with Tuscan décor house food that is unconventional and totally delicious. Scope out veal ragu adorned with chunks of pumpkin and juicy steaks accompanied with amazing caramelized onion salad. Jovial happy hour, raw bar, DJs in front, quiet room in back. -$35

Turkish Kitchen 386 3rd Ave. (27th & 28th Sts.) (212) 679-6633 Turkish. We'd spend more than 1,001 nights at this Arabian paradise, with wall-to-wall flying carpets illuminated by candlelight. Delicious iskender kebab, grilled fish, lamb chops and save room for crisp, sticky baklava. Live music on Tuesdays makes for a true Turkish delight. +$25

Vatan 409 3rd Ave. (29th St.) (212) 689-5666 Indian. Traditionally garbed foot servants and lavish decorations bring authentic flava. Hunker down to be served like a maharaja, with vegetarian cuisine from the state of Gujarati, perfectly spiced dosas and samosas. Toss a nickel in the well and wish for gastronomical nirvana. -$25

Wolfgang's Steakhouse 4 Park Ave. (33rd St.) (212) 889-3369 Steakhouse. After cutting his chops with steakmaster Peter Luger, headwaiter Wolfgang Zweiner left to start his own high-end meat house. Exceptional porterhouse, unbelievable filet mignon, and tasty sides that include German potatoes and creamed spinach. The makings of a modern classic, well-done. -$75.

NIGHTLIFE Murray Hill & Kips Bay

Aubette 119 E. 27th St. (Lexington Ave. & Park Ave. So.) (212)686-5500 Soho-style loft space looks out over 27th, with plush candlelit retreat in back. Rowdy young professionals leering at classy females, drunken lounging, get suavely lit. French flair until four in the morning, so we're using up our sick days.

Cherry at the W Tuscany Hotel 120 E. 39th St. (Park & Lexington Aves.) (212) 519-8508 Gets yours popped at this very dark, incense-laced lounge that cloaks a mix of hotel guests and locals. Walls, curtains, lights, and drinks will have you seeing red, so be a rebel and drink a white cosmo in the grey room.

The Cabin Club at Pinetree Lodge, 326 E. 35th St. (1st & 2nd Aves.) (212) 481-5490 The Hill's hidden gem off the Midtown Tunnel, surreal summer camp vibe mixes Kamp Krusty and David Lynch. Lots of woodwork and decapitated trophy animals, appropriately kooky crowd. Ideal backyard hideaway, we've got cabin fever. **BlackBook**

Ginger Man 11 E. 36th St. (5th & Madison Aves.) (212) 532-3740. Heaven for hops lovers. Girls get outnumbered by the mostly male crowd, but with over 66 brews on tap, thirsty singles still find great head. If you can't decide between chocolate stout or amber ale, consult the tomes by suds expert Michael Jackson.

Jazz Standard 116 E. 27th St. (Lexington Ave. & Park Ave. So.) (212) 576-2232 Laid-back by NYC's stuffy jazz standards, but solely for cats looking to drop serious money. Wailing bebop provides the backdrop for casual boozing at the multi-level hall downstairs from Blue Smoke, feel free to improvise.

Mica Bar 587 3rd Ave. (38th & 39th Sts.) (212) 661-3181 Candlelit, art deco lounge gets crammed with moneyed Midtown office crowd, who've gone from formal to normal by simply untucking their shirts. Aggressive singles mating scene and feverish office gossip abound, escape to the rooftop porch on hot summer nights.

Morgans Bar at the Morgans Hotel 237 Madison Ave. (37th & 38th Sts.) (212) 726-7600. Velvety subterranean lounge is cozy, costly, good for a mature drink and casual affair, if a bit kitschy. Runway-primed staff grazes their lovely heads on crystal chandeliers while spiriting your spirits, try not to gawk.

Rare View at the Shelburne Hotel 303 Lexington Ave. (37th St.) (212) 481-1999 Striking rooftop panorama of the Chrysler and Empire State will have you humming Gershwin. Draws a mix of business travelers and youngish Murrays. Plenty of space, plenty of chairs and plenty of clever cocktails to blur the view. Tasty blood orange cosmo is a rare treat.

Rodeo Bar 375 3rd Ave. (27th St.) (212) 683-6500 The ghost of Johnny Cash floats through Murray Hill's own roadhouse, blessing every last drop of whiskey. Hold on tight and drink hard while chewing on a tasty wad of Skol and toasting a Texas that has nothing to do with George W.

Under the Volcano 12 E. 36th St. (5th & Madison Aves.) (212) 213-0093 Spanish poetry along the walls, wonderful margaritas and Dos Equis erupting on tap, we'll run the risk. Same owner as Ginger Man, this smaller sibling holds all the charm with leather banquettes, red lamps, and Mexicana decoration.

Wet Bar at the W Court Hotel 100 E. 30th St. (Lexington & Park Aves.) (212) 592-UN44 Another Randy Gerber production gets you soaked. Brown armchairs, red velvet sofas, a little bamboo and a vicously loud system. So dark, you can barely make out all the suits flashing their corporate cards.

WEST 30s & GARMENT DISTRICT

(map p. 203)

Some people call it the Garment District, the Fashion Center or Koreatown, while basketball fans know it as **the traffic frenzy they hurried through to catch Starbury at the Garden**. With an eclectic mix of publishing and record company offices, rehearsal spaces and a high concentration of recording studios, you never know when you'll catch Damon Dash and posse tumbling out of their custom Roc-A-Fella humvee. Sure, the neighborhood has more than its share of winos, crazies, thugs and depressive suits hoofing it back to **Penn Station** to catch the last train home to Jersey. As long as you can avoid the smell of garbage/McDonuts outside of the McDonald's on 34th Street, you can survive this area of town, and **even stumble across some of its hidden gems**. Catch us having drinks in one of **Koreatown's far-out lounges**, or on a romantic date at **Market Café**. Everyone knows icing is one of the five food groups, so for dessert let's hit up the **Cupcake Café** before making it with the models at **Lobby**.

RESTAURANTS West 30s & Garment District

Cheyenne Diner 411 9th Ave. (33rd St.) (212) 465-8750 American. Perfect pit stop if you've got a few hours to kill 'til your bus leaves, or your just fond of the area. One of the last true diners left comes to life at 4am. A burger for every nation: red, dyed or feather. And Re-Run on the wall still gets no cheeseburger love from Shirley. -$15

Cho Dang Gol 55 W. 35th St. (5th & 6th Aves.) (212) 695-8222 Korean. Authentic "Seoul food" dishes infused with a house specialty Korean tofu, or dobu, yo. Delicate flower-lamps, traditional Korean unies on the waitresses, quasi-rustic. Full of real, live Koreans—the best endorsement possible. $30

Cupcake Café 522 9th Ave. (39th St.) (212) 465-1530 Coffeeshop & Bakery. Once again voted better than the Village's Magnolia. No-frills establishment save for the decorative pastel icing on the thick cupcakes. But that doesn't make the food, or the ambiance, any less sweet. Great coffee, too. Gets busy on weekends, best for take-out. +$5

Han Bat 53 W. 35th St. (5th & 6th Aves.) (212) 629-5588 Korean. Dishes orbited by plates of banchan like so many moons, pots of broth simmer aesthetically in the stone-lined enclave in back. Wash it down with an O.B. All-night bright stop especially good for carbo-loading after a night of Midtown clubbing. $25

Keens Steakhouse 72 W. 36th St. (5th & 6th Aves.) (212) 947-3636 Steakhouse. Welcome to the boy's club. Choose from hundreds of whiskeys and pick your poison: single malts, single stockbrokers. Old-school class in the restaurant, rowdy times in the pub. Believe the burger, don't believe the pipe. $35

Kum Gang San 49 W. 32nd St. (Broadway & 5th Ave.) (212) 967-0909 Korean. Think Disneyland Korea, with much better food. Personal tabletop barbecues make up for gaudy décor. Arguably the city's top bi bim bop. Fun, loud atmosphere, great for large groups. +$20

Mandoo Bar 2 W. 32nd St. (Broadway & 5th Ave.) (212) 279-3075 Korean. It's all about the dumplings: delicious, copious, multi-colored dumplings stuffed with various goodies. Long, narrow rectangle has some design-y touches, and the young Koreatown crowd chatters about the latest developments at Dad's store. $10

Market Café 496 9th Ave. (37th & 38th Sts.) (212) 564-7350 American. Chill 50s-modern atmo contrasts the grit, grime and noise of area. Phenomenal steak frites, burgers and coq au vin, but in truth, everything's good. We wish we could keep this place to ourselves. Sedate spot with the apropo architectural touches raises the classiness quotient of the 30s a few notches. $25 **BlackBook**

Plantain 20 W. 38th St. (5th & 6th Aves.) (212) 869-8601 Caribbean. Going back to the island, Mon. Haute Latin fare attracts throngs of hungry lunch-goers, most wishing they were somewhere a little more tropical to properly enjoy jerked island dishes. Big nighttime scene: Chi-chi's del Bronx in biz cas attire throw back guava coladas and work it to Thalia tracks. $25

Sandwich Planet 534 9th Ave. (39th & 40th Sts.) (212) 273-9768 Sandwiches. Kindergartner's dream feast. Nearly 100 sandwiches saturated in Play-doh primary colors. French dip and the mini-Christo might be the best lunch option in the area. Take pity on the poor girl… $10

Splashlight Studios Restaurant 529-535 West 35th St. (10th & 11th Aves.) American. (212) 268-7247 While the models stick to their Camel Lights and Fiji water, feast on salmon, hanger steak and black-eyed peas. Open for lunch in the clean, well-designed, loft-like setting of your dreams. $35

Tagine Dining Gallery 537 9th Ave. (40th St.) (212) 564-7292 Moroccan. Arabian Nights-themed harem complete with candle light and cushions. The fragrant spring lamb tagine is nice, but we dig on the grilled marguez, fed to us by hand, slowly. Could that really be the Port Authority across the way? $20

NIGHTLIFE West 30's & Garment District

Andalucia 533 9th Ave. (39th & 40th Sts.) (212) 736-9411 Not-in-NY feel, though getting all up on the Port Authority. Drink an Estrella with Guillermo and ask him to recount his well-traveled life story, then ask for the fresh tapas he makes till the wee hours. Nonchalant vibe. Good juke, too. **BlackBook**

Bellevue Bar 538 9th Ave. (39th & 40th Sts.) (212) 760-0660 Home to the best jukebox in the West 30s and strewn with obscure discarded camp, this gateway to Hell's Kitchen is appropriately dimly lit. Ms. Pac-Man meets G.G. Allin, and Big Buck Hunt for prime stress relief: capping defenseless bambies is almost better than Xanax! Try it! You'll like it!

Club Shelter 20 W. 39th St. (5th & 6th Aves.) (212) 719-4479 House of soulful house. Multi-chambered and acoustically blessed. Shelter is the big name jam, but nights come in other assorted dance flavors too. Dance 'til Sunday morning or 'til that go-go girl in the g-string and vinyl pants is carted off in an ambulance. Whichever comes first.

Copacabana 560 W. 34th St. (11th Ave.) (212) 239-2672 Arriba! Alive and well, even post relocation and revamping. Redone exactamente like the first one, but please don't sing Manilow, please do dance salsa, merengue, and dress to impress the copa girls. Expect long lines and high energy.

Holland Bar 532 9th Ave. (39th & 40th Sts.) (212) 502-4609 The consummate dive bar. While away your waking hours in Bukowskian fashion. Stick to the cheap beers and do go asking for anything fancy in your drink. Like a lime.

Lobby 330 W. 38th St. (8th & 9th Aves.) (212) 465-2200 Decked-out VIP girlies keep the private soirees well-sauced at this huge, multi-leveled, popular clubby club. Big enough for private events, with the requisite velvet ropes and bottles service and silhouetted shenanigans in back. Jeremy C. keeps the party in check.

MBC Music Box 25 W. 32nd St., 3rd fl. (5th Ave & Broadway) (212) 967-2244 Down a few and get over your stage fright. Cause if we all must sing Madonna covers, let us do so at MBC, where the rooms are private and the disco balls are plentiful. Oh and they're open 'til 6am.

"There is a great tango of eye contact between men and women on the streets of New York."

—Joseph Giovanni

MIDTOWN WEST & HELL'S KITCHEN

(map page 204)

The mass transit crossroads of the city, Times Square is also the nexus for the variety of dynamic forces that have shaped the city over the past half century, and has gone from glitzy to sleazy and back again with astonishing speed. Where classy proletariat drinking gardens once stood, 80-foot animated billboards now dominate the vista, selling ad time at five grand per second. Behind those signs lurk the monumental office towers of the giants of publishing, broadcasting and banking, the inhabitants of which stream out onto the area's restaurants at night, expensing everything in sight. **Times Square is New York's heart in need of a triple bypass, but it's the only ticker we've got**. Midtown West is also home to Fashion Avenue, where the captains of catwalks scratch their way to the top. Depending on who you ask, the Broadway theater scene is either rejuvenated or decaying. Regardless, it's where all young actors must come to cut their teeth, and where you can see excellent theater in all its incarnations. **Hell's Kitchen is still a bit seedy, but we wouldn't want it any other way.** Ninth Avenue is bursting with new eateries, bars and lounges drawing the Chelsea crowd northward. We'll be dining at the resplendent **Aquavit**, slurping shakes down the street at **Island Burgers**, then descending to the subterranean **Single Room Occupancy**, or imbibing the strong pours at **Siberia**.

RESTAURANTS Midtown West & Hell's Kitchen

Acqua Pazza 36 W. 52nd St. (5th & 6th Aves.) (212) 582-6900 Italian. Luxe. A verified Midtown heavy hitter, featuring a sparkling interior infused with subtle detail. Class, style and sophistication, all the way. Everything on the menu is spectacular, but opt for the namesake dish: an entire fish cooked in a bath of seawater, Sicilian sea salt, white wine and cherry tomatoes. Finish with an espresso and biscotti. $50

Alain Ducasse 155 W. 58th St. (6th & 7th Aves.) (212) 265-7300 French. Luxury in excess, enough to make the Sun King blush with envy. An almost entirely gilded décor is the setting, and the cuisine lives up to it, of course. A set of increasingly spectacular dishes, served on an phalanx of wheeled carts, comes one after the other, unrelenting. Secret: lunch is a real "bargain." $300

Aquavit 65 E. 55th St. (Madison & Park Aves.) (212) 307-7311 Scandinavian cuisine can be bland, but Marcus Samuelsson has given it an adventurous twist. Herring and gravlax are accounted for, but tandoori-smoked char with goat-cheese parfait and Osetra caviar is the real star. Finish with the tart apple sorbet. Stunning presentation, clever staff and a futuristic dining room complete the picture. +$70 **BlackBook**

Asiate at the Mandarin Oriental Hotel 80 Columbus Circle (60th St.) (212) 805-8881French/Japanese. Don't let you 35th floor vista of Central Park, the Biography sign (Ben Stiller this Thursday), or Trump's tauntings distract you from Norie Sugi's culinary innovations. Namely, Caesar salad soup and the cote de boeuf. Finish with mango soufflé. $55

Blue Fin at the W Times Square 1567 Broadway (47th St.) (212) 918-1400 Seafood. Generally included in most "best NYC seafood" discussions, order off the fresh catch board, let them do the rest. Another Steve Hanson creation, with a floor-to-ceiling glass front affording a prime view of the tourist parade, draws a discerning crowd. Again, all about the fish. $45

Bar Americain 152 W. 52nd St. (6th & 7th Aves.) (212) 265-9700 American. Whether you consider Bobby Flay a total genius, or kind of annoying, you have to admit this place is impressive in all ways. From the cocktails, to the spice-rubbed steak, to the David Rockwell design, to the eye-popping prices, it's all there to drink in. Big-night-out kinda place. $55

Bond 45 154 W. 45th St. (Seventh Ave.) (212) 869-4545 Italian. Oscar Hammerstein's old digs, used to be the Olympia Theater. Large two tiered room with very unassuming crowd, not bad for keeping it low key or grabbing a pre-theater bite. Appetizers are the key, and their mozzarella barata is worth dying for. Leave the leftovers, take the cannoli. $35 ✮

Brasserie 8 1/2 9 W. 57th St. (5th & 6th Aves.) (212) 829-0812 French. A Midtown favorite, although the setting trumps the food. Léger stained glass mural looms overhead, while you eat an abundant poached lobster salad. Menu features some delicious underage eating options like grilled baby octopus and roasted baby pig. Always a big scene, retreat to the dual downstairs lounges. +$60

The Burger Joint at the Parker Meridien Hotel 119 W. 56th St. (6th & 7th Aves.) (212) 245-5000 American. The home of the cheapest, tastiest lunch in Midtown, anachronistic in the grand lobby of the Parker Meridien. Tiny brick burger den drops juicy, satisfying burgers and fries, which were apparently much appreciated by Snoop and his posse. -$6

DB Bistro Moderne 55 W. 44th (5th & 6th Aves.) (212) 441-2400 French. Momorably threw down the gauntlet with a proclamation of "best burger on earth." It seems smallish, but you'll have a hard time finishing it: juicy, savory and perfect with ding-dong style interior of truffles. Setting is a bit stuffy and neat for a "bistro," humanized by excellent service. Gorgeous photos by Christopher Beane on the walls. $75

Eatery 798 9th Ave. (53rd St.) (212) 765-7080 American. Like a Cafeteria clone, comfort food in minimalist setting, but menu has evolved nicely. Chef Mario Arnero brings it with tasty barbecued duck and seared tuna on soba. A nice, clean option in this dirty hood. Can't go wrong with the spicy meatloaf. $30

Island Burgers & Shakes 766 9th Ave. (51st & 52nd Sts.) (212) 307-7934 American. A gem. Feels like a Malibu surfer shack, colorful and kooky with an appropriately chill staff. The sheer number and variety of toppings on the superb burgers is a bit daunting, we keep it simple with cheddar and purple onion. Churrasco chicken is of note as well, as is the delicious black & white shake. -$15 **BlackBook**

Masa at the Time Warner Center 10 Columbus Circle (59th St.) (212) 823-9800) Japanese. Masa is indeed the masta, and has announced his arrival in NYC with extraordinary sushi, kaiseki and haute Japanese in a delicate setting to match. Throws down the gauntlet to Nobu, Blue Ribbon and other NY daimyo with unsurpassed quality and attention to detail. +$400

Michael's 24 W. 55th St. (5th & 6th Aves.) (212) 767-0555 American. Oft-touted power lunch scene has cooled off a bit, still more publishing and media big shots than you can shake a stick at, us included. Dry-aged NY strip and humongous salads are the dish of choice and, of course, multiple martinis. Surprisingly pleasant in the evening. +$55

Modern at the MoMA 9 W. 53rd St. (btwn 5th & 6th Sts.) (212) 333-1220 French. Danny Meyer strikes again, this time bringing Gabriel Kreuther over from the Ritz to set up shop. We desperately wanted to hate this place, with its uber clean lines, unabashed flamboyance and air-kissing culture whores, but dammit it's all so beautiful and the food so spectacular… Get the roast duck or the special. $65

Nobu Uptown 40 W. 57th St. (5th & 6th Aves.) No Phone. Just like the downtown Nobu, on steroids and powerful hallucinogens. Thirteen-thousand square feet: wow, that's big even by NY standards. Expect more of the same creative and colorful cuisine, here devoured by Uptowners unwilling to venture down to the Tribeca outpost. $60 ✮

Océo at the Time Hotel 224 W. 49th St. (Broadway & 8th Ave.) (212) 262-6236 Eclectic/Global. Flows seamlessly from the Time lobby. In a word, sleek. Shane McBride, formerly of Lespinasse, imbues his dishes with unabashed creativity: lobster soup gets even more decadent with fois gras floating in it. Delicious biscuits n' gravy reveal Shane's southern roots. $40

Per Se at the Time Warner Center 10 Columbus Circle (60th St.) (212) 823-9335 American. Discrete and intimate, with stunning attention to detail by Thomas Keller of Napa Valley's much-revered French Laundry. Warm elements of stone and wood contrast sharply with the buildings' harsh mirrored architecture, ideal setting for the meticulously conceived and crafted dishes. Go ahead, break the bank. $100

Petrossian 182 W. 58th St. (7th Ave.) (212) 245-2214 French. A New York landmark around the corner from Carnegie Hall, where many of that venue's world-class performers come for opening night after parties. Grand entrance gives way LaGuardia-era art deco interior, neatly attired staff bring incredible bellini and champagne. Time warp. +$70

Ruby Foos 1626 Broadway (49th St.) (212) 489-5600 Chinese. Big fun from Steve Hanson just off the epicenter of Times Square, mentioned in half-a-dozen musicals about our fair city. Crispy stir-fried shrimp are a necessity, and the wok-steamed lobster impresses. The real treat though is descending the resplendent Mamescent staircase: Jazz hands, Jazz hands! +30

Sosa Borella 832 8th Ave. (50th St.) (212) 262-8282 Argentine & Italian. Chintzy 8th Avenue is uplifted by this Italo-Argentino high concept kitchen, cousin of the Tribeca branch. Housed in a tiny, elegant townhouse, home to sizable steak cuts, savory bruscetta and bounteous pastas. Garden patio is a nice respite. $32

Trattoria dell'Arte 900 7th Ave. (56th & 57th Sts.) (212) 245-9800 Italian. Enormous barn-like space, echoing with the voices of jovial diners and singing waiters. Frequently repped as some of the best Italian restaurants in the city, fresh sea bass and linguine with clams, and the city's best antipasto bar has us convinced. Perfect for big, boisterous celebrations. $50

21 Club 21 W. 52nd. St. (5th & 6th Aves.) (212) 582-7200 American. Jacket and tie required in this infamous former speakeasy, protected out front with a cache of lawn jockeys. Bankers and various Fortune 500 clientele settle into big leather banquettes, devouring juicy steaks and copious martinis. Amazing steak tartare is prepared tableside. Atmospheric wine cellar below. +$70

V Steakhouse at the Time Warner Center 10 Columbus Circle (59th St.) (212) 823-9500 Steakhouse. You knew that Georges would throw his hat in the ring here, and give thanks he did. Amidst the TW's somewhat rarified culinary stars, this place keeps it old school. Generous cuts, porterhouse, filet mignon, NY strip in appropriately musty rococo digs. $55

NIGHTLIFE Midtown West & Hell's Kitchen

Ava Penthouse Lounge 210 55th St. (Broadway & 7th Ave.) (212) 956-7020 Named for Ava Gardner, an expansive midtown duplex occupying the top two floors of the Majestic hotel. High design space is a maze of glitzy nooks. Soak in the incredible view of Times Square humming far below.

The Carnegie Club 156 W. 56th St. (6th & 7th Aves.) (212) 957-9676 Thick with old school New York history and atmosphere, right down to the collection of rare books. Bi-level arrangement and comfy chairs, perfect for sipping Scotch and planning hostile takeovers.

Hudson Bar at the Hudson Hotel 356 W. 58th St. (8th & 9th Aves.) (212) 554-6343 An incredible space taken straight from that ending scene in "2001: A Space Odyssey," unfortunately shamed by a cheesy Euro-crowd. Nice nooks if you can grab one, those in the know escape to the veranda.

Japas 55 253 West 55th St. (Broadway & 8th Ave.) (212) 581-2240 Low key after-work joint to take the edge off. Authentic Japanese staff sets up the sake as you jot down the karaoke ID number for your favorite Stevie Nicks jam. Enjoy the latest pop videos from Nippon while the salaryman at the end of the bar sings "Sweet Caroline." Half off sushi before 7pm.

K 30 W. 52nd St. (5th & 6th Aves.) (212) 265-6665 Quietly the top hang in Midtown, still largely undiscovered, thankfully. Backed by the offspring of Deepak Chopra, hazy, windowless rooms contain one of the most unique atmospheres in the city. A Hindu temple replete with Kama Sutra wall diagrams, recline in the plush, pillowed back room with your harem. **BlackBook**

The Living Room at the W Times Square 1567 Broadway (47th St.) (212) 930-7444 A gorgeous, soft-lit space of white leather banquettes and booths, gets slammed with an odd mix of tourists, business travelers and rock bands in town for shows at the nearby Roseland Ballroom. Scantily clad waitresses teeter precariously, almost spilling your pricey martini. Self-conscious vibe, but fun.

Paramount Bar at the Paramount Hotel 235 W. 46th St. (Broadway & 8th Ave.) (212) 764-5500 A living metaphor for the city, décor blends 1920s speakeasy elegance with wonderfully tacky disco stylings. Mirrored ceilings, crystal chandeliers, leggy blondes, and loads of celebs all dazzle the eye. Clever, if overly sweet cocktails get you swizzled.

Penthouse Executive Club 603 W. 45th (11th Ave.) (212) 245-0002 What's wrong with this city, when there's only one place left you can feast on Kobe steaks while getting a $300 lap dance? You've gone soft, NY. Slick silver façade houses Guccione's decadent scene within. Private shows in the plush back rooms.

Pentop Bar at the Peninsula Hotel 700 5th Ave. (55th St.) (212) 956-2888 Great view, wack crowd. It's really that simple. Twenty-three floors above the city, mid-level execs with cell phone holsters slug expensive, watery drinks. Close-up vista of midtown architecture does impress, though, and you can work on your tan.

Russian Vodka Room 265 W. 52nd St. (Broadway & 8th Ave.) (212) 307-5835 Flavored vodkas behind the bar are a rare treat: pepper, pineapple, strawberry, ginger, etc. Take your pick, or get a taster's menu. Either way you'll be nicely sauced before the show at Roseland across the street. Supposedly haunted…

Show 135 W. 41st St. (6th Ave. & Broadway) (212) 278-0988 Synonymous with Britney before she got hitched, now lacking in tacky celeb appeal, but still fun. Expansive dance floor chock full of sweaty bodies, snazzily-dressed staff and young celebs put it on the NY club-scene map. Cabaret shows feature Ami Goodheart and her Go-Go Gal revue.

Siberia 356 W. 40th (8th & 9th Aves.) (212) 333-4141 Remember the TV show "Nightcourt"? That's what the crowd looks like here, mingling with the cast of "Taxi" and the actual cast of "Rent" after they finished their last show around midnight. Lots of strung-out journalists and committed alkies, too. Big space, trashy in a good way, with strong pours. Beloved.

Single Room Occupancy 360 W. 53rd St. (8th & 9th Aves.) (212) 765-6299 Keep looking, Sherlock, and you'll find it. Follow the blue light. Basement nook is long and narrow, long on class and sophistication. Splurge on the shiraz or the Potent Monster, nosh on choco Teddy Grahams in lieu of pretzels. Candle lit, mysterious air, a Midtown jewel. **BlackBook**

Town at The Chambers Hotel 15 W. 56th St. (5th & 6th Aves.) (212) 582-4445 Minimalist hotel bar with a clever lighting scheme and seductive atmo. Peopled with young professionals who make mint off their artist clients, smirking dubious, meticulously prepared drinks. Thoroughly modern.

MIDTOWN EAST

(map page 205)

We'll gladly trade some of our choice UN oil for food at some of the Midtown East's rarified eateries, just don't tell our dad, Kofi. Home to the corporate headquarters of the world's evilest companies, Midtown East is a daunting maze of soul-crushing concrete and glass urban canyons, best described as a "beautiful disaster." Fifth Avenue is prime retail, a row of luxury mega-stores guarded by intimidating men in designer suits, who gladly open doors for another Iowan tourist in daisy-dukes. To escape the bustling Midtown chaos, take a stroll around beautiful Tudor Park to see dapper urbanites and UN delegates living life on the other side. **Grand Central** is a magnificent commuter hub, home of the **Oyster Bar** and the **Campbell Apartment**, with their grand décor reminiscent of a bygone era. Like Lower Manhattan, Midtown East is a scary wasteland at night, unless you find yourself in one of the classy bars like the timeless **King Cole Bar**, or the uptown Decibel: **Sakagura**. If you can get a table, lunch at inimitable **Four Seasons**, where you'll be accurately seated according to your up-to-the-minute standing in the power rankings. **Power, truly, is the ultimate aphrodisiac** . For a more subtle form of seduction, sample the delicate creations from the expert chefs at **Sushi Yasuda**.

RESTAURANTS Midtown East

BLT Steak 106 E. 57th St. (Park & Lexington Aves.) (212) 752-7470 Steakhouse. The name can be a little confusing, BLT standing for Bistro Laurent Tourondel, formerly of fondly remembered Cello. Steak in every cut imaginable; strip, porterhouse, Kobe, etc. The Interior is simple, effective and warmly lit—perfect in helping you digest that 40oz. piece. +$55

Chikubu 12 E. 44th St. (5th & Madison Aves.) (212) 818-0715 Japanese. Authentic Japanese cuisine with authentic clientele. The Zen rock garden is the much needed office meditation break. Great service, and clean environment make this a popular choice. Teriyaki, noodles, sashimi and omakase dinner where the chef does his best to confuse and excite diners with a convoy of distinct dishes. $45

Chola 232 E. 58th St. (2nd & 3rd Aves.) (212) 688-4619 Indian. Bollywood starlets serve sizzling Indian favs to a crowd of locals and the occasional group of lost tourists. Specialties are divided by region and mix traditional Indian recipes with dishes from the lesser-known regions. Try the lamb specialties. Beat the weekday work masses and make it for the much worthy weekend buffets. $35

Django 480 Lexington Ave. (46th St.) (212) 871-6600 Mediterranean. Named after the world's greatest jazz guitarist. The interior is amusing and charming although a table outside is always worth the extra hassle. Middle Eastern flavors mingle with raw oyster bar; Medi-staples from Cedric Tovar. Dressed-to-the-nines crowd delights when the excellent tagines arrive, and are possibly cool enough to have known the late Mr. Reinhardt himself. $50

57 57 57 E. 57th St. (Madison & Park Aves.) (212) 758-5757 American. The fabulous Four Season's fabulous A-List sister. The foie gras from upstate under a light gingered fig-cutney, roast duck with pomegranite syrup, crab cakes with bell pepper oil are exquisite. The scene is interesting: starlets, grumpy PR women, media moguls and the occasional rap star... $60

The Four Seasons 99 E. 52nd St. (Lexington & Park Aves.) (212) 754-9494 American. Uptown dinning as it should be. Exquisite decor from wall to wall, attentive and reliable service, creative food of the highest rank. Carefully thought-out seating hierarchy. Choice of rooms for every occasion: the grill room for grillin' or the pool room for chillin'. $75 **BlackBook**

Le Colonial 149 E. 57th St. (Lexington & 3rd Aves.) (212) 752-0808 Vietnamese. Lush foliage and photos of colonial Vietnam taken straight from The Quiet American. One of New York's original fusion experiments doesn't dazzle as it once did, but the spring rolls are a great start before dropping into their more refined dishes. $40

Lever House 390 Park Ave. (53rd St.) (212) 888-2700 Creative European. The decor is at once ornate and demure, and the food is meticulously prepared yet unimposing. Entrees trumped by appetizers and masterful pastries. Real estate moguls power lunch and power dinner . $60

March 405 E. 58th St. (1st Ave. & Sutton Pl.) (212)754-6272 American. Sushi Hamachi with olive oil. Foie Gras with garam masala. Like Soon Yi and Woody without the incest. High prices worth it for those with pioneering taste and the appropriate bulge in the wallet. Garden and slim rooms enhance the sleek, impressive nice time. +$55

Mr. Chow's 324 E. 57th St. (1st & 2nd Aves.) (212) 751 9011 Chinese. Used to be a Warhol/Factory hang Nowadays Creative elite of greedy rap CEOs come and discuss what to flog next. Still has the disco feel of it's golden days. Food comes so fast, we suspect it was hastily delivered from Chinatown. $50

Opia 130 E. 57th St. (Lexington Ave.) (212) 688-3939 French. Young pros, pre-theater crowds and self-aware movers n' shakers opiated on copious amounts of booze and eye contact. Mediterranean and separate Asian influenced menu a curious, but good choice during a lively scene. Where Brazilian and Argentine models catch their homeland's futbol games. $45

Oyster Bar at Grand Central (42nd St. & Vanderbilt Ave.) (212) 490-6650 Seafood. After reenacting the baby pram scene on the stairs of Grand central, slip into this gorgeous space for a glamorous old school feel. Make sure you have a later train planned cos' you don't wanna be rushing. Exquisite cocktails, more oysters than you can handle. Kick back, relax.... if only cigars were still allowed. -$40

Palm 840 2nd Ave. (44th & 45th Aves.) (212) 687-7698 Steakhouse. Has a bit of a reputation as the flagship of the successful chain. Serves Italian and seafood specialties but success definitely lies in the meat. Filet mignon, New York strip or rib eye. Lunch scene of local suits talking contracts. $60

Pampano 209 E. 49th St. (2nd & 3rd Aves.) (212) 751-4545 Creative Mexican. More refined than the average Mexican joint, bi-level airy space feels more like a trendy hotel restaurant. Chef owner Richard Sandoval offers food that lives up to the decor. Whole red snapper, pan-weared pompano, albondigas, spicy ceviches, chocolate tacos and fresh margaritas all astoundingly good. $45

Patroon 160 E. 46th St. (Lexington & 3rd Aves.) (212) 883-7373 American. Big headed junior execs pack this clubby bar. The Maine lobster is as big said execs egos, although most portions tend to be on the small and pricey side. Skip the meal and head directly for desert -the ice cream sundae is our favorite $70

Pietro's 232 E. 43rd St. (2nd & 3rd Aves.) (212) 682-9760 Steakhouse. Quality steak since '32, keeping regulars satisfied before there was such a thing as a generator. The steaks are cooked to perfection. Try some of their pasta sides like the shells or the mouthwatering homemade gnocchi. $45

Q56 65 E. 56th St. (Madison & Park Aves.) (212) 756-3800 Seafood & Creative. Classy space age seafood-focused diner inside the Swissotel. Open three meals a day and bustling straight thru each. The fish menu is rather limited but the cocktails are fabulous (like their own version of the Cosmo) and the wine list is extensive, not expensive. $50

Savannah Steak 12 E. 48th St. (5th & Madison Aves.) (212) 935-2500 American & Steakhouse. Sweet Georgian leans in favor of delicious beef and seafood. BIG, sexy lounge spot with plus furniture perfect to chill with the taste of sirloin in your mouth. The seafood selection is of surprising high standards, still we're all about the meat, like the porterhouse or prime rib. Juicy. $45

Smith & Wollensky 797 3rd Ave. (49th St.) (212) 753-1530 Steakhouse. Possibly Manhattan's most classic steakhouse with meat in every incarnation. Big men in expertly tailored suits keep the world at bay in this neatly latticed, window-less bunker. The service in experienced and unintrusive. Try the filet mignon, nature, or better yet, with smoky Cajun spices. +$50

Sushi Yasuda 204 E. 43rd St. (2nd & 3rd Aves.) (212) 972-1001 Japanese. Thirty kinds of raw fish, five types of eel and a floor you could eat off. Hip Sushi joint in unhip area. Comes in handy of you wanted to show off your recently purchased Pradas, although it's rarely packed. Minimalist, trendy-Zen interior. Detail orientated: sake served on a miniature mat of bamboo. $40 **BlackBook**

Tao 42 E. 58th St. (Madison & Park Aves.) (212) 888-2288 Pan-Asian. New York rip off of Paris' famous Buddha bar. The size is there, as is the fusion cuisine and the giant Buddha weighing over the all-looks crowd. This is the kind of place that has or could have it's own 'chill out' compilation. The upstairs caters to a younger drinking crowd. The sexy hostesses are worth getting to know better. $65

Vong 200 F 54th St. (3rd Ave.) (212) 486-9592 French & Thai. Chef Jean Georges churns out another fusion formula winner. The decor is best described as designer tiki kitsch. The food blends Thai and French cuisines with dishes like a mango and ginger foie gras or the salmon with galangal sauce. $65

NIGHTLIFE Midtown East

Au Bar 41 E. 58th St. (Madison & Park Aves.) (212) 308-9455 Big, plush, cheesy, can't shake the 90s fun, but still goes off some nights. Also goes by the moniker Club 58, hosts big hip-hop mogul parties. Eurotrash lament the loss of their fromer mecca. Ask Stratis about his love for the Hayden family.

Branch 226 E. 54th St. (2nd & 3rd Aves.) (212) 688-5577 The Metronome Woods Project. A party of youngsters pay the gown at the door and get lost in a maze of with Bourbon, woodland barriers, a dance floor bar and kicking sounds. Sure to be a private party destination and rambunctious good time, if it avoids the Bermuda triangle of midtown clubs which snatches off customers before they get to the velvet rope.

The Campbell Apartment at Grand Central 15 Vanderbilt Ave. (43rd St.) (212) 953-0409 Feels like an older NYC. Serious suits sipping cognac or bourbon on the rocks discuss stock exchanges and business ventures. Watch 'em loosten the tie as they get to their fourth round. No sneakers or jeans, btw.

King Cole Bar at the St. Regis 2 E. 55th St. (5th & Madison Aves.) (212) 339-6721 Utmost style and service, contested inventor of Bloody Mary, cozy mahogany and leather, attractive but quiet, selective crowd. We think it deserves a bigger following -although in the meantime you won't hear us complaining. Thick with NY history: make some of your own. **BlackBook**

LQ 511 Lexington Ave. (47th & 48th Sts.) (212) 593-7575 Murder Inc. lived up to their name with drive-by earlier this year… but don't let that stop you from slammin' Latin nights. Upscale, so-called ghetto-fab crowd. Lots of events, you might catch J-Lo trying to get cred without actually having to visit said uptown block .

Sakagura 211 E. 43rd St. (2nd & 3rd Aves.) (212) 953-7253 Turn the Decibel uptown and here's what you get, no split eardrums just sake aplenty, and if you can't decide betwixt the supai or amae, have the $15 tasting set. Wise to befriend the Japanese salaryman next to you: he's probably worth more than some small countries… **BlackBook**

Subway Inn 143 E. 60th St. (Lexington & 3rd Aves.) (212) 223-8929 Super old-timey dive, derelict looks and characters inside. Random Hunter College kids skipping class, old dudes at the bar possibly skipping life in exchange for cheap beers from wrinkled rockstar Charlie. Check it out before they tear it down and make a Quiznos.

The World Bar 845 United Nations Plaza (E. 47th St.) (212) 935-9361 set in a timely location. In all honesty this is a classy, nice joint but do you really want to put more money into Trump's pocket, especially when he shamelessly sells the "world's most expensive cocktail" at $50? Bring an Evian bottle full of gin and order a $6 tonic water instead.

"There is a great tango of eye contact between men and women on the streets of New York."

—Joseph Giovanni

UPPER EAST SIDE (map p. 207)

Once called the Gold Coast, the Upper East is home to the toney mansions of the old money barons of industry, the new money hedge fund managers, and is still the neighborhood of choice for those with the means. **Downtowners may complain about getting nosebleeds for coming up this high**, but there's more classy spots than you can shake a jewel-encrusted finger at. **Nothing epitomizes a high-class New York night than sipping scotch at the resplendent Bemelman's Bar**. While most of the creative culinary action seems to be happening downtown, don't sleep on newcomer **Geisha** or trendsetter **Daniel. J.G. Melon** still kicks one of the city's best burgers. After that posh opening the Met, find us summoning Geeves for a quick ride in the Bentley over to greet our friend **Nello**, before settling in for a brandy or two at **Mark Bar**.

RESTAURANTS Upper East Side

Atlantic Grill 1341 3rd Ave. (76th & 77th Sts.) (212) 988-9200 Seafood. Large, clean white space. Steve Hanson sails the seven seas and emerges with more tropical booty than a Sean Paul video. Does raw and cooked in big, raucous space. Upscale bar scene. Delish seafood like nori-wrapped yellowfin tuna and bamboo-steamed shrimp. ⊢ $40

Aureole 34 E. 61st St. (Park & Madison Aves.) (212) 319-1660 American. Charlie Palmer's house of indulgence set inside old, wood-paneled residence previously owned by Orson Welles. Leather banquettes and blooming bouquets throughout . It's all about the seafood here. From tuna sashimi to pan-roasted halibut. Desserts are flawless in both presentation and taste. Staff is attentive without butting in. + $75

Barbaluc 135 E. 65th St. (Lexington & Park Aves.) (212) 774-1999 Italian. Fresh from the pages of Wallpaper, standard for downtown but stands out up here. Excuse me miss, who's driving your plane? Risotto del giorno and an extraordinary white wine selection from Friuli. Drink enough and feel like Barbaluc, the wily wine elf himself. $50

Brasserie 200 E. 60th St. (3rd Ave.) (212) 688-8688 French & Japanese. Gaul on bottom, Nipponese on top - sure to have good looking babies. Large duplex, paint-by-numbers French theme down to the Brigitte Bardot pictures. If you can't decide on what cuiz you desire till you're actually inside a restaurant, this is your place. $40

Café Sabarsky at the Neue Galerie 1048 Fifth Ave. (86th St.) (212) 288-0665 Austrian. Viennese café, marble tabletops, black cafe chairs and waiters looking sharp in black and white. Flowered patterned sofas in muffled colors, dark parquet flooring, grand piano in the corner. Coffee served in cups on little silver trays with a petit glass of water. Terrific strudel a hit with posh art dealers. -$20

Centolire 1167 Madison Ave. (85th & 86th Sts.) (212) 734-7711 Tuscan. Elegant welcome from hostess in little black dress and pearls. Upstairs/downstairs Italian comes complete with elevator. Generous portions of Prince Edward Island Mussels, seafood stews arriving in earthenware crockery. With 100 lire you can go to America, and for forty Euros you can eat here. $45

Coco Pazzo 23 E. 74th St. (5th & Madison Aves.) (212) 794-0205 Tuscan with the nice rack of lamb, from Pino Luongo. Discreet exterior, parquet floors, light color scheme in a medium-sized room. Earthy farrotto ai funghi amid the famous, fabulous and the simply European. +$45

Daniel 60 E. 65th St. (Madison & Park Aves.) (212) 288-0033 Superstar French making dramatic entrances via the stunning staircase. Almost hate to touch the food it's so incredibly constructed. But hey, you're hungry, somebody else is paying, and there are plenty of utensils on the table to dismantle that edible sculpture on your plate made from seared foie gras with sliced kumquats. Archetypal. +$85

Dumonet at the Carlyle Hotel 35 E. 76th St. (Madison Ave.) (212) 744-1600 French. Posh like an English manor. Chocolate sofas and walls, delicate china, amazing floral arrangements. Wealthy people, diplomats and Hollywood execs dining on rich steaks and such. +$60

Elaine's 1703 2nd Ave. (88th & 89th Sts.) (212) 534-8103 Continental. Classic literary haunt. Homey, red walls, old-school Italian feel. Though the chow isn't the lure, get the veal saltimbocca and pour some vino out for the late George Plimpton. You'll feel unloved unless you're Woody Allen, but worth going once. NY institution. +$30

Fred's at Barneys 660 Madison Ave., 9th fl. (60th St.) (212) 833-2200 American. Top floor of superlative designer department store, room caked in light. Hoard of socialites mobs it at lunch to pick at fresh, large salads. Pastas, pizzas, and a helluva burger also on tap should you not care about fitting into that size 0. Glorious brunch requires reservation. Don't skip the chicken livers! $40

Geisha 33 E. 61st St. (Madison & Park Aves.) (212) 813-1113 Asian fusion. Japanese seen through the looking glass. Slick, bi-level space with smooth, buttery booths. Miso consommé comes with New Zealand cockles, and the chicken Kinoko is stuffed with more exotic fungi than your average high school locker room. Not as attentive as a good concubine should be, but definitely energetic and down for whatever. $50

J.G. Melon 1291 3rd Ave. (74th St.) (212) 744-0585 American. Incredible cheeseburger puts the crease on your khakis. And the chili will tickle you pink and green. Preppy classic with the watermelon motif, Otis on the juke, and nicest staff in the hood. Cottage fries washed back with brew in unpretentious digs. $25

Kai 822 Madison Ave. (68th & 69th Sts.) (212) 988-7277 Japanese kaiseki with French influence. Minimalist Asian, slate, concrete, bamboo. Drop some yen on tea time with more flavors than Baskin Robbins. Take the elevator to the private room and catch the sixth Beatle, Yoko, dining here several times a week. Shizukani desu... know this. +$50

Mezzaluna 1295 3rd Ave. (74th & 75th Sts.) (212) 535-9600 Amazing Italian. Look up for the soothing baby-blue firmament, down for serene terracotta floor and to your plate for wood-oven pizzas and absolutely perfect Italian fare. Has their own cookbook and is big with UES families. MT's favorite. +$35

Nello 696 Madison Ave. (62nd & 63rd Sts.) (212) 980-9099 Italian. Attracts the super famous, the ridiculously rich, the divinely beautiful, the notoriously "connected", and the just plain awestruck. If you are a true player, George greets you by name when you enter, Lenny takes you to your table in the front, and you get a shout out from Nello himself before you break. Oh, and the food's pretty damn good, too. +$50 **BlackBook**

Payard Patisserie & Bistro 1032 Lexington Ave. (73rd & 74th Sts.) (212) 717-5252 French. Pastries in the front, bistro in the back. Bouloud's project with Monsieur Payard is a smash. Crowd of older regulars on weekdays, Hello Kitty set on weekends who come to consume the best cakes around. Movie set looks and tasty sorbet drinks. +$40

Post House 28 E. 63rd St. (Madison & Park Aves.) (212) 935-2888 Steakhouse. Elegant refuge in Lowell hotel, patriotic art on walls, jacket required. References available upon request. Money. Power. Beef. Quality. It's what's for dinner. Much more refined than expense-account deal-closers, but still slings sick sirloin. +$55

rm 33 E. 60th St. (Madison & Park Aves.) (212) 319-3800 Seafood. Series of elegant, well-lit, rooms. Drowned in shells, seahorses, and photos of the ocean. Delicious start to finish. Prix-fixe is the only way to proceed. Rick Moonen does it again. Hit the smoking lounge upstairs for some a la carte options. +$55

Sarabeth's 1295 Madison Ave. (92nd & 93rd Sts.) (212) 410-7335 American. Connecticut's embassy in the UES. Think Martha Stewart pre-disgrace. Homemade jams to be savored with easy-listening jams. Eggs benedict renowned, beloved chocolate chip cookies. Bring the kids or borrow some to make sure you fit in at brunch. +$25

Scalinatella 201 E. 61st St. (3rd Ave.) (212) 207-8280 Italian. Yacht-owning Euro-jetsetters and their ilk ordering off the menu and buying new pal Mick Jagger drinks. You think you're a P.I.M.P. when you break out the Benjamins as you hit Diddy on his two way? These cats flex Woodrow Wilsons and have the Pope on speed dial. Get the veal chops and look out for cuddly, trust-funded bears. +$60

Serafina 29 E. 61st St. (Madison & Park Aves.) (212) 702-9898 Italian. You need to get on the terrace and check out this scene if you want a real taste of the bourgeoisie. Amex-black rockin, Fendi-totin' Dalton girls just out of puberty looking way too sophisticated for their age discuss first Brazilian wax. +$30

Serendipity 3 225 E. 60th St. (2nd & 3rd Aves.) (212) 838-3531 American. Looks like freaky Tom Petty video of yore with Mad Hatter throwing phat jam full of foot-long dogs and frozen hot chocolate in oversized bowls. Classic to dazzle any little kid in your life, they will freak the f out when they see the size of that peanut butter sundae. Buy some kitschy gifts on the way out. +$18

Skyline Restaurant 1055 Lexington Ave. (75th St.) (212) 861-2540 Diner. Hey, McFly we're talking to you! American throwback for shakes. The old man says you're always safe here. Even when Tom Ridge announces Code Fluorescent Orange. Cheap for the area, immense menu. -$12

Swifty's 1007 Lexington Ave. (72nd & 73rd Sts.) (212) 535-6000 American. Ahh, yes, we'll be at the club with Muffy, Biff, and Bunny. Discreet elegance, society gals and pals in leather chairs. Tiny tables in railroaded rooms. Heiresses lunch on crab cakes and chicken hash, discuss the fabulous benefits they're throwing/attending later in the week. $45

NIGHTLIFE Upper East Side

Great Hall Balcony Bar at the Metropolitan Museum of Art 1000 5th Ave. (82nd St.) (212) 535-7710 Toss the door girl a shiny nickel and take the elevator to the area's best daytime watering hole, or rooftop garden, as the case may be. The drinks aren't the greatest, but the views are intoxicating enough that you might actually stumble into an exhibit on the way out and get some culture for a change. Closes at 8pm.

Bar@Etats-Unis 247 E. 81st St. (2nd & 3rd Aves.) (212) 396-9928 Where the Yorkville white hats go to impress dates. See honey, I don't need a beer bong to have a good time. Sick selection of vino on list, sicker selection of chinos on guests. Quaint, intimate digs and a benevolent personnel.

Bemelman's Bar at The Carlyle Hotel 35 E. 76th St. (Park & Madison Aves.) (212) 744-1600 Named after Madeline creator, Ludwig, whose murals enliven one of Manhattan's classiest drinking experiences. It's the fucking bar at the Carlyle, do you think it's going to be anything but phenomenal? This kind of money bridges all generation gaps as twenty-three old with gazillion dollar trust fund talks new Vertu plan with aging, face lifted baroness. **BlackBook**

Club Macanudo 26 E. 63rd St. (Madison & Park Aves.) (212) 752-8200 Latin brings you pre-Fidel Havana, puros and some single-malt swank. Drink to drink is the Havana Martini. The real players rent their own humidors. Oh, did we mention you can LIGHT UP INSIDE? That's right, no more grubby sidewalks. Just smoke inside like a normal civilized person.

Lexington Bar & Books 1020 Lexington Ave. (73rd Sts.) (212) 717-3902 Formal yet cozy, armchairs, shelves of books, top-shelf cognacs and single malts from sexy librarian Aimee. Stogie sales equal loophole in Bloomberg's ban, thus smoking is permitted...in fact, it's encouraged. Take that Dr. C. Everett Koop!

Mark's Bar at the Mark Hotel 25 E. 77th St. (5th & Madison Aves.) (212) 744-4300 In fave hotel, best in wee hours for nuts and muted elegance. The yacht cabin you've always wanted. Perfect drinks, class acts behind the bar. Cool spot and one of the best hotel bars in the city. **BlackBook**

Sushi Hana 1501 2nd Ave. (77th & 78th Sts.) (212) 327-0582 Get the good stuff. Cozy, small, you've probably walked by it a million times and not noticed it. Some serious Asian talent at work, on any level. Need any more persuasion? Melange of sakes good on their own or complimented by sibling Sushi Hana. No relation to Beni.

Scores 333 E. 60th St. (1st & 2nd Aves.) (212) 421-3600 We'll take that dessert a la Scores, with two generous scoops of silicone: vanilla, chocolate or that butter pecan Puerto Rican from the Boogie Down. Haute pole dancing. A wad of singles isn't gonna cut it, twenties and higher only please. Lots of suits, fake tits and Knicks. Shouldn't you guys be practicing or something?

"A car is useless in New York, essential everywhere else. The same with good manners."

—Mignon McLaughlin

UPPER WEST SIDE

(map p. 206)

Those who love to say they'd never travel above 14th Street don't seem to be in very good company. Still amass with Bugaboo strollers and the nannies pushing them, **the Upper West Side continues to draw the rich and fabulous uptown for its deluxe high-rises, park views and gastronomic delights**. (Word on the street was that even Spike Lee would have ditched his native Brooklyn for the comforts of the UWS.) And few nabes have been captured on celluloid like this one—see "Rosemary's Baby," "Seinfeld," and many Woody Allen flicks. Probably the cleanest part of Manhattan, blending sophistication and hominess, New Yorkers who can afford it move here for the comfort of swanky doormen buildings—the granddaddy of which, **The Dakota**, still draws tourists—personal trainers and dog walkers. Meanwhile, uptown, the **Ding Dong Lounge** is attracting more than just the Columbia kids, what with all the Lower East Side hipsters heading up in droves, complaining their hood isn't seedy and punk enough anymore. Lincoln Center is ringed with luxury residential apartment towers, television studios and tons of notable restaurants, namely **Shun Lee**, while **Central Park** acts as a center of serenity amidst the tall buildings. A lakeside beer just tastes better and a trip to **The Boat Basin** is worth even the masses of tourists and yuppies racking up their bar bills. **Jacques-Imo's** brings its Big Easy flavor north and serves up finger lickin' fried chicken. The up-market gastronomy trend lives on, notably at Tom Valenti's **Ouest**. And we seem to find ourselves drawn again and again to **Aix**, followed by chilled sake at **Sushi Hana**.

RESTAURANTS Upper West Side

A 947 Columbus Ave. (106th & 107th Sts.) (212) 531-1643 Caribbean/ French. Popular with locals and the fresh-faced Columbia crowd, this pocket-sized storefront serves up fresh organic fare in a casual BYO setting. Chef-owner Marc Solomon cooks nearly as fast as he talks – your order arrives almost before you're done giving it. Don't miss the escargots or curried lamb pie. -$20

Aix 2398 Broadway (88th St.) (212) 874-7400 French. French-country rustic meets Manhattan chic in this supremely elegant bi-level Provencal palace. Sit upstairs and overlook the beauties taking in the butter-walled ambience, cooing over chef Didier Virot's coolest dessert: liquored cotton candy. $55

@SQC 270 Columbus Ave. (72nd & 73rd Sts.) (212) 579-0100 New American. A coveted window seat inspires envy from passersby's—or maybe it's the "Life in a

Cup" hot chocolate you're sipping. Scott Campbell's "deconstructed" menu appeals to creative types, offers pre-assembled options like grilled duck and beef tenderloin. Great weekend people-watching as the young and hangover pick through their brunch. +$30

Awash 947 Amsterdam Ave. (106th & 107th Sts.) (212) 961-1416 Ethiopian. Expel your inner carnivore with a heaping plate of spicy yellow lentils, or sample a Sambusa – a kind of Ethiopian egg roll. Order a sturdy side of collard greens and mop it all up with baskets of velvety African bread. A friendly, patient wait staff talks you through the exotic menu. -$30

Bello Sguardo 410 Amsterdam Ave., (nr. 79th St.) (212) 873-6252 Mediterranean. Not a bad compromise: small plates, big dictators. Italian and Spanish tapas. Quick fare with Turkish influences and shiny bar. Surprisingly sleek décor for such old school Mediterranean snacking. Stick with the candlelight and meze and try to ignore the spillage from the Crane Club next door. $35

Big Nick's 70 W. 71st St. (Columbus Ave) (212) 799-4444 Pizza/Burgers. With its 24/7 schedule, happy hour–priced $1 drafts, you'd almost expect a frat house to be lurking around the corner, rather than a Theory store and muffin shop. Hot slices, burgers, gyros and even baklava are available anytime, attracting the neighborhood mommies, daddies and hard-partying nannies alike. Get the gorgonzola stuffed burger. -$10

Bistro Ten 18 1018 Amsterdam Ave. (110th St.) (212) 662-7600 American. Get lost in the wine list, chill in the sedate, relaxing atmosphere and enjoy upscale comfort food like Cobb salad, crab cakes or warm pastrami on sourdough. Attentive but unobtrusive service makes it great for an intimate anniversary or other quiet celebration. +$30

Café des Artistes 1 W. 67th St. (Columbus Ave. & CPW) (212) 877-3500 French. More big questions get popped here than on Who Wants to Be a Millionaire. Starry-eyed couples book well in advance for a Big Night Out among exuberant paintings of nymphs and nereids. Slip her the ring over foie gras and Dom, or wait for the dreamy crème brulee dessert. +$55

Café Lalo 201 W. 83rd St. (Broadway & Amsterdam Ave.) (212) 496-6031 Eclectic. Eat your entrée elsewhere and stroll in here to catch your second wind. Pick from the luxurious dessert menu: the chocolate mousse comes thick as fudge cake, and the tiny portions can last you a good long while. Few better options for an evening jolt of sugar and caffeine. -$10

Café Luxembourg 200 W. 70th St. (Amsterdam & West End Aves.) (212) 873-7411 French. The first of the upscale eateries uptown, it still shines. Drink in the murmur of sophisticated conversation in a pre-Balthazar classic bistro setting. Try the minted beet salad with haricot vert and steak frites and sip from the extensive wine list among white tile and flickering candles. +$45

Calle Ocho 446 Columbus Ave. (81st & 82nd Sts.) (212) 873-5025 Pan-Latin. Get acquainted with the ceviche and yucca fries, tip back that glass of white sangria and sway to the rhythm of salsa music. The high-ceiling dining room's colorful décor compliments the menu's bright flavors in dishes like plantain-crusted mahi-mahi. $35

Carmine's Uptown 2450 Broadway (90th & 91st Sts) (212) 362-2200 Italian. Bring on the carbs and prepare to walk out of here fat, happy and hoarse. The huge portions and casual atmosphere seem to encourage loud, raucous parties. But after a few jelly glasses of the stout house red you won't much care about the noise. $25

'Cesca 164 W. 75th St. (Columbus & Amsterdam Aves.) (212) 787-6300 Italian. Ouest's Tom Valenti gets in touch with his Italian side and looks to dominate the Upper West Side. The grilled sardines and lamb shank are reliably good, and the pasta dishes outshine the seafood options. Save room for the honey goat milk gelato. $35

Citrus Bar & Grill 320 Amsterdam Ave. (at 75th St.) (212) 595-0500 Asian-Latin fusion. Pretty plates of sushi and Mexican, Caesar salad and yam fries. Bi-level, well-lit, non-annoying army of waitresses. Overarching decorating principle: modern cactus fusion. Grab a booth and order the trio of dips and a blood orange margarita. $25

Compass 208 W. 70th St. (Amsterdam & West End Aves.) (212) 875-8600 American. If you don't have a visa to travel below Canal Street, drink in the downtown cool at this swankily minimalist joint. The prix-fixe dinner—heavy on fresh seafood—is one of the best bargains around. And don't skip the cheese plate. +$35

Fujiyama Mama 467 Columbus Ave. (82nd & 83rd Sts.) (212) 769-1144 Japanese. You say it's your birthday? Watch the wasabi-fueled boys and bachelorettes fight it out for disco domination. One of the first wave of hot NY sushi spots continues to serve up fresh fare. White-shrouded chairs glow under black lights while Japanese techno throbs and anime plays on the plasma screens. +$25

Gennaro 665 Amsterdam Ave. (92nd & 93rd Sts.) (212)-665-5348 Italian. Get in line—it's the UWS at its best, sans a reservation policy. Warm, wobbly, wooden tables piled high with pear salads, antipasto, fresh gnocchi, and vino. The service may be slow, but tip 'em high for memorizing seven-minute orations on tonight's specials. Cash only. $40

Haru 433 Amsterdam (80th & 81st Sts.) (212) 579-5655 Japanese. Reliable if rushed, Sun Tsu-quoting biz-boy types like to show off their Japanese pronunciation at this blonde-wood haven. Hefty slabs of maki and tako perpetually pack the place with faithful regulars. +$25

Isabella's 359 Columbus Ave. (77th St.) (212) 724-2100 Mediterranean. The people-watching spot of the nabe and the perfect finish to a day of visiting dinos. Deco touches complement the polished Euro style at this two-tiered celebrity fave. Let attentive staff point out the menu's perennials, like a camembert and pear salad or pumpkin ravioli. +$35

Jacques-Imo's NYC 366 Columbus Avenue (77th Street) (212)-799-0150 Cajun. About the only place around to find a shrimp and alligator sausage cheesecake. Stick around for the crawfish and BBQ shrimp. Loud and funky with friendly staff, stuffed alligators and Spanish moss hanging from the rafters. Drinks at the bar will have you sitting in table #5's Creole creation. $35

Jean Georges 1 Central Park W. (60th & 61st Sts.) (212) 299-3900 French. Pricey, sure, but worth every penny. Tucked in the base of the brass-and-glass Trump International condo tower, this lofty French eatery gives the Donald a much-needed infusion of elegance by association. Pawn a favorite heirloom for a taste of the lamb. +$75

Kitchenette Uptown 1272 Amsterdam Ave. (122nd & 123rd Sts.) (212) 531-7600 American. Down home cooking. The shabby-chic SoHo standby gets Northern exposure in this uptown extension. Taste their take on the crème-filled cupcake and you'll never go Hostess again. The breakfast is enough to get you out of bed early… but they serve it till 4:30 just in case. $20

Land Thai Kitchen 450 Amsterdam Ave. (81st & 82nd Sts) (212) 501-8121 Thai. This ain't your Uncle Pongpat's Thai joint. Forgo the pad thai and try the drunken noodle chicken. The locals couldn't keep quiet and the waits are getting longer. Grab a beer next door and the friendly staff will call when your table is ready. Be sure to check out the bathrooms. -$25 ★

Mama Mexico 2672 Broadway (101st & 102nd Sts.) (212) 864-2323 Mexican. Let the margaritas flow but save room for the guacamole. Ample portions of fresh avocado and spices are prepared tableside at this vibrantly cheerful outpost of the Midtown original. If you're very, very good, the manager may pour some top shelf tequila straight down your craw. $20

Max SoHa 1274 Amsterdam Ave. (123rd St.) (212) 531-2221 Italian. Cash-strapped Columbia kids as locals line up for the meatballs, sausage and Italian bread and this uptown take on the East Village original bustles with a no-fuss good cheer. Ample, inexpensive pasta dishes pack the tiny dining room but it's best in the summer, when outside seating allows for more elbowroom. $25

Neptune Room 511 Amsterdam Ave. (84th St.) (212)-496-4100 Mediterranean. Bright, fantastically designed spot on otherwise barren block. Bring a date or parent for the scallops with blueberries and various under the sea treats. Oysters for a buck Mon-Fri. A secret door leads to a bathroom bigger, cleaner and better decorated than your whole apartment. +$30

Nice Matin 201 W. 79th St. (Amsterdam Ave.) (corner of 79th St.) French. A Pastis clone with a remarkably similar vibe down to the front doors but tamer. French Riviera cuisine from Andy D, celeb-spotting sidewalk complete with candles in bags, goat cheese salads and fennel mackerel. Meet friends for drinks inside and feel all relaxed and Euro. $35

Nussbaum & Wu 2897 Broadway (at 113th St.) (212) 280-5344 Bakery. Lives up to law-firm-like name: efficient and clean. Columbia kids with laptops come for the breakfast, lunch, smoothies, knishes, and birthday cakes. "You've Got Mail" scene filmed here (but cut), exemplary of quaintness levels. $12

Ouest 2315 Broadway (83rd & 84th Sts.) (212) 580-8700 American. Beautiful people flock to sample chef/owner Tom Valenti's deservedly famous New American fare. Backdrop is clubby, yet warm. The lamb shanks are legendary and the pan-roasted rabbit is the best of the city's few serious game offerings. +$50 **BlackBook**

Pampa 768 Amsterdam Ave. (97th & 98th Sts.) (212) 865-2929 Argentine. Perpetually packed Latin steakhouse. Head right out to the garden for les hectic atmosphere and ordered up a glass of malbec Diez puntos. Skip the so-so ensaladas and go right for the meat, particularly the piquant grilled chorizo. +$30

Picholine 35 W. 64th St. (Broadway & CPW) (212) 724-8585 French/Mediterranean. Jewel of Lincoln Center and deservedly so. The cheese course here is proof that God loves you and wants you to be happy. Assuage your choice anxiety with the pricey tasting menu, or enjoy the more affordable prix-fix options. +$50

Quintessence 566 Amsterdam Ave. (87th & 88th Sts.) (212) 501-9700 Healthy. The raw food fad hasn't surpassed. Featuring the lowest ConEd bills in the city: nothing boiled, processed or nuked. Ordering out will leave you ample time to ponder your dogma: 40 minutes minimum to not cook your dinner. Surprisingly tasty desserts. $28

Radio Perfecto Uptown 1187 Amsterdam Ave. (118th St.) (212) 932-8555 American. Comfort food mixed in with more Christmas lights than the Griswolds. Trying too hard to be hip? Maybe. But homey American fare fits in fun dishes and introduces hops-hounding undergrads to citified phrases like "sesame-seed crusted." +$25

Rigaletto 208 Columbus Ave. (69th & 70th Sts.) (212) 721-2929 Italian. Gourmet pizza spot of the block. Wide triangles of spinach and ricotta will run you a pretty penny, but it doesn't matter. After a slice of life here, you won't be able to fit into the skimpy Intermix threads next door, anyway. -$10

Sabor 462 Amsterdam Ave. (82nd & 83rd Sts.) (212) 579-2929 Latin American. Mojitos may be so two summers ago, but Sabor's version is worth a second taste. The unassuming décor belies a sophisticated menu, which includes everything from traditional peasant fare like corn cakes to elegant grilled tuna in coconut-ginger broth. $30

Saigon Grill 620 Amsterdam Ave. (90th St.) (212) 875-9072 Vietnamese. Menu goes on and on, and whiles it's not much on looks, the simple dining room is justifiably crammed for its consistently good specialties. Sweet and sour combo soars with the deep-fried shrimp paste wrapped in sugar cane. Pick any of the spicy soups and you'll come up with a winner. $25

Shun Lee West 43 W. 65th St. (Columbus Ave. & CPW) (212) 595-8895 Chinese. 80's-chic version of its sedate East Side sister spot, the extensive menu stars such delights as pickled jellyfish and a mouth-watering Peking duck. Celebs love the grown-up Chinese food in the company of the immense good-luck dragon encircling the dining room. Dim sum café next door rocks too. $25 **BlackBook**

Sushi Hana 466 Amsterdam Ave. (82nd & 83rd Sts.) (212) 874-0369 Japanese. Graze on tasty appetizers at the bar on a whim, or call ahead and order the lobster. Fresh, delectable cuts of sashimi, impeccably presented. A life without a taste of this kitchen's wasabi pork dumplings is a life half-lived. Worth the fuss. +$25

NIGHTLIFE Upper West Side

Abbey Pub 237 W. 105th St. (Broadway & Amsterdam Ave.) (212) 222-8713 The late-afternoon Penguin paperback bar crowd gives way to grad students on a tear as the evening progresses. The fun begins when the local drunks arrive. Possibly Columbia's best dive.

Amsterdam Billiard Club 344 Amsterdam Ave. (76th & 77th Sts.) (212) 496-8180 Take a quick lesson or two in shooting stick and soon you'll be hustling for beer money before you can say "rack 'em up." Frequent league nights can mean a long wait for a table, but the lively bar crowd makes the time pass quickly.

Boat Basin Café 79th St. @ the Hudson River (212) 496-5542 Locals come to drink beer, chow on burgers, and, oh yeah, there's that sunset, lake, nature thing happening, too. Sprawling, breezy and pleasantly loud. The café is for fair weather friends only— it's closed November through May.

Café del Bar 945 Columbus Ave. (105th & 106th Sts.) (917) 863-5200) A laidback scene plus as dope a Jamaican vibe as you'll get North of Kingston, mon. Friendly vibe, always packed. This roots reggae spot offers frosty Red Stripes but no, the barkeep won't help you score any herb. **BlackBook**

Dead Poet 450 Amsterdam Ave (81st & 82nd Sts.) (212) 595-5670 Throw on your dirtiest jeans, and screw your laundry. Your quarters are better spent on the nabe's best juker. The bartenders at this classic Irish pub have followings to rival Sun Myung Moon's.

Ding Dong Lounge 929 Columbus Ave. (105th & 106th Sts.) (212) 663-2600 Sort of like the East Village when it was cool. Disaffected Columbia kids, hipsters and motor city peeps now head uptown. Brave the crack-alley sidewalk and mourn the memory of punk amid. Get a little misty as the DJ spins hardcore 80s faves.

Dive 75 101 W. 75th St. (Columbus & Amsterdam Aves.) (212) 362-7518 Cheap drinks, check. ESPN, check. Rabid sports fans and the girls who love them? Mercifully, no. Just a young neighborhood crowd kicking it with a Bud and brushing up on their Connect Four moves (a set at every table). Faux pas to poke at the fish.

Fez/Time Café 2330 Broadway (85th St.) (212) 579-5100 Now that the downtown outpost is no longer, sink into a plush booth with Cosmo's Moroccan cousin, Fez. DJs rock the Kasbah on weekends. Post-Symphony Space destination on the weekdays. Candles and cast-iron lamps cast a sexy, mysterious light on the singles mixer.

Hudson Beach Café 103rd St. (Riverside Dr.) (212) 567-2743 More relaxed backyard barbeque feel that uptown sib of Boat Basin Café. Sip electric lemonade and watch beach volleyball the way New Yorkers play it – on hard, unyielding concrete – and bask in a Hudson River sunset. Summertime only.

Makor 35 W. 67th St. (CPW & Columbus Ave.) (212) 601-1000 What Jdate.com would be if people didn't hide behind computers. The hub of the young, Jewish UWS scene, but better than it sounds. Great bands (including BlackBook favorite The Lascivious Biddies) add to the cultural center's lineup of events.

Night Café 938 Amsterdam Ave. (106th St.) (212) 864-8889 Locals drink their Buds and tolerate the slumming Columbia brats pretending to play pool in the back. The two cultures manage to co-exist without clashing, but overheard conversations about Godard and some guy's last jail stretch can make for cognitive dissonance.

Northwest 100 Columbus Ave. (79th St.) (212) 799-4530 Grown-up spot, even if you're not one yet. The quiet booths and view of the Natural History Museum's pretty little park are perfect for a glass of wine on an autumn evening. A tad on the yuppie side, we admit…

Shalel 65 W. 70th St. (Columbus Ave.) (212) 799-9030 Underground delights await in one of the UWS' most seductive haunts. Low lights and secluded crannies make for a safely decadent atmosphere. Bop to the hypnotic Moroccan music and try not to let the secret out.

UPTOWN

UPPER WEST SIDE

"The New York waiter...knows more than you do about everything. He disapproves of your taste

in food and clothing, your gauche manners, your miserliness, and sometimes

it seems, of your very existence, which he tries to ignore." —Kate Simon

HARLEM & WASHINGTON HEIGHTS

(map page 208)

Take the A train up to Harlem as Duke Ellington so sweetly advised, and step into a storied neighborhood that has been the source of some of the most important artistic and political movements in American history. Besides Duke, legends such as Louis Armstrong, Bessie Smith, Billie Holiday and Ella Fitzgerald all lived and worked here, performing at the Cotton Club, the Savoy, and the legendary **Apollo Theater.** Black nationalists Marcus Garvey and Malcolm X found their voice, as did W.E.B DuBois and Thurgood Marshall, who each lived in the brownstone at 409 Edgecomb, check it out. More recently, Harlem has experienced the inevitable onslaught of jaded downtowners and artists looking for cheap rent and more space. Like the streets themselves, **the cuisine and nightlife in Harlem and Washington Heights have rapidly evolved.** This new renaissance reflects the forces of gentrification, and features the flavors of Mexico and Morocco, Jamaica and the Dominican Republic. Find us eating burgers at the **Willie's**, power-lunching with Bubba at **Flash Inn**, or on our way to check the jazz at the awesome **Lenox Lounge.**

RESTAURANTS Harlem & Washington Heights

Bleu Evolution 808 W. 187th St. (Ft. Washington & Pinehurst Aves.) (212) 928-6006 Mediterranean. Funk-opulent dining room with a spacious patio for al fresco summer dining. Someone in your party orders the mussels: a huge pile, swimming in beer, bacon and goat cheese. $22

Charles' Southern Style Kitchen 2841 Frederick Douglass Blvd./aka 8th Ave. (151st & 152nd Sts.) (212) 926-4313 Soul Food. Non-descript take-out joint in the middle of a looong block has some of the best fried chicken, collared greens and sweet tea in the world, all-you-can-eat for $10 at brunch. Perfect post-Rucker celebratory spot. $12

Dinosaur BBQ 646 131st St. (12th Ave.) (212) 694-1777 Barbecue. New Yorkers transplanted from all points south of the Mason-Dixon love to complain long and loud about the lack of good BBQ in these here parts. Your wait is over: get the meaty pork ribs, drizzled in sweet/spicy sauce, slow cooked in their customized pits. -$20 ☆

Flash Inn 107 Macombs Pl. (155th St.) (212) 283-8605 Italian. Choice spot for area's art and political intelligentsia, thick with history and tradition. Classy soul: think '69 Baraka supping with Sly Stone and Clyde Frazier in a dark leather banquette. Steakhouse menu is solid, regulars go with the veal medallions zingarella. $40

Hispaniola 839 W. 181st St. (Cabrini Blvd.) (212) 740-5222 Dominican. A trendy, arty little scene is developing up at the top of the island, and this is where it's at. The red snapper in papaya sauce está diez puntos, but locals rave on the seasoned scallops with fresh pico de gallo and the red wine marinated grilled quail. ¡Ay por Dios! $23

Hot Spot 2260 7th Ave. (133rd St.) (212) 491-5270 West Indian. Owner Joy Boyd's been doin' it proper for over 20 years. Old walls graced with Martin and Malcolm, Huey and Nina, and all those that have come through Harlem. We'll just throw this out there, then duck and cover: the jerk chicken here is the best in the city, BK included, son. $15

M & G Soul Food Diner 383 W. 125th St. (Morningside Ave.) (212) 864-7326 Soul Food. Corner spot with awesome gospel/funk jukebox. The salon girls next door are obviously diggin' on some chicken; it's as crispy and crunchy as the pancakes are soft and fluffy. $12

Mookie's No Pork on My Fork 2093 Adam Clayton Powell Jr. Blvd./aka 7th Ave. (125th St.) (212) 866-4061 Take-out. Hands down the best restaurant name in NYC. Basic greasy spoon options, burgers, turkey bacon-and-egg sandwiches, etc, all served up with a little Harlem 'tude. DO NOT talk shit about the Yankees/Knicks/Giants in here. $8

The New Leaf Café at Fort Tryon Park, 1 Margaret Corbin Dr. (212) 568-5323 American. Bette Midler's joint. 1930s stone building transformed into one of the most tranquil spots in our on edge city. Food lives up to the leafy setting and gorgeous view: try the filet mignon, roast chicken or amazing sautéed pork tenderloin. $28

Rancho Jubilee 1 Nagle Ave. (194th St.) (212) 304-0100 Dominican. Authentic home cooking, but bring your Spanish-English Dictionary. Real island flava and attitude in a real island setting. Carribean gourmet: pinchos langosta, canoa de mariscos, stewed guinea hen, broiled rabbit all impress. La playera for la playas. $30

Rao's 455 E. 114th St. (Pleasant Ave.) (212) 722-6709 Italian. The prospect of getting plugged here hasn't deterred celeb diners one bit, in fact, may have enhanced their rep. Make a reservation if they'll let you, which they won't, unless you've already been "made." Supposedly great pastas... +$50

Willie's Burgers 274 W. 145th St. (7th & 8th Aves.) (212) 368-6912 American. Uptown burger shack is a great grease fix, year after year unjustly left off "Best NYC Buger" lists. We recognize. The fish sandwich is good, too, as is the generous portion of fries. Crazy good milkshakes, get a "half and half" to go with a cheeseburger. $12 **BlackBook**

NIGHTLIFE Harlem & Washington Heights

The Den 2150 5th Ave. (131st & 132nd Sts.) No phone. Hip hop, soul, R&B, clasics, rare grooves, house, reggae—this place is hoppin, courtesy of former Brand Nubian DJ Alamo. Funky little spot, rap luminaries like Nas and Diddy swing by to give props. Crazy food menu is pretty tasty.

Lenox Lounge 288 Lenox Ave. (125th St.) (212) 427-0253 Malcolm hung here, as did Billie, Miles and Coltrane. Recently restored to original 30s art deco splendor: gorgeous tile, banquets and baby grand make the Zebra Room one of the finest spaces around. Right off of bustling 125th, find a dark corner, settle in, chill and take care of business.

Moca 2210 8th Ave (119th St.) (212) 665-8081 Leon's intimate lounge with dark colors and soft soul music is the perfect setting for a D'Angelo video. Good lookin' crowd on weekends, and the best drink name in NYC: the booty-call martini.

The Monkey Room 589 Ft. Washington Ave. (187th St.) (212) 543-9888 New to the neighborhood, this simian little space has already developed quite a following. Coffee and pastries by day, a hang out for music lovers at night. Take your pick of live bands, DJs (no jungle, though), and yes, karaoke, on Thursday.

"New York is the perfect town for getting over a disappointment, a loss, or a broken heart."

—Shirley MacLaine

WILLIAMSBURG & GREENPOINT

(map p. 209)

Each spring, when the next round of Suzies, Sloanes and Carolines graduate from Penn and make their way to the city to live out their little "Friends" fantasy, they're as likely to set up shop in Williamsburg as they would on the Upper East Side or Murray Hill. And why shouldn't they? It's safe, convenient to the city and still relatively cheap, as these things go. And are they so different from their artistically inclined hipster forbearers, who originally claimed these dingy blocks a decade back? Either way, Dad's footing their bill. But we're not here to hate, rather, appreciate. **We love this neighborhood, dearly**, even though you're increasingly more likely to find a stroller-clogged boutique than a family-owned bodega, and even though the nightlife been thoroughly uncovered not only by the usual slumming Manhattanites, but now by Jersey and L.I.'s finest. The chain-free ordinance is brilliant (although we suspect it's days are numbered...), and **smart restaurants like Moto and Bonita and savvy bars like Larry Lawrence and Supreme Trading ooze sophistication** that rivals anything the island to the left has to offer.

RESTAURANTS Williamsburg & Greenpoint

Acqua Santa 556 Driggs Ave. (N. 7th St.) (718) 384-9695 Italian. Nice place to eat, especially with one of whom you have impure thoughts. Best Italian in the 'hood for creative apps, brick-oven pizza with artichokes and capers. A guilty altar boy—the owner himself—presides over the comfortable dining room. $35

Allioli 291 Grand St. (Roebling & Havemayer) (718) 218-7338 Spanish. Comfortable place with beautiful garden and full bar ruled by Robbie. Authentic paella on Thursdays. The seared calamari are perfect, but get them to make the apple/manchego cheese dessert ravioli for you. Obviates the need, but instills the desire, to move to Spain forever. +$20

Anytime 93 N. 6th St. (Berry St. & Wythe Ave.) (718) 218-7338 Eclectic. Whoa, this place grew up in a hurry. One minute it's a tiny take-out/delivery counter, full of heartily stoned locals sloppily devouring egg n' cheese sandwiches, now it's all upscale n' shit. Tasty burger. $15

Ashbox 1154 Manhattan Ave. (Ash & Box Sts.) (718) 389-3222 On the farthest reaches of the Greenpoint gentrification frontier, steps from the Pulaski Bridge. For most of you, this place might as well be on Mars. That's just fine for the

Greenho locals, who can sip good coffee and iced drinks in relative peace and obscurity, for now. Good sandwiches, too. -$8

Aurora 70 Grand St. (Wythe Ave.) (718) 388-5100 Italian. Sweetest new Italian with perfect homemade pasta and a really nice garden. THE place to take your new vegetarian boyfriend: tell him all about the difference between maltagliati and tagliatelle. For the m-eaters: duck liver parfait, you won't need dessert. +$18

Black Betty 366 Metropolitan Ave. (Havemeyer St.) (718) 599-0243 Mediterranean. South Billyburg fusion at its finest: spiky hairstyles make the transition from hat head to Bedouin head. World beat flavors with serious soul: pitzas, merguez sausage, grilled chicken and samboosak. +$14

Bleu Drawes Café 97 Commercial St. (718) 349-8501 Jamaican. Hard to find, but oh so worth the trek. Fish, oxtail, butter beans supplement the amazing jerk chicken. No voodoo shack, but a much needed change from the Greenpoint/Williamsburg Thai-assault. Cozy to the nth degree. +$15

Bonita 338 Bedford Ave. (S. 2nd & S. 3rd Sts.) (718) 384-9500 Mexican. Thanks to its next-door neighbor, God, you can't get tequila. So no 'ritas, kids, the amazing white wine sangria will have to suffice. Besides that, more perfection from the Diner peeps. Low lit, cool staff, fresh and creative Mexican cuisine including mole chicken and grilled fishes. $15 **BlackBook**

Brick Oven Gallery 33 Havemeyer St. (N. 7th & N. 8th Sts.) (718) 963-0200 Italian. One-hundred-thirteen year-old oven is good luck for us. Artistic pizza for artistic locals. In our opinion, the only good pizza to be found on the west side of the BQE. Spicy sauces, eclectic toppings, rich pastas, warm vibe, all proffered by a super-friendly owner. +$15

Christina's 853 Manhattan Ave. (Milton & Noble Sts.) (718) 383-4382 Polish. Low-cost, high flavor Polish grub, less than gorgeous atmo. Try potato pancakes with beef goulash, pierogis and blintzes. Hottest staff this side of Scores West (check the matching mini-skirts), but you'll need your Polish-English dictionary to make headway. -$15

D.O.C. Wine Bar 83 N. 7th St. (Wythe Ave.) (718) 963-1925 Italian. Rustic wine bar feels like Sardinia without the Mediterranean, sidewalk overflowing with the new Bburg set. Interchangeable selection of little plates and wines keeps 'em coming back. Try the cascatta, and, of course, the chianti. +$20

Diner 85 Broadway (Berry St.) (718) 486-3077 American. The hottie wait staff scribbles the specials on your table; pay attention since they're almost always better than the regular menu. Delicious bowl of polenta highlights the brunch, spherical burger for dinner. Just don't get stabbed by the woman in the cowboy hat knitting at the next table. +$22

Dumont 432 Union St. (Metropolitan Ave.) (718) 486-7717 Bistro. Reasonable French and American eats for the mature young Williamsburger. Friendly service, beautiful back patio. Noteworthy, and stinky, mac et fromage. Good coq au vin, the scallop ceviche's delish, great beat salad. +$25

M. Shanghai Bistro & Den 129 Havemayer St. (Grand St. & S. 1st St.) (718) 384-9300 Chinese. Wong Kar-Wai film-set interior with communal benches and eclectic selections of fortune. THE place for dim sum, Shanghai-style, and try the salt and chili pepper shrimp. Many offerings for vegetarians. Leo's mu-shu is, in fact, fabulous. +$13

Marlow & Sons 81 Broadway (Berry St.) (718) 384-1441 American. From the Diner and Bonita peeps, with ultra "fish-shack cred." Cold cuts, cheese, raw vegetables and cold fish, available á la carte, are so puritan in their preparation, almost repressed. Raw radishes with cold butter anyone? It's like a picnic, only inside and for more $$$. $25

Miss Williamsburg Diner 206 Kent Ave. (Metropolitan Ave. & N. 3rd St.) (718) 963-0802 Italian. They have t-shirts that are kinda barfy, and the service is, ahem, a trifle on the ditzy side. Which is part of why we love this self-proclaimed 'Burg stand-by with dining-car look and delightful backyard. The food is good, vote Yes! on the butter and sage ravioli. $22

Moto 394 Broadway (Hooper St.) (718) 599-6895 Eclectic. We crave the pressed sandwiches, super dainty "French-style" salads and other delicacies despite internalized metrophobia. Feels a little like a cramped, Parisian, David Lynch-esque reform-school (check out the dungeon bathrooms) for "29" year olds. We love Moto, especially at night. +$25 **BlackBook**

Oznot's Dish 79 Berry St. (N. 9th St.) (718) 599-6596 Mediterranean. Home to one of the best brunches in Williamsburg: flavorful couscous, Moroccan steak, lentils, eggs barbarossa and feta cheese. Smoke a little hash and the colorful 50s Marrakesh interior dazzles, but can turn scary and insanely loud come eventide. $25

Peter Luger 178 Broadway (Bedford & Driggs Aves.) (718) 387-7400 Steakhouse. Simply put: where one eats steak in New York City. Confident, old school, no-nonsense waiters deliver on all promises: steaks are juicy, perfectly charred and expensive. The Secret: they grill on ovens older than NY. +$60 **BlackBook**

Planet Thailand 133 N. 7th St. (Bedford Ave. & Berry St.) (718) 599-5758 Thai. Hope the giant boat doesn't fall on you. Vaulted ceilings, 45-minute waits, 250 menu items, decent sushi and Thai food churned out by the gross ton. Reliably good pad thai, fresh papaya and Thai beef salads and spicy curries. Change it up and cop the beni-hana style hibachi option. $22

The Queen's Hideaway 222 Franklin St. (Green St.) (718) 383-2355. American. Nonchalant, squatter-chic, looks like you're in someone's kitchen. Chef Liza Queen makes whatever she feels like it on the constantly rotating menu. Full of creative G-point types in the yard, though the Times blew it up so Manhattanites arrive by the cab-load. $20 **BlackBook**

Relish 225 Wythe Ave. (N. 3rd St.) (718) 963-4546 American. Coach-car chrome and color-love are helped by well-mixed cocktails from the backlit bar and smartish comfort food like fabulous southern-style catfish. Lovely outdoor area is great at night and the motorcycle repair shop across the street provides the opportunity for some class betrayal. $30

SEA 114 N. 6th St. (Berry St. & Wythe Ave.) (718) 384-8850 Thai. Astoundingly over-designed Brigitte Bardot sex-club meets Mariko Mori theme park interior with frankly decent food, cute-as-a-button menu, and shockingly reasonable prices. Get the drunken noodles, a lychee martini and dance all night long in the three-urinal cylindrical pisser. $20

Sparky's 135 N. 5th St. (Bedford Ave & Berry St.). (718) 302-5151 American. Burgers and dawgs made from organic, grain-fed beef, with all the fixins your heart could desire. Ideal for late night cravings. Sparse minimalist interior, a little brightly lit, but you're drunk ass won't mind. $7

Thai Cafe 925 Manhattan Ave. (Kent St.) (718) 383-3562 Thai. Small, unpretentious, always crowded, recently redesigned. Best Thai in Brooklyn, with robust curries mad spicy like their 'sposed to be: get the coconut kind. Fun staff puts up with you and your drunk buddies. $25

Union Picnic 577 Union Ave (N. 10th) (718) 387-3800 Southern. Clapboard roadside haven transplanted from Val Dosta, GA straight to industrial wasteland. Do yourself a favor, get yourself some buttermilk fried chicken, mashed potatoes and cornbread. Grilled sandwiches, FRIED OKRA, homemade cobbler: the solution to the plight of modern man. +$15

NIGHTLIFE Williamsburg & Greenpoint

Artland Bar 609 Grand St. (Leonard & Lorimer Sts.) (718) 599-9706 Open in Williamsburg for four years, this remains The Bar that No One Ever Talks About. Ambitious programming notwithstanding (e.g., tango lessons on Wednesday nights), this is our #1 favorite bar to hide away in. Cheap, strong pours.

Bembe 81 S. 6th St. (Berry St.) (718) 387-5389 Totally anti-Colonialism grass-roots free-thinkers from Sarah Lawrence mix it up with Afro-Latino lovelies at this outpost of convergent world music. Location under the Williamsburg Bridge, right across the street from Busta Rhymes' new penthouse may make it the new seat of Hip-Hopcracy.

Blu Lounge 197 N. 8th St. (Driggs Ave.) (718) 782-8005. Hip-hop karaoke, anyone? Comfortable seats, cool beats, low-key joint for special sake and Asian apps. Decent enough place to have a drink. Watch the parade of life (...on Driggs?) from the miniscule sidewalk patio.

Boogaloo 168 Marcy Ave. (Broadway & S. 5th St.) (718) 599 8900 A space-station of cool in Billyburg's mini-Bronx. The 2001/Soylent Green sci-fi aesthetic makes you think twice before ordering those Midori Sours. Rearrange the red sectionals for optimum play, climb up the Captain's hatch to escape to... ? Order the Commodore. Mixed bag of DJs.

Bozu 296 Grand (Havemayer & Roebling Sts.) (718) 384-7770 Ichi-ban sunken bar. Dark, swank, and lovely. Daruma everywhere peep while you nibble on grilled eel sushi BOMBs and kataifi-encrusted shrimp. It's so Japanese you feel like you're in L.A. When they are finally able to legally vend their rare infused vod-kas, we will never, EVER leave.

Enid's 560 Manhattan Ave. (Driggs Ave.) (718) 349-3859 The girls wear white boots and big earrings, the boys have band shirts and scruffy tattoos. North of McCarren Park, a safe distance away from slumming Manhattanites on Bedford strip. The weekend brunch, its existence doubted by many, is quite good.

Europa 98 Meserole Ave. (Manhattan Ave.) (718) 383-5723 Saturday night fever strikes the young Polish set. Strictly techno with a dress code straight from Soho. Catch up on what's crackin' in Krakow while you speak the International Language of Love. Body building nights are the hottest shit ever.

Galapagos 70 N. 6th St. (Kent St. & Wythe Ave.) (718) 782-5188 Quintessential Williamsburg bar/performance space/theater still looks good and has righteous programming like Bluegrass Wednesdays and film/video screenings in the back room. Make a point of not "baptizing" yourself in the reflecting pool on the way out.

The Greenpoint Coffee House 195 Franklin St. (Green St.) (718) 349-6635. Daytime lures in the arty locals by the best coffee around, the better to hone their screenwriting skills. Nighttime, switches back to a laid-back wine bar, ideal for chatting up Rozyczka, Wiktorja, Nazwiska or Krystynka.

Iona 180 Grand St. (Bedford Ave.) (718) 384-5008 Imported beers and imported bartenders (hot damn!) rule this Irish outpost. Footie onscreen and eclectic music—Outkast meets Paul Weller—give way to HI-NRG ping-pong in the crumbling back patio. If the decent sandwiches aren't to your taste, ask the bartenders (*sigh*) to help you order a pizza.

Laila Lounge 113 N.7th St. (Berry & Wythe Sts.) (718) 486-6791 Singer/songwriters struggle along on-stage, weakish pour in your glass. Despite flaws, friendly vibe rules—especially late nite. Open mic, open screen, "jazz jam," movies. Cheap hot toddies in winter are a nice touch, just remember that Hot Buttered Rum = rum + butter.

Larry Lawrence 295 Grand St. (Roebling & Havemayer Sts.) (718) 218-7866 James Bond in Scandinavia, entrance in cognito: look both ways before slipping past the gray metal door (marked "bar"). Check out our butts as we head to the elevated smoking patio to watch the sleek and lovely bar (and beauties) from above. Scalding hot-spot late. **BlackBook**

Lucky Cat Lounge 245 Grand Ave. (Driggs & Roebling) 718-782-0437 Coffeeshop by day, bar by night, home of the "Monday Chess and Go Club for Wayward Men and Ladies". The coffeeshop aesthetic comforts... almost as much as the stiff pour. A haven anytime, especially late at night when you check your mate in the tiny, jammed patio out back.

Metropolitan 559 Lorimer St. (Metropolitan Ave.) (718) 599-4444 Brooklyn's only full-time gay bar. Decidedly low-attitude, friendly crew on both sides of the bar help you while away the hours. Fireplaces in the winter, multi-level backyard in the summer. Sunday brunch includes free Lucky Charms, smokin' Lesbian Wednesdays…just don't tell the breeders.

Northsix 66 N. 6th St. (Kent & Wythe Aves.) (718) 599-5103 This music venue's been here forever though it looks like it's not finished, which is just fine for the self-conscious indie-rockers who watch TV on the Radio. Go downstairs for the freshest LIVE indie beats, or slouch around outside and pretend like you lost your crew.

The Pencil Factory 142 Franklin Ave. (Greenpoint Ave.) (718) 609-5858 Irish pub for local artists. Put the pints away as dogs tread underfoot. Watch film crews getting blitzed after shooting at the creepy warehouse down the block. Just don't run with that thing for chrissakes—you'll put somebody's eye out.

Pete's Candy Store 709 Lorimer St. (Frost & Richardson Sts.) (718) 302-3770 Number one for quality live tunes, number one bar. Twisty space with a sexy side hallway. Artistic, talented, alcohol-dependent cuties, and retro shoes everywhere you look. Back patio is just-right run-down. Why go anywhere else? Just make sure you can find your way home.

R Bar 541 Meeker Ave. (Graham Ave.) (646) 523-1813 Italian locals are punk rock, queers are punk rock, hipsters are punk rock, Harley guys are punk rock: at R Bar, you too can be PUNK ROCK. More Austin/Chapel Hill/Athens than New York, we wear our PJs on Tuesdays for free drinks and are totally grody famous.

Royal Oak 594 Union Ave. (Richardson St.) (718) 388-3884 Hot indie-girls with boyfriends prettier than they are break it down for you at this surprisingly large and sophisticated fave. Curling up in the powder-blue make-out room is a million bucks, just don't shake your money-maker too hard or they'll get shut down for dancing...again. **BlackBook**

Southside Lounge 41 Broadway (Kent & Wythe Aves.) (718) 387-3182 Not much has changed in this cozy dark dive, least of all Lucy the beer-drinking dog. A relief after trying to get someone to serve you a drink at Giando's eerily staffless mafia compound down the street (which overlooks the river…)

Spuyten Duyvil 359 Metropolitan Ave. (Havermeyer St.) (718) 963-4140 Knowledgeable barkeeps guide you through bewildering list of beers, and dispense meticulously prepped chacuteries. We love sitting in the wilderness garden out back and playing this game: "ok, I'm gonna order a Spkyttr Bsnchausen... think they got that?"

Stinger Club 241 Grand St. (Driggs Ave. & Roebling St.) (718) 218-6662 Especially if you like the danger. Good juke, better DJs, best MCs with the crowds changing schizophrenically to match the entertainment. Polka Dots to thugs. Catch sight of the new kids in town. Hip-Hop nights are beyond the "milky" way. Hurts so good.

Supreme Trading 213 N. 8th St. (Driggs Ave. & Havermeyer St.) (718) 599-4224 Large and cleverly-designed bar has a friendly neighborhood vibe, ideal for chillin' on weeknights, or full-on ridiculous revelry on weekends. You'll probably attend some type of magazine event here, if you haven't already. Dope jukebox. **BlackBook**

Sweet-Ups 277 Graham Ave. (Grand St.) (718) 384-3886 When Barbara Krueger tells employees to wash their hands, you bet your ass they do it. Cute neighborhoodies sing karaoke on Tuesday and get loaded on sweet'n'freshness the rest of the week. Get yourself a mojito, my lassie... Soviet-bloc-style "smoking lounge" through the bathroom out back.

Trash 256 Grand St. (Driggs Ave. & Roebling St.) (718) 599-1000 The second reincarnation on the site of once-Berliniamsburg famous Luxx. Completely revamped now looks like a caricature of 'the' indie rock club. Good entertainment promises, but until further development, we'll continue to call it Ex-Luxx.

Union Pool 484 Union Ave. (Meeker St.) (718) 609-0484 Slick corner cooler is essentially, one ongoing party, perpetually packed and fun on weekdays and weekends alike. Live music space in back, outdoor smoking lounge, and an unparalleled view of the BQE. Late-night last-chance hook-up spot.

Warsaw 261 Driggs Ave. (Eckford St.) (718) 387-0505 We got 31 flavas. Shows range from electronica, the best names of indie rock to polka. Call or check your listings, kids, crowds vary in a big way. QT-scene at the long bar on off-nights: Poles in loud arguments, all set to the latest Timbaland joint. Huh?

BROOKLYN

WILLIAMSBURG

"I want to wake up in a city that never sleeps." —Frank Sinatra

BROOKLYN SOUTH
(includes Brooklyn Heights, Carroll Gardens, DUMBO, Fort Greene and Red Hook)
(map p. 210)

We've grouped these five distinctive areas together for their proximity to one another. Although you'll need wheels or ninja skills to get to Red Hook, it's worth the haul. Stop into **Red Hook Bait & Tackle** and glimpse nautical relics dangling above the bar while you consume as many Swedish fish your greedy guts can handle. Brooklyn Heights is scenic and serene. Stroll along the Promenade, stepping past a few Asian wedding party photo ops, then grab a romantic dinner at **River Café**, while the seagulls scream your soundtrack to love. Fort Greene is one of the best kept secrets in the city, and the much beloved home of Spike Lee, so Do the Right Thing and savor some Jamaican eats at **Brawta**. The Carroll Gardens restaurant scene shows no signs of slowing down, and is beginning to look like Epcot's Paris, **with more bistros per square inch than you can shake a baguette at**. We're digging on Mexican joints like **Luz** to light our fires with spicy bites and **Pacifico** to quench them with fruity margaritas. As the sign says, you can live work and play in DUMBO, but still carry your pepper spray. Party at **Pedro's** with cheap drinks, watch the sunrise at the waterfront, then head to **Bubby's Brooklyn** for a brunch: don't forget the awesome apple pie.

RESTAURANTS Brooklyn South

Alma 187 Columbia St. (Degraw St.) (718) 643-5400 Mexican. Slick wood interior with colorful lights and a rooftop lovefest, lit by lanterns and the everlasting fire in your eyes. Chef Gary Jacobson of Zarela fame, whips up creative Mex like pork stuffed ancho relleno. The mole sends us into orbit, so does the house-infused vanilla-pineapple tequila. $30

Aqua 174 Smith St. (Warren & Wyckoff Sts.) (718) 643-1589 Seafood. Dramatic wooden beams feel like you're in the belly of a ship. Delectable seafood dishes, prepared by chef Belinda Ber with Mediterranean flair. Inventive Bouillabaisse for a fresh twist on a French classic or have an intimate tobiko caviar four-way with your friends. $35

Banania Café 241 Smith St. (Douglass & Butler Sts.) (718) 237-9100 Bistro. Corner spot composed of copper and tin, always crowded with Carrollites. Hugely popular brunch spot for banana pancakes. Dinner is candelit with luscious lamb shanks and burgers on brioche, lots of family-friendly options. Banana filled wontons for dessert, and yes, that is a banania in our pocket. +$35

Bar Tabac 128 Smith St. (Dean St.) (718) 923-0918 French. Kitschy spot is French to the core, right down to the haughty wait staff. Walls adorned with interesting bric-a-brac. Foosball in the front, rusty vintage moped in the dining room, sophisticates sipping Bourgogne in the midst. Bistro bites like juicy burgers or moules frites. $28

Brawta 347 Atlantic Ave. (Hoyt St.) (718) 855-5515 Caribbean. Recognize the patty size. Neon green spot, decorated with Bob Marley posters. Ten tables, always packed with folks lovin' on the "big tings" or the "likkle tings." Goat Roti that kicks ass. Try Jamaica's national dish of ackee and saltfish, wash it down with bloody sorrel juice. $25

Bubby's Brooklyn 1 Main St. (Plymouth & Water Sts.) (718) 222-0666 Breezy and countrified, just like its Manhattan counterpart, but lacking in celeb sightings. Instead, we focus on the buttermilk fried chicken or pulled pork. Best brunch in the 'hood is a yum-fest of assorted pies and Atkins enemies. $25

Butta Cup Lounge 271 Adelphi St. (DeKalb Ave.) (718) 522-1669 Asian & Southern Soul. Tucked in two floors of a townhouse, snootier soul food lures y'all to Fort Greene. Dark, cozy atmos helps us get wild in swank cheetah-print booths. Wacky day-glo cocktails in the upstairs lounge. Fun to order "lil' Big Daddy's Fried Chicken". -$24

Cafe Luluc 214 Smith St. (Butler & Baltic Sts.) (718) 625-3815 French. Homey bistro for everything fantastically French, so hone your double-cheek kissing technique. Tantalizing apps and classic entrees like Hangar Steak with frites. Starry-eyed couples in the corners nursing glasses of Merlot. Sunday brunch to wear off your Saturday night hangover. $20

Chez Oskar 211 DeKalb Ave. (Adelphi St.) (718) 852-6250 French. Corner spot with laid back vibe and sweet ambiance. Calls itself "Le funky French Bistro de Brooklyn", whatever that means. Bistro-fied menu accented by dishes like mustard rabbit. Tuesdays are all you can eat mussels- line your purse with plastic and take a trip on the D train. $30

Downtown Atlantic 364 Atlantic Ave. (Hoyt St.) (718) 852-9945 American. Three Franks attempt to recapture the lost spirit of Brooklyn in a wood dining room lined with old school boro photos. Polenta app is a must, unbeatable burgers. Cheesecake that rivals Junior's famous. 20 wines under 20 bucks. Sunday night jazz and black cherry soda. -$25

Faan 209 Smith St. (Baltic St.) (718) 694-2277 Pan-Asian. Cute college-types congregate for Pan-Asian fusion. 200 dishes from nearly every Asian country. Pad Thai is solid. Stir frys are huge spicy mounds of yummy. Order a lychee martini and represent with the cucumber and crab Brooklyn roll. -$15

Five Front 5 Front St. (Old Fulton St.) (718) 625-5559 American Bistro. Quaint townhouse nestled under the Brooklyn Bridge. Aged wooden floors, exposed brick, mushy banquettes. Sophisticated clientele dine on rib eye, mahi mahi. Order zucchini blossoms stuffed with manchego. The gorgeous garden literally sits under the bridge, so watch out for those pigeons. -$30

Grimaldi's Pizza 19 Old Fulton St. (Front & Water Sts.) (718) 858-4300 People are passionate about these pies. One of the older ovens in the city, still spitting out some delicious pizza, old school Brooklyn style. Sinatra over the speakers, while devotees form lines out the door and down the block. Get it to go and hit the waterfront, beat the lines of tourists. $20

The Grocery 288 Smith St. (Sackett & Union Sts.) (718) 596-3335 American. Nothing to do with C-Town. Pale green walls to soothe your soul and orgasmic eats to rev it back up again. Smith St's pioneering restaurant, still the best for a reason. Sharon and Charles select the freshest local ingredients for their seasonal menu. Try the local duck or peekytoe crab. $35

Henry's End 44 Henry St. (Cranberry & Middagh Sts.) (718) 834-1776 American. Ye olde bizarre food place. Wooden, dark, dingy and delicious. Been around a long time, since the knights of yore. In the fall, Society of Creative Anachronists gather for the Wild Game Festival with venison, rabbit and duck. Black bottom pie is all you gotta say. $30

Hill Diner 231 Court St. (Baltic & Warren Sts.) (718) 522-2220 An Improvisation on traditional diner food with an eclectic crowd to match. Shiny retro diner décor in an organic atmosphere. Lots of vegetarian options for the soy-minded and good old cow for the carnivores. $8 prix fixe brunch packs the back garden. Soon to be open 24hours on weekends. $20

Hope & Anchor 347 Van Brunt St. (Wolcott St.) (718) 237-0276 American. Brick and mirrors on weekdays, smoke and mirrors for weekend drag queen karaoke. Diner faves with additional flaves, meatloaf and mashed potatoes or something more creative like a ham-wrapped tuna steak. Hanging art and sailor motif spice up the metallic retro-diner decor. -$25

Jacques Torres Chocolate 66 Water St. (Main & Dock Sts.) (718) 875-9772 Café. Learn what love is all about. Endless varieties of chocolate drinks to accompany your chocolate truffles. Take a tour of the chocolate factory, but be on the lookout for oompa loompas. A ultra indulgent PMS extravaganza, bring your Clearasil. -$10

Joya 215 Court St. (Warren St.) (718) 222-3484 Thai. Industrial décor with dreamy techno. Extensive drinks list, we love the mango martini. Papaya salad, massaman curry takes you back to your Thailand backpacking trip, when it was just you, your llama and a dream. Cute garden in the summertime, packed with hipster cuties. $12

Junior's 386 Flatbush Ave. (DeKalb Ave.) (718) 852-5257 Diner. Flashy, chintzy old-school cool with Crooklyn's finest cheesecakes. Try not to get trampled in the intense rush to bakery counter. Egg creams, malts and gargantuan sandwiches for two. Been here forever, so the waitstaff knows your dad, your dad's dad and all their friends. $15

Kino 1 Main St. (Front & Main Sts.) (718) 243-9815 Italian & French. Huge bi-level loft space, picturesque bridges and Manhattan views. Draws a hip clientele for it's great drinks. Food is great, too. Especially the creamy fettucine, but the spot's the draw. -$28

Little Bistro 158 Court St. (Amity & Pacific Sts.) (718)797-5778. American. Chef Cheung of Jean Georges and Nobu wants to have some fun, okay? He kicks ass with sweet and sour baby back ribs, mac and bleu cheese and the giggle-inspiring banana brownie sundae. Wash it all down with one of the gazillion micro brews off the extensive list. $30 ★

Luz 177 Vanderbilt Ave. (Myrtle & Willoughby Aves.) (718) 246-4000 Latin. Settle into a colorful banquette, nurse a watermelon martini and let Luz. Creative Latin with several ceviches, red snapper is super good. Empanadas are delicious, lemongrass flan is creamy and refreshing. Gracias chef Lopez, you blow our minds. $30 ★ **BlackBook**

Madiba 195 DeKalb Ave. (Clinton & Adelphi Sts.) (718)855-9190 South African. Kick off your Brooklyn wilderness safari at one of Madiba's wood picnic tables, but don't carve your name in, okay? Instead, enjoy the colorful paintings of Africa while you stick your head into a delicious ostrich steak or the more traditional bobotie. Loved by locals. $20

Mancora 176 Smith Street (Warren & Wyckoff Sts.) (718) 643-2629 Peruvian. Simple decor, adobe-like walls and a large fishing mural. Brooklynites with a spicy side, dine on pork tamales, yummy ceviches, shrimp en risotto de quina, paella. FYI: The chocolate empanada is better than the choco taco from the Mr. Softy Van. $25

Noodle Pudding 38 Henry St. (Cranberry St.) (718) 625-3737 Italian. Just like grandma never made. Italian in the Heights, loved by locals. Prepare to be moon-struck. Mushroom risotto is creamy and delightful, venison ragu is an offbeat treat. Mahogany dining room with pale yellow walls, chock full o' quirky antiques, sweet service. Now that's amoré! $25

Pacifico 269 Pacific St. (Smith St. & Boreum Pl.) (718) 935-9090 Mexican. Cute cantina with a sweet fireplace. Burritos for five bucks, lots o' alcohol, and a large outside deck to revel while waiting for your table. Feels like a party in a stranger's backyard, but the drinks are better and the crowd is hotter. $20

Pedro's 73 Jay St. (Front & Water Sts.) (718) 625-0031 Spanish & Mexican. Mándale, manito. Holdover from back in the day, pre-gentri DUMBO. Luckily, now you can leave behind your pepper spray and stroll to this awesome spot. Great tacos with dirt-cheap drinks. The way Mexican should be. Occasional live bands get you groovin'. $12

Pete's Waterfront Ale House 155 Atlantic Ave. (Clinton & Henry Sts.) (718) 522-3794 Pub. Free popcorn while you sip scotch and wait for your venison chili. German wurst platter is a genuine heap of meat for carnivorous alkies. Fifteen beers on tap rotated weekly. Take home Pete's house hot sauce- by the jug. +$14

Quercy 242 Court St. (Kane & Baltic Sts.) (718) 522-9060 French. Mon dieu! A rustic French bistro with elegant modern finish. Deep red walls, black-and-white photos of European villas. Chef Jean-Francois Fraysse named this spot for his hometown. Exquisite rustic entrees, like a dense and dangerously delicious cassoulet. Pear tarte tatin with crème fraiche for dessert. $35

Rice 81 Washington St. (Front & York Sts.) (718) 222-9880 Pan-Asian. Unpretentious, understated, sophisticated blend of Caribbean, Thai, Indian and Mexican. And that's just the waitress. Got Indian chicken curry on Thai black rice. Much meaner than Nolita version packs in twice the hipsters. Gorgeous patio and Low Bar below. $15

River Café 1 Water St. (Old Fulton St.) (718) 522-5200 American. Jackets required. Sorry folks, that means shoes, too. But no one's checking for undies, so bring a hot date. Rack of veal is amazing, we also love the lamb shank. Be mesmerized by the B-Bridge's lights and the smell of nature as the river dribbles by. +$55

Robin des Bois 195 Smith St. (Baltic & Warren Sts.) (718) 596-1609 French. Stealing from the rich, and hooking up the Smith row poor. Oh wait, all these people are gainfully employed. But there is a leafy garden, old church pews, and mod artifacts. Winter fave: croque monsieur and hot spiced red wine. Sit in the display window, survey the Smith Street scene, keep your eyes peeled for Maid Marion. $22

Sammy's 391 Henry St. (Verandah Pl. & Warren St.) (718) 625-4333 Bistro. Heights' hidden gem. Quaint, tucked away café with a cozy atmo a cross between mom's kitchen and an eclectic antique shop. Menu is heavy on the seafood, with killer crab cakes and an fragrant oyster stew with fresh ginger. BYO. $25

Sample 152 Smith St. (Bergen & Wyckoff Sts.) (718) 643-6622 Preserved foods. For really lazy people who can't open a jar by themselves, have your server do it for you! A kitchenless food joint with everything cold, canned, bottled. Like a tapas bar, pick a plate, a wine, grab a book and dig in. Try the Serrano ham with hazelnuts or the citrus smoked salmon. -$15

Saul 140 Smith St. (Bergen & Dean Sts.) (718) 935-9844 American. Saul Bolton has been soothing the savage Smith Street beast since '99, before the boom. Buttery yellow walls, exposed brick, tin ceiling for the perfect Brooklyn atmo. The coriander-crusted sirloin steak is delicious, but we have two words: Baked Alaska. $30

Schnack 122 Union St. (Columbia St.) (718) 855-2879 American. An amalgamation of favorite childhood fast-food restaurants with a home cooked twist. Beer milkshakes is a dare we're willing to take. All meats straight from Brooklyn butchers, kielbasas and schnakie sliders. Try the shoestring onion rings. $15

Scopello 63 Lafayette Ave. (Fulton St.) (718) 852-1100 Italian. From the bottom of the boot with a hint of Sicily. Breads and pastas homemade daily, cheese imported from the motherland. The pastas are delicious, but it's the osso buco we love. Drink at the glowing blue bar hit the spacious back room under an orange hue with live music. $25.

Shinjuku 177 Atlantic Ave. (Clinton & Court Sts.) (718) 935-1300 Japanese. High ceilings with steel beams and an industrial aesthetic. Sit at the brass and stainless steel sushi bar and try the empire roll. Kick off your shoes in a private tatami room and get some lovin' while sharing a "loveboat" behind closed doors. $25

Taku 116 Smith St. (Pacific St.) (718) 488-6269 Creative Japanese. Gorgeous earthy interior by Jewel Bako designers. Breezy garden feels like home. Chef Adam Shepard rocks the green tea soba like no other, but be adventurous and try the ginger-seared scallops or yuzu chicken. Crazy sake list is a bargain. $30

Thomas Beisl 25 Lafayette Ave. (St. Felix St. & Ashland Pl.) (718) 222-5800 Authentic Viennese. Solid wood bar straight out of Cremaster 3 and Viennese style dining room with parquet floor and golden lights. Chef Thomas Ferlsesch slings schnitzels, beef gulash, spaetzle. After your lovely linzer tortes, hop over to BAM for a Fassbinder flick. $28

360 360 Van Brunt St. (Wolcott St.) (718) 246-0360 Bistro. You never thought you'd be hookin', but now you can't stop. Foodies travel from distant Manhattan to remote red hook for Sebastien Smits' scallops in lobster coulis and frog's legs. Modern sky-lit setting. The crux of Red Hook's burgeoning restaurant scene. $35

Village 247 Smith St. (Douglass & Degraw Sts.) (718) 855-2848 A little bit of small town USA, done boro-style. Faux store facades line the walls, illuminated by street-lights. Muffaletta sandwiches and juicy burgers served by Serial Mom. Speakeasy pub downstairs for no-holds-barred nationalism of domestic brews and old school rock 'n' roll. $30

NIGHTLIFE Brooklyn South

Ambar 179 Smith St. (Warren & Wyckoff Sts.) (718) 522-2820 Caribbean paradise if you can't afford that couples resort in Jamaica. Glowing amber bar is a perpetual sexy sunset, so hold hands and drink the Mama Juana, rumored to be an aphrodisi-ac. Wait: any drink consumed in large quantities produces an aphrodisiac effect, or at least amnesiac sensations. Be forewarned.

B-61 187 Columbia (Degraw St.) (718)643-5400 Named for the bus line that stops outside the door, so you never have to call for directions. Downstairs from Alma, so quench the fire from your spicy meal. Indie and professional types mingle to a fun jukebox. Dogs are encouraged, especially beer-drinking breeds.

Boat 175 Smith St. (Wykoff & Warren Sts.) (718) 254-0607 Sister bar of Great Lakes in the Slope, but this ship is scurvy-free. Aspiring novelists, garden-variety hipsters, neighborhood types warm up by the fireplace in winter. Excellent indie rock jukebox is some geek's pride and joy, so appreciate it, buster.

Boudoir Bar 273 Smith St. (Sackett & Degraw Sts.) (718) 624-8878 Have you been naughty? Busty bar wenches in negligees provide drinks for artsy crowds. Lipstick red walls, gilt mirrors for a dangerous liaison. Please refrain from putting your waitress' tip in her cleavage. This is a classy joint, ya hear? Live music, open mic nights.

The Brooklyn Inn 148 Hoyt St. (Bergen St.) (718) 625-9741 Creaky, haunted and the old schoolest around the way. Like stepping into a time warp, 150-year old bar with classic wood details. Draws cool crowds of hipsters and ghosts. Best bloody mary, just don't say it three times in front of the mirror. Jazzy jukebox. And there's a pool table in the back.

Brooklyn Social Club 335 Smith St. (1st St.) (718)858-7758 Former Italian social club turned hipster hang, minus those sly guys puffing cigars. Tin ceilings, cream colored walls and a beautiful wooden bar. Invoke old blue eyes and try old school drinks with a twist: try a ginger old-fashioned while snacking on an awesome sandwich.

The Duplexx 46 Washington Ave. (Park & Flushing Aves.) (71 643-6400 Sexy & swanky. Far from the G(hetto) train, but worth the walk. Hidden industrial loft space. Look for the pink lights, hit the reggae nights. Very diverse crowd reflects what Fort Greene is all about. The new home of legendary Bang the Party with E-Man.

Floyd 131 Atlantic Ave. (Henry & Clinton Sts.) (718) 858-5810 Chill neighborhood hangout with comfy antique couches, patchwork walls of tin, brick and wall paper. An old worn bar and a bocce court so you can further embarrass your drunken self as the night wears on. You will be a regular, we promise.

Frank's Cocktail Lounge 660 Fulton St. (S. Elliot St.) (718) 625-9339 World famous, but just in Brooklyn. Tons of drunken cuties waiting for you to arrive from your Jarmusch flick at BAM. Best R&B jukebox we can think of and plenty of booze to get the party going. It just ain't Ft. Greene without Frank's.

Gowanus Yacht Club 323 Smith St. (President St.) No phone. At attention, Sailor: drop anchor at this biergarten perfect for smoking and summertime brews served in styrofoam cups. Dollar PBRs pulled from a sad looking cooler, hot dogs on the grill, and strings of 75-watt light bulbs illuminate from above. Weathered wooden bar, nautical decor, beach party atmosphere.

Hank's Saloon 46 3rd Ave. (Atlantic Ave.) (718) 625-8003 What's a dazzling urbanite like you doing in a rustic setting like this? Country music dive with $2 beers attracts lots of tats. Great for a laugh and for some serious drinking, too. Hipsters mix with bikers mix with hard-core alkies from dusk til yawn.

Kili 81 Hoyt St. (State St. & Atlantic Ave.) (718) 855-5574 Vaguely mountain-sounding name and a somewhat ski-lodge feel (well, they have a fireplace). Exposed brick, wooden beams and 20-somethings lounging on mushy red sofas. Super popular with locals and lovers of soul music. Leave your skis behind and float home.

Last Exit 136 Atlantic Ave. (Clinton & Henry Sts.) (718) 222-9198 Last exit off the Lost Highway. Kitschy interior, bizarre drink concoctions. Original Cobble Hill lounge. Deep Brooklyn vibe. In summer, chill outdoors in tiki garden with a Gowanus martini. Nice, subtle DJing all weekend long.

Lillie's 46 Beard St. (Dwight St.) (718) 858-9822 Former longshoreman bar out in the middle of nowhere, and the Hookers like it that way. Super-friendly owner Lillie is at the bar and the dogs are at your feet. Red Hook classic. Backyard BBQs make for a great Sunday in the summer.

Low Bar 81 Washington St. (Front & York Sts.) (718) 222-1LOW A "smart" bar. Beneath Rice, dope little spot that looks unfinished in a good way. Hot crowd, DJs, burlesque, retro-futuristic beats, scratched-up jazz records, and all with a happy stomach from a great meal upstairs and a Red Stripe in your hand.

Lunatarium 10 Jay St. (John St.) (718) 813-8404 Huge, cool loft is a haven for brilliant DJs like DJ Spooky and Holmar Filipsson. Ever-changing parties that bring hundreds of hipsters. Huge space supported by columns could hold an army, but never feels too crowded. Amazing locale overlooks the skyline from the Manhattan bridge.

Magnetic Field 97 Atlantic Ave. (Hicks & Henry Sts.) (718) 834-0069 Hipsters unite and pay tribute to their mod roots at this unpretentious little joint. Red walls and disco balls alter your perception of time. Bands and DJs during the week and an old jukebox that plays free old punk and indie 45s.

Moe's 80 Lafayette Ave. (S. Portland Ave.) (718) 797-9536 Sweet & laid back corner space. Tons of windows with pretty Ft. Greene views, but duh, the eye candy is inside. Singles vibes to the occasional DJs and lounge on vintage couches, pretty curtains. "Duff" beer on tap and a pyrotechnic "Flaming Moe" to drink yourself yellow. Warm and cozy on winter nights.

Quench 282 Smith St. (Sackett & Union Sts.) (718) 875-1500 Chic 70's atmo for that insatiable thirst. Former topless bar revamped: now serving sexy cocktails on Smith St. Orange walls, shiny mirrored ceilings and retro music. Chill vibe attracts hipsters on dates. Pants no longer optional.

Red Hook Bait & Tackle 320 Van Brunt St. (King St.) (718) 797-4892 A fallen tree was salvaged from the street and turned into the actual bar. Fishing tackle, harpoons, mermaids and toys dangle from the ceiling. Looks like a junk shop with younger Hookers getting loaded. Unlimited goldfish and Swedish fish. ★ **BlackBook**

Red Hook Blue 18 Commerce St. (Columbia & Richards Sts.) (718) 522-9400 If you build it, they will come. If you give them a shuttle bus to remote Red Hook, they will come by the droves. Old school-feel in new spot. Live jazz and blues in a laid-back but sophisticated spot. Ample bar, and really strong drinks.

Roxy Bar 144 Smith St. (Bergen St.) (718) 802-9686 Simple recipe: Indie rock on the jukebox, the usual neighborhood hip-stahs, alcohol – shake n' serve. Not to be confused with massively gay Chelsea nightclub. Former jewelry store revamped by people behind Great Lakes. Dour looking young men in Pixies t-shirts and cute girls in vintage dresses.

Stonehome 87 Lafayette Ave. (S. Portland & S. Elliot) (718) 624-9443 Classy wine bar where sophistos unite. Extensive list, heavy on the French and Cali wines. Tasting flights from $20, small plates of fromage to accompany. Yuppies jiggle to latin beats, wax moronic over the abstract paintings, re-enact their favorite scences from Sideways.

Sunny's 253 Conover St. (Reed and Beard Sts.) (718) 625-8211 Because I'd rather have a bottle in front of me than a frontal lobotomy. An awesome place, like walking into a Tom Waits song. No frills atmosphere. Salty dogs waiting for their ships to come in, drown in Jameson's instead. Waterfront institution for three generations. Out of the way, but worth it.

Vegas 135 Smith St. (Dean & Bergen Sts.) (718) 875-8308 Colorful windows attract artsy bohemians, punks, and drunks alike. Cavernous and dim exposed brick space, punctuated with much beloved pool tables and Victorian couches. What happens here, stays here. Badass bartenders make sharp drinks.

BROOKLYN

BROOKLYN SOUTH

"The City of New York is like an enormous citadel, a modern Carcassonne.

Walking between the magnificent skyscrapers one feels the presence on the fringe of a howling,

raging mob, a mob with empty bellies, a mob unshaven and in rags." —Henry Miller

PARK SLOPE & PROSPECT HEIGHTS

(map p. 211)

Longtime stronghold of the Stroller Mafia, this neighborhood is home to legions of grad students, dog lovers, lesbians, vegans, indie guys with Asian girlfriends, joggers, bloggers, BoBos, babies, trannies, nannies, and the entire editorial community of New York City. And wait, is that Jennifer Connelly? A laptop on one hip and a toddler on the other, these residents hike the tree-lined blocks toward **500-acre Prospect Park** in search of barbeques, softball and playgrounds, or perhaps a shady place to crack open the new Jonathon Franzen novel. **Seventh Avenue's** the place to find a gift for that baby shower, or a Wi-Fi connection to go with your chai latte. But the cool kids know that **these days it's all about 5th Avenue, where new bars and restaurants are popping up from the South Slope all the way to Flatbush.** Not long ago 99-cent stores and bodegas dominated the edges of this strip, but today we're getting our drink on in the South End at **Buttermilk** and **Royale**, or gettin' tipsy up north at **Total Wine Bar** and rock club **Southpaw**. Whether you think it's better than Bedford Ave., or just starting to look like **Smith St.**, it's good to be in this neck of the woods on the weekends. Catch us splurging at **Al Di La**, or savoring that late night duck club at **Blue Ribbon**. For brunch we're at **Beso** sampling tropical mimosas and mangu con huevos, ordering the short ribs and eggs at **Stone Park Café**, and wondering when was the last time we ate in Manhattan.

RESTAURANTS Park Slope & Prospect Heights

Al Di La 248 5th Ave. (Carroll St.) (718) 783-4565 Italian. Some of the best Northern Italian in the whole city is served up by Emiliano and Anna, the fabulous Venetian and Brooklynite duo. Casual, rustic-elegant, romantic by accident. Everything here is delicious, magical and worth the long wait for a table. +$35

Applewood 501 11th St. (7th Ave.) (718) 768-2044 American. This homey mom and pop joint sates your Earth Day alter ego with organic, antibiotic-free cuisine. Be assured that the succulent beast on your plate lived a natural life of wild abandon before it was braised and served with a fava-basil puree. Excellent, cruelty-free dinner, killer brunch. $35 ☆

Bar Minnow 444 9th St. (7th Ave.) (718) 832-5500. Seafood. Exit the F train and you're practically ordering already. Nurse a pale ale and take in the foot traffic on 7th while you wait for those fried oysters. Large dinner crowds make for slow service, but the raw bar delivers and the classic cheeseburger won't disappoint. $20 ☆

Bar Toto 411 11th Street (6th Ave) 718-768-4698 Casual enoteca. Off the beaten path, so sit on the sidewalk without having to see a bus go by. Brilliant reverse happy hour (11pm-2am daily) keepin' you sassy when it counts. Pizzas, pastas, panninis, and the beloved Toto burger, all under $10. Classy looking date spot that won't mock your tax bracket. $20

Belleville 330 5th Ave. (5th St.) (718) 832-9777 French Bistro. A solid French Bistro done in a French Bistro style serving French Bistro food. Cheerful canary yellow corner space with mosaic floor, high ceilings, and lots of sidewalk seating. Perfectly charming and kid-friendly. $30

Beso 210 5th Ave. (Union St.) (718) 783-4902 Nuevo Latino. Creative, flavor-packed spot that's rarely crowded weeknights. But come Sunday brunch-time you better put your name in quick cuz those folks outside aren't waiting for the bus. Laid back waiters in guyaberra shirts supply fresh guava mimosas and dulce de leche French toast to kick off your siesta in the park. $20 **BlackBook**

Biscuit 367 Flatbush Ave. (Park & Sterling Pls.) (718) 398-2227 BBQ. Motto: Save a Cow, Eat a Pig. Baby back Ribs that melts off the bone. A pulled pork sandwich that tugs at your heartstrings. Fingerlickability rates off the charts for the fried chicken and the mac n' cheese. The freshest biscuits. We would bathe in this BBQ sauce, for real. $20

Bistro St. Marks 76 St Mark's Ave. (Flatbush Ave.) (718) 857-8600 Bistro. You just saw that early Altman film at BAM. You're sophisticated, seeking sleek, modern spaces, delicious food served by a vacuous staff. Come for Wednesday's Carnivore's Ball to savor filet mignon with a fine cabernet. That's just lovely, isn't it, darling? Now return to your brownstone. $35

Blue Ribbon Brooklyn 280 5th Ave. (1st St. & Garfield Pl.) (718) 840-0404 American. Already a Brooklyn institution, restoring our faith in humanity at all three meals: brunch, dinner and 2am duck club sandwich. Excellent raw bar with a wide assortment of oysters. Shareable steaks and fragrant paella magdalena. Chocolate chip bread pudding is unreal. Prepare to wait on weekends. +$40 **BlackBook**

Blue Ribbon Sushi 278 5th Ave. (1st St.) (718) 840-0408 Japanese. Because it's near midnite and you want to eat super fresh, ultra creative raw fish, not another greasy slice. Zen confidence, heavy on the wood, looks almost like a sauna but cooler. Thank you Bromberg bros for serving up another reason to stay in Crooklyn thin woolmond +$40

Bonnie's Grill 278 5th Ave. (Garfield Pl. & 1st St.) (718) 369-9527 American. Gourmet diner where there's a Polenta of the Day. Extensive beer menu and cute waitresses. Drool as Mike and Anthony hook up the Slope's best burger. We'd walk barefoot in a snowstorm, uphill both ways- just for these fries with chipotle mayo. $18

Brooklyn Fish Camp 162 5th Ave. (Douglass & Degraw Sts.) (718) 783-3264 Seafood. Another Manhattanite who now has more space and a backyard. Brooklyn's branch of Mary's Fish Camp is roomier and since you're not a total whore for dining in an elite closet, this is a good thing. Same fingerlickin' lobster roll, same succulent oysters. New convenient location. $35 ☆

Café Steinhoff 422 7th Ave. (14th St.) (718) 369-7776 Austrian. Crowds gather nightly at this South Slope spot for schnitzel, speatzle, and an unrivaled variety of Czech/Austrian beers. Snag a seat on the sidewalk next to the grad degree crew and hip young transplants who showed up for the $5 Goulash on Monday night and never left. $25

Chip Shop 381 5th Ave. (6th St.) (718) 832-7701 Fish & Chips. Fancy a newspaper cone of deep-fried anything? Quaint, corner locale, busy with young lads and lasses. Buttery cod and big fries are perfect hangover helper. Inventor of deep-fried candy bars and Twinkies – who says the English can't cook? $12

Corn Bread Cafe 434 7th Ave. (14th & 15th Sts.) (718) 768-3838 American. Don't inhale that whole basket of corn muffins before sampling Bettina Harris's savory North Carolina BBQ and crawfish etoufee´. Catfish po'boys and hominy grits to make your pants tight. Weekends, your ultimate comfort brunch and Sade soundtrack await you on the back patio. $20

Long Tan 196 5th Ave. (Berkeley Pl. & Union St.) (718) 622-8444 Thai. Ultra-mod Slopestah hang. Wacky cocktail specials for a late-night rendezvous with that dude that looks like that dude from The Strokes. Sprawling, dynamic, yet ultimately intimate once you're in a booth. Green curry seafood stew leaves your lips burning. It's a good kind of pain. -$20

Maria's Mexican Bistro 669 Union St. (4th & 5th Aves.) (718) 638-2344 When you hop off the R train, there's always that daunting uphill climb before you reach restaurant row. Be lazy and hit Maria's at the foot of the hill. Start with a Tecate and a ceviche. The cool staff will direct you from that point on. $25

Nana 155 5th Ave. (St. John St. & Lincoln Pl.) (718) 230-3749 Pan-Asian. After a few exotic cocktails, gaze into the glowing fish tank and disappear. Sprawling trendster zen, chic and ultra-mod, complete with a lovely garden. Get the rib-eye steak apps. Feels like you're in Manhattan, down to the blazing staff. $25

Pepperoncino 72 5th Ave. (St. Marks Ave.) (718) 638-4760 Italian. Nowadays Key Food isn't the only place for sustenance at this end of 5th. Forget the groceries and head up the block for memorable wood-fired pizza topped with edible gold leaves. The service leaves something to be desired. Maybe that something is a pie topped with mussels and calamari. $25 ☆

Press 195 195 5th Ave. (Union St. & Berkeley Pl.) (718) 857-1950 Sandwiches. Unofficial meeting ground for the Stroller Mafia. Mouth-watering paninis made with fresh local ingredients. Cute garden for sipping Mom's Sangria in summer. You're having roast beef and onions on a pressed knish while the baby's busy with PBJ. -$15

Rose Water 787 Union St. (5th & 6th Aves.) (718) 783-3800 Mediterranean. Sweet, down-to-earth staff awaits you for serene dinner and excellent brunch. Now your girlfriend's parents really like you. Seasonal menu, grilled octopus and tuna excel. Some portions are a little small, but never disappoint. Juicy pork chops. Valrhona chocolate Pot de Crème like religious ecstasy. $32

Sette Enoteca e Cucina 207 7th Ave. (3rd St.) (718) 499-7767 Italian. New spot for solid, interesting Italian: if you don't mind dining next to your parents and all their friends. Sleek, calculatingly inviting décor; think IKEA does Tuscan villa. Pretty patio for sharing a bottle from the Venti per Venti (20 wines for $20 each) and looking at the photos from Zach's bar mitzvah. +$40 ☆

Stone Park Café 324 5th Ave. (3rd St.) (718) 369-0082 American. Charming the pants off Park Strollers and Slopesters alike with casual sophistication. Munch on marrowbones and bluefish cakes, brunch on the Hangtown fry (a Gold Rush-era recipe of oysters, eggs and hash). What your waitress lacks in know-how she makes up for with those cute green plastic frames. ☆

Tom's Restaurant 782 Washington Ave. (St. Johns & Sterling Pls.) (718) 636-9738 Deli & Diner. "It is always nice to see you," says the man behind the counter. Amazing egg creams, ice cream sodas and cherry lime rickeys. Hyper-busy weekend brunch. If you get in, get the mango pancakes or a beef brisket sandwich. Free cookies and lollipops. -$12

12th St. Bar and Grill 1123 8th Ave (12 St.) (718) 965-9526 American. Classic on the corner. Charming date spot with class. White tablecloths, cute lanterns, great seafood and bloody burgers. Friendly staff, typical Slope residents relaxing after a long day of editing. Consistent, although a touch predictable. $35

Two Toms 255 3rd Ave. (President & Union Sts.) (718) 875-8689 Italian. Rumored to be the longest running Italian restaurant in Brooklyn. Stripped-down, no-frills, bare-essentials Italian. Devoid of décor, no dessert, not even menus, so pray you can decipher your waiter's thick Brooklyn accent. Phenomenal pork chops, ricotta-stuffed veal cutlet and perfect manicotti. $25

NIGHTLIFE Park Slope & Prospect Heights

Bar Reis 375 5th Ave. (5th & 6th Sts.) (718) 832-5716 If you can squeeze through the door, we love this neighborhood hang, packed like the F in the morning. For Great Lakes graduates who need a little more ambience. One of the best gardens in the Slope, two rooms in front and three levels.

Barbès 376 9th St. (6th Ave.) (718) 965-9177. Named for a North African neighborhood in Paris, this intimate spot has a devoted following of Francophiles and music lovers. Your cutie's lookin' cuter in this lighting but don't let the Pernod do all the talking. The back room's got great jazz and foreign flicks, so check your local listings. **BlackBook**

Buttermilk 577 5th Ave. (16th St.) (718) 788-6297 Pretty people slummin' it. Divey hub of young Slope scene. Companion bar to Great Lakes. No old dudes drooling in their beers, just a sick indie-rock jukebox and free pizza nights. Around midnight you and the bartender light up – now you're on fire, you'll be smokin' all night!

City Lighting 307Flatbush Ave. (Prospect Pl.) (718) 230-3321 Brought to you by the crew of Boat in Carroll Gardens. Former lighting shop: retained its name but none of the glow or glory. Strong, cheap drinks served by boys in Pixies t-shirts. Gloomy, indie, loud, grungy, Christmas light-lit and perfect for late-night drunken eats.

Commonwealth 497 5th Ave. (12th St.) (718) 768-2040 Story goes that when this joint's proprietor stopped bartending at Great Lakes he took every cd in the juke with him. Because they were all his. Explains the Malkmus-heavy soundtrack here. Shiny new spot for drinks after a grueling day of working from home. Sunday Scabble tournaments, finally. ✦

Ginger's Bar 363 5th Ave. (5th & 6th Sts.) (718) 788-0924 Epicenter of the Dyke Slope scene, which is the center of the Dyke Universe. Shoddily painted wood stuff, acoustic music. Debonair ladies with crew cuts and tats hoist pitches in the park, then hoist pitchers in the garden.

Great Lakes 284 5th Ave. (1st St.) (718) 499-3710 Dark, smelly and indie: just like your dream date. Everyone starts singing along when "Wave of Mutilation" inevitably gets played on the jukebox. Disaffected bartenders serve up big, strong drinks. Be sure to check the bathroom walls for the latest Slope gossip.

Half 626 Vanderbilt Ave. (Prospect Pl.) (718) 783-4100 Sexy wine bar, another addition to the booming bar scene in Prospect Heights. Great date place, warm and comfy atmo. Very crowded weekends. Nothing to do with legendary Brooklyn streetballer Half-Man Half-Amazing.

O'Connor's Bar. 39 5th Ave. (Dean & Bergen Sts.) (718) 783-9721 Once you get your head 'round the idea of $3 beers and cocktails, realize that you're basking in the sickly neon glow of the best jukebox in NYC. Deep Brooklyn atmo. Befriend the moose's head above the bar, commune with the notorious ghost of the ladies room.

Patio 179 5th Ave. (Sackett & Degraw Sts.) (718) 857-3477 Suffering from a lack of imagination? Or maybe you are sick to death of the indie kids at Great Lakes? A small lounge that's perfect for a glass of wine on a balmy Brooklyn evening. Good chill-out for low-key nights.

Royale 506 5th Ave. (12th & 13th Sts.) (718) 840-0089 The irony of cheap vintage-Vegas decor isn't lost on you and your Friendsters. Red velvet booths and animal prints enhance loungey effect. Nightly Djs inspire impromptu dance parties while you enjoy a Redneck special from the Value Menu. We recommend the can of PBR and shot of Jim Beam for $6.

Soda Bar 629 Vanderbilt Ave. (Prospect Pl) (718) 230-8393 Former 40's soda foundation turned microbrew heaven. Cute vintage-inspired interior, sweet outdoor garden. Jukebox heavy on morbid 80s bands: which is a plus. A dash of Morrissey and a whiskey will cure whatever ails you. We'll be in the bar with my head on the bar.

Southpaw 125 5th Ave. (Sterling & St. Johns Sts.) (718) 230-0236 Another Anglophile name for a Park Slope indie rock spot. The neighbors complain about the noises above. Intimate club with a serious sound system. Same booker as legendary Maxwell's in Hoboken, gives Crooklynites yet another reason to avoid Manhattan.

Total Wine Bar 74 5th Ave. (St. Marks Ave.) (718) 783-5166 Not long ago the only hoppin' spots on this stretch of 5t.h were the Pentecostal churches. These days, we're making a pilgrimage north to get tipsy at this smart, sexy wine bar. Low-key crowd, inspired wine list, savory cheese menu. Glowing u-shaped bar keeps it intimate. Totally. ✫ **BlackBook**

BROOKLYN PARK SLOPE & PROSPECT HGTS.

BAY RIDGE & REST OF BROOKLYN

(map p. 212)

There is so much more to Brooklyn than the 'Burg, the Heights and the Slope. The tight-knit neighborhood of **Bay Ridge**, depicted in Saturday Night Fever and Summer of Sam, is home to one of hands-down best Italian restaurants in the city (country? world?) **Areo Ristorante**. In **Flatbush**, the sounds, smells and flavors of the Caribbean are alive at **Junior Sylvestor's**, where local rastas spit Island patois over bun & cheese. **Coney Island** is prime for big guts, packed beaches, bad tattoo choices, minor league ball games and the odd hipster taking it all in with ironic detachment. We'll be lining up for a classic hot dog from **Nathan's**, before puking it out after a turn on the historic Cyclone. After another pleasant day of sailing the lovely waters of Sheepshead Bay, **we'll be carbo-loading on guido food at L & B Spumoni Gardens** before some BK-style revelry at the **Salty Dog**.

RESTAURANTS Bay Ridge & Rest of Brooklyn

Areo Ristorante 8424 3rd Ave. (85th St.) (718) 238-0079 Italian. Bay Ridge locals love this place. A Valentine's Day favorite for ladies with big hair, dudes with fat wallets. Think: Moonstruck. Long wait, good pastas, Sicilian salad, swordfish steaks, amazing antipasti. And they take requests. Crowded, Noisy, Fun. The beginnings of a Brooklyn romance. +$45

Caribbean Delicacy 575 Lincoln Pl. (Bedford & Franklin Aves.) (718) 788-7558 Vegan & Caribbean. Cheap, healthy and delish. Rice and peas, dumplings, curried veggies, tofu treats and a cleansing tonic of maubi bark! Lawdavmercy! Niceness guaranteed by Diarmuid. -$8

Chadwicks 8822 3rd Ave. (88th St.) (718) 833-9855 American. Classy joint with old-school 40's atmo- cool by accident. Though they've had a spot on the Food Network, it's mostly just Bay Ridgers chowing down on the delicious Veal Saltimbocca or Pistachio Crusted Pork Chops. Inventive menu, romantic date spot, if you're into that kind of thing. $40

El Greco Diner 1821 Emmons Ave. (14th & 15th Sts.) (718) 934-1288 Diner. Hot Russian girls flipping standard diner menu in old timey, hipster fave diner. The Russian equivalent of polska-run Kellog's in Williamsburg. The staff speaking strictly Slavic. Tight people watching, a-ight eats and did we mention how fine Svetlana and her waitress friends were? This place is really ridiculous, you have to go. -$15

Embers 9519 3rd Ave (718)745-3700 Steakhouse. Not exactly Luger's, but carnivore worthy, indeed. Lots of loud, outer-Brooklynites with thick accents are quieted by the succulent T-Bone or the juicy Filet Mignon. "Oh my gawd" is heard throughout the room as the special sauce is poured. We're just kvelling over this place. $40

Gina's Café 409 Brighton Beach Ave. (Brighton 4th & 5th Sts.) (718) 646-6297 Russian. Let us introduce you to the Blini-bling bling. Coney Island hipster hang with snazzily-dressed immigrant kids, all to a Russian hip-hop soundtrack. Potato pancakes and caviar blintzes will fill you up, comrade. $13

Henry Grattan's 8814 3rd Ave. (88th & 89th Sts.) (718) 833-6466 American. A Brooklyn Italian's demented vision of an Irish Pub. Tacky lighting, lots of wood stuff. Bossman Frankie's delicious burgers are the big draw here, 2 for 1 on Mondays. Bossman Frankie goes to Hollywood for Thursday night karaoke. Must be seen to be believed.$15

John's Deli 2033 Stillwell Ave. (86th St.) (718) 372-7481 Deli. Dudes with gold chains, stone wash jeans & elaborate Nikes live for this famous old-school spot that gets packed on Wednesdays, Thursdays and Saturdays. The reason: a mound of paper-thin slices of roast beef, sautéed onions, and mozzarella on a French roll. Sublime guido food. -$10

Junior Sylvester's 1695 Utica Ave. (Aves. H & I) (718) 338-2968 Jamaican. One of the hottest spots in the 'Bush. Much beloved by locals, warrants a trip from the city for the atmo alone. They got the jerk chicken and tings, but what local heads go for is the bun & cheese. -$8

L & B Spumoni Gardens 2725 86th Street (718) 372-8400 Italian. Dyslexic pizza never tasted good so! Glorious epicenter of Bensonhurst guido culture serves up one of the most unique pies around: huge spongesquares with the sauce on top. Complete genius. Afterward, suck on some spumoni. $12 **BlackBook**

Nathan's Famous 1310 Surf Ave. (Stillwell Ave.) (718) 946-2202 Hot Dogs. Home of the freakiest hot dog eating contest on earth. No trip to Coney would be complete without some dogs from Nate's. Eat several then puke 'em up on the Cyclone after watching NY's truly local team kick ass. -$5

Odessa 1113 Brighton Beach Ave. (Brighton 13th & 14th Sts.) (718) 332-3223 Russian. Easily one of the weirder nights-out in NYC: sick Rockettes-style shows, huge Russian families, little kids rockin' Armani and Fendi like their parents. An endless prix fixe that includes bottle after bottle of Absolut. Bring your wallet, don't dispute the bill. +$65

Randazzo's Clam Bar 2017 Emmons Ave (21st St.) (718) 615-0010 Look for the neon lobster. Classic Sheepshead Bay seafood joint, all things fried and frittered; better than pricey stalwart Lundy's across the way. Tables of construction workers pounding beer and yelling for more fried clam strips. Bossy waitresses with Brooklyn charm bringin' 'em with haste. A truly cultural experience. $30 **BlackBook**

Roll N' Roaster 2901 Emmons Ave. (29th St.) (718) 769-6000 American. True Brooklynites remember the late night commercial jingle "They got the best at Roll N' Roaster". Kaiser rolls dunked in gravy then loaded with succulent roast beef. If you like, a squeeze of cheez. Served on paper plate with a mound of fries. Fake plants and molded plastic booths. Truly addictive. $10

Totonno Pizzeria Napolitano 1524 Neptune Ave. (W. 15th & W. 16th Sts.) (718) 372-8606 Pizza. Take it from Tony on their 3 am commercials: some of the finest pies in Brooklyn. Coney institution has been serving the masses since 1924. Sausage and anchovies are nice, but ask for the white pizza. Closed Mondays and Tuesdays. Why, you ask? Shut uppa your face, they make the rules. $18

NIGHTLIFE Bay Ridge & Rest of Brooklyn

Blue Zoo 8402 3rd Ave. (84 & 85) (718) 745-2721 From the depths of your wildest nightmares to the streets of Bay Ridge. A jungle-themed dance club, replete with leopard couches, glowing tropical fish tanks and murals with snarling tigers, glaring lions. Moronic monkeys on the dance floor, dressed as neophyte mobsters with their pleather pants and slicked back hair. Don't feed the animals.

L'amour 1545 63rd St. (718) 837-9506 The original heavy metal hangout. Poison's first tour landed them here: and there we were, fake ID in hand, desperately trying to get a glance at Rikki Rocket's ass in chaps and Brett Michaels' fake bulge. Back when girls reeked of Paul Mitchell hairspray and guys with eyeliner had a babe on each arm. Nope, not much has changed here.

Muses 8320 3rd Ave. (83rd & 84th Sts.) (718) 745-2721 Sophisto-guido chillout spot. Warm, familiar wine bar appeal, dotted with comfy couches. Kick-ass Espresso Martinis. Live Blues, Jazz, Swing bands on the weekends. Word around town: "This is where ya wanna take a chick, ya know?" $5 cover.

Rasputin 2670 Coney Island Ave. (Avenue X) (718) 332-8333 If you crave a tad of Vlad or a dash of Dasha, here's the joint for you. Double-breasted Armani suits and iced vodka. Be on your best behavior, because the Russian mob does not fuck around: You bring a knife, they bring a gun. You bring a gun, they bring a rocket launcher.

Salty Dog 7509 3rd Ave. (75th & 76th Sts.) (718) 238-0030 The true Brooklyn: cramped, cheesy, unintelligent, fun. Dudes: gel your hair to a hard crunchiness, paint on your lycra shirt and go for a swim in the cologne. Ladies: dust off the fake ID, get the glitter out, put vaseline on your freshly-inked lower-back tattoo (the pictionary version of "Every Rose Has Its Thorn"), and squeeze into those jeans. Make sure to pronounce the name "suoltie dawg". **BlackBook**

"A hundred times have I thought New York is a catastrophe...it is a beautiful catastrophe."

—Le Corbusier

QUEENS

(Map p. 213-214)

If the unbelievable culinary diversity isn't enough to convince you, gentle reader, to make an occasional trek to this oft-overlooked if not downright forgotten borough, how about the beautiful parks and tree-lined blocks of brownstones, the **small but high-quality nightlife scene**, the **cool museums highlighted by PS1 and the Noguchi Sculpture Garden**, an all-around friendly vibe and a **pleasant lack of hipsterness**? While Manhattan marches mindlessly into total coporatization, and Brooklyn follows lockstep with it's planned boondoggle skyscrapers, **Queens still feels like New York, gritty and real**. Still unconvinced? OK, Queens also has more sleazy titty-bars than the rest of the boroughs combined, led by the epic **Goldfinger's**. Find us there, or sipping a frosty draught at **L.I.C.** in L.I.C., savoring the tagines with Mustafa at **Mombar's** in Astoria or devouring the best Thai in NY at Jackson Heights' **Sripraphai**.

RESTAURANTS Long Island City

Lil' Bistro 33 33-04 36th Ave. (718) 609-1367 French. Definitely on the small side, but this lil' French-Asian combination has sophistication to spare. Chef Anza' seamlessly and subtly blends east and west: get the duck confit spring rolls to start. Upmarket and romantic, raises the class of the neighborhood by itself. +$35

Lounge 47 47-10 Vernon Blvd. (46th Rd. & 47th Ave.) (718) 937-2044 One of the better spaces in L.I.C., with an especially nice back garden. Interesting menu includes tasty apps like wasabi devilled eggs, solid sandwiches and the occasional clever martini. Best burger in the 'hood. $15

Sage American Restaurant 26-21 Jackson Ave. (44th Dr.) (718) 838-2257 American. Little walk-in sandwich spot in the shadow of the Shitibank building, caters to nearby P.S. 1 and the L.I.C. gallery/studio scene. All ingredients are fresh and organic, how the art-types like it. Nothing small about the Little Miami, the best Cuban in Queens, ma. $12

Ten 63 10-63 Jackson Ave. (48th & 49th Aves.) (718) 482-7679 Coffeehouse. Huge, lofty space, nicely reconfigured with clever architectural detail. Draws out the local freelancers, models, artists, Japanese punk bands and other glamorously underemployed with the best coffee in the 'hood, as well as buttery pastries and fresh salads and soups. -$10

Tournesol 50-12 Vernon Blvd. (50th & 51st Aves.) (718) 472-4355 French. Pascal and Pat's country bistro, anachronistic in the warehouse wasteland of L.I.C. Warm, gorgeous interior, the better to savor creative soups, a perfect duck breast, impeccable terrines of rabbit and fois gras, and coq au vin like your grandmere used to make. Look for the sunflower. $35 **BlackBook**

NIGHTLIFE Long Island City

L.I.C. 45-58 Vernon Blvd. (46th Ave.) (718) 786-5400. A nicely weathered corner bar thick with neighborhood history, resurrected by the folks behind Greenpoint's Pencil Factory. The hood deserved a bar of this character, with excellent imports and Brooklyn on tap. Low-lit, dark wood interior illuminated by live jazz many nights. Head to the back garden for smokes and conversation. **BlackBook**

Tupelo 34-18 34th Ave. (35th St.) (718) 707-9588 A real find, if you can find it. Awesome front doors you could tack your 95 theses to, give way to low-lit atmospheric haunt, stiff pours and plentiful cheap beers. Inclusive scene within is mercifully free of irony and electro. Also has screenings and a gallery.

RESTAURANTS Astoria

Elias Corner 24-02 31st St. (24th Ave.) (718) 932-1510 Greek. When in line, pay close attention to the refrigerated display counter, and the panoply of fish contained therein. You'll be quizzed on it later. Garish turquoise interior abuses the eyes, loved by locals nonetheless. All about huge platters of grilled fish and Hellenic beer. $25

Esperides 37-01 30th Ave. (37th St.) (718) 545-1494 Greek. Astoria mainstay with the full panoply of Greek cuisine on show. Airy interior, reminiscent of your island home on Zakynthos. The roasted suckling pig is a massive feast, or go with any of the grilled fish, all fresh. No kissing after the especially garlicky tzatziki. -$30

Girassol Churrascaria 33-18 28th Ave. (33rd & 34th Sts.) (718) 545-8250 Brazilian. Astorio-Brazilians are loyal to the food, so no need to decorate. Fab feijoada and picanha, among other Brazillian classics, all richly spiced and fragrant. Give props to Ronaldo, and applaud as brave staff leaves for deliveries on infamous duct-taped Vespa. -$20

Mombar 25-22 Steinway St. (25th & 28th Aves.) (718) 726-2356 Egyptian. No menus, no sign outside, tiny cinnamon-scented room of tapestries, mosaics, stained glass and happy regulars. Forget that dry flavorless falafel ubiquitous to Manhattan; everything here is fresh, richly spiced. Try the chicken tagine and nicely scented couscous. $28 **BlackBook**

Sabry's Seafood 24-25 Steinway St. (25th Ave. & Astoria Blvd.) (718) 721-9010 Greek. Friendly Muslim owned spot disallows booze, but no worries, you'll be so slap-happy about the food, it don't matter. Delicious tagines served in earthenware bowls simmering with cumin and fragrant spices, fresh fish are grilled to perfection. $25

Zlata Praha 28-48 31st St. (Newtown Ave.) (718) 721-6422 Czech. The best Czech restaurant in all of NYC. A little slice of malastarna under the authentic décor harkens back to quaint, Commie-era Czechoslovakia. Fried cheese and pivo like you're streetside on Wencelas Square. Great beers on tap and a nice courtyard. $20

NIGHTLIFE Astoria

Athens Café 32-07 30th Ave. (31st & 32nd Sts.) (718) 626-2164 Astoria triangle intersection is prime people-watching locale. Sit outside in the shade of the N train with the Greek talent, their boyfriends, and their boyfriends' friends. Frappés and tight shirts for everyone.

Bohemian Hall & Beer Garden 29-19 24th Ave. (29th & 30th Sts.) (718) 274-4925 Awesome summertime diversion, sippin' Spaten in the best beer garden in New York, a throwback to a long-forgotten era. Munch on Czech sausage and lots of other robust snacks and drinking foods. **BlackBook**

Café Bar 32-90 36th St. (34th Ave.) (718) 204-5273 Casual spot serves pastries and brunch, including a great roast pork and haloumi sandwich, but owner Monica Contantinides's spot is best after-hours. Astorian hipstahs, continental kids right from Laguardia, hot girls with unpronounceable names, all nudge and nustle in retro-boho hang.

Cavo 42-18 31st Ave. (41st & 42nd Sts.) (718) 721-1001 Even the competition admits that this is the center of Astoria nightlife. Eurohouse/Eurostyle on the deca-dent dance floor, interesting finger foods and cocktails in the decadent Hellenic gar-den. Greeks with velvet ropes, so dress to impress.

Lounge 32 32-03 Broadway (32nd St.) (718) 204-7010 Come lounge with some suds in hand, scoping all the Greek hotties in tight jeans under the low lights. A true outer-borough nightclub experience. Rock Night is Tuesday, no matter what the sign says. Greek rock, that is.

Rapture Lounge 34-27 28th Ave (35th St.) (718) 626-8044 Why Astorians never come to the city. Greek hotties, Asian hipstahs, Italian suits: Astoria's multi-culti mix cozy up, have Sex on the Sofa(s). Corner spot on a quiet block has plenty of late night diversions: DJs, live local bands, tarot card readings, and good people-watching.

RESTAURANTS Jackson Heights, Sunnyside, Woodside & Rest of QNS

Afghan Kabob House #4 74-16 37th Ave. (74th & 75th Sts.) (718) 565-0471 Afghan. Warm hospitality in a simple, calming setting. Owner Mohammed Mian suggests the fish or chicken kabobs, followed by amazing fried boulanee: tiny pumpkin turnovers served with a minty yogurt dip. One of several in the city, this one's got the coziest vibe. $18

Ariyoshi 41-13 Queens Blvd. (41st & 42nd Sts.) (718) 937-3288 Japanese. Oishi means delicious. Yasui means cheap. Kuweenuzu means Queens. Family-style bentos are everything Nobu isn't, thankfully, and the sushi, sashimi and assorted snacks and side dishes are all fresh, robust and delicious. $18

Eddie's Sweet Shop 105-29 Metropolitan Ave. (718) 520-8514 A Norman Rockwell scene: malts, shakes, egg creams, sundaes w/homemade ice cream and big gobs of nostalgia, all from a century old soda-fountain. Queens classic is much-beloved in the neighborhood, perfect pre/post Mets games or U.S. Open. $5

Inti Raymi 86-14 37th Ave. (86th & 87th Sts.) (718) 424-1938 Peruvian. The purple stuff everybody's drinking? Cold chicha morada. You can make your own at home! Chill, colorful little family spot around the corner from big Indian joints, get with some hella fresh (and cheap!) ceviche, and a great papa rellena. Big futbol watching contingent. $15

Jackson Diner 37-47 74th St. (Roosevelt & 37th Aves.) (718) 672-1232 Indian. Bully of the banghra block. The bangin' lunch buffet is still dominant, check all the midtown heavy hitters who hop on the 7 train just to take advantage. We like the creamy saag paneer and perfect tandoori, then raita cools the palate. After, head around the corner for hot Bollywood action. $22 **BlackBook**

La Flor Bakery and Café 53-02 Roosevelt Ave. (53rd St.) (718) 426-8023 Mexican. Welcoming Mexican bakery with the imaginative French and Italian touches, highlighted by the insane, ornate, mouth-watering pastry displays. Locals love the imaginative brunch by chef Vilto, including the bourbon-vanilla French toast, huevos rancheros and amazing trittata. -$15

QUEENS

La Porteña 74-25 37th Ave. (74th St.) (718) 458-8111 Argentine. Apparently an all-meat diet is what makes Argentines so fine. Authentic country-style digs, dig into enormous, endless plates of perfectly cooked and sliced beef. Top it off with a calming, yet strangely stimulating mate tea. Gauchos give chase if you utter the name Beckham. ¡Aguanten los pibes! +$25

Nick's Pizza 108-26 Ascan Ave. (Austin & Burns Sts.) (718) 263-1126 Pizza. Forest Hills hideaway. Queens natives scoff at the lines at Grimaldi's, Lombardi's, et al. This is the real deal Holyfield, right here: thin pies with incredible fresh sauce and imported mozzarella are addictive. Nice array of toppings include fresh mushrooms and olives, but keep it simple. $16

Sripraphai 6413 39th Ave. (64th St.) (718) 899-9599 Thai like they do it in Thailand, not that cute, fusion-y Manhattan stuff. Upbeat, friendly spot will have you reminiscing about the Kha Sahn road, without all the lady-boys. They expanded to accommodate growing fan-base, all clamoring for bowls of green curry, chicken coconut soup and spicy duck. Huge menu demands multiple visits. $12 **BlackBook**

NIGHTLIFE Jackson Heights, Sunnyside, Woodside & Rest of Qns

Goldfinger's 92-77 Queens Blvd. (Harris Harding Expressway) (718) 997-8661 If Whitesnake were a place instead of a band. Everything's big (10,000 sq. ft.) and artificial: the screens, the stage, the buffets, the tits. Check out AV star Tera Patrick! Downtown needs one of these sooo badly.

Kilmegan's 60-19 Roosevelt Ave. (61st St.) (718) 803-9206 ...Then hide her body's. Loved by locals for years, thankfully resisted the temptation to modernize. Yeats, perfectly greasy shepherd's pie, frosty Guinness, Arsenal vs. Chelsea on the telly and lots of nooks and crannies for serious imbibing: pubbing at it's finest, mate.

"I moved to New York City for my health. I'm paranoid and New York was the only place where my tears were justified." —Anita Weiss

HOTELS

New York hotels offer everything the discerning traveler requires: fancy addresses, high-end amenities, fine bars and restaurants, attentive clerks that you can throw phones at when it's 4am and you're trying to call Australia. Though the fabled Plaza shut it's fast-fading doors, majestic warhorses of yore like the **St. Regis**, the **Pierre** and the increasingly trippy Carlye continue to dazzle. Designer downtowners like the **Mercer**, **60 Thompson**, and the **SoHo Grand** ooze casually fabulous celeb cred, while hip sproutlings like the Gansevoort, **Soho House** and **Hotel on Rivington** capitalize on fashionable lands once reserved for transvestite hookers and drug dealers (though Soho House has probably seen its share of both). Find us at the **Hotel Chelsea** with a bottle and a ouija board, eavesdropping on the ghosts of Mark Twain and Sid Vicious.

HOTELS Downtown

Abingdon Guest House 13 8th Ave. (12th St.) (212) 243-5384 As close to West Village townhouse experience one can get without buying a small dog and an Equinox pass. Two beautiful, historic homes with a mélange of rooms from romantic to too-cutesy. Open to all, but prefers the type that's gonna be respectful and ain't gonna make a lot of racket. $150-225

The Cosmopolitan Hotel 95 W. Broadway (Chambers St.) (212) 566-1900 Downtown and clean, but low in the frill department. Holds it's own as low maintonance option during Tribeca film festival. Smallish rooms with double beds and white and purple color scheme. Area is nice to walk around in, but can deserted streets and proximity to Ground Zero makes it a little eerie at night $100-159

East Village Bed & Coffee 110 Ave. C (7th & 8th Sts.) (212) 533-4175 Puts the B&B into Alphabet City. The place is clean, quirky and boasts ethnically themed room like the Mexican or the Afghani. Chill common areas and free local calls (though most are probably dialing international). Recently expanded to nine rooms. The incredibly warm owner Anne keeps the younger crowd cozy. $80-110

Holiday Inn Downtown 138 Lafayette St. (Howard St.) (212) 966-8898 Wins points for location near nightlife-heavy LES and shop-heavy SoHo as well as being temporary crash site for dazed-looking Chinese businessmen and Bowery Ballroom-bound rockers on budget-conscious indie labels. Loses points for not having pool like HI's midtown branch. $120-235

Hotel Chelsea 222 W. 23rd St. (7th & 8th Aves.) (212) 243-3700 New York treasure. Trod in footsteps of Twain, Dylan, and Christo, eclectic charmer has inspired all manner of artist since 1884. Storied past rife with creative bursts, celebrity conceptions and legendary misbehavior, retains aura of endless possibilities. High ceilings, relaxed, bohemian atmo. The unique rooms run gamut from jackpot to double whammy, but still better bet than roulette. $175-485 **BlackBook**

Hotel Gansevoort 18 9th Ave (Little West 12th & 13th Sts.) (877) 426-7386 Glowing beacon in the meatpacking district. Proof that New York has become sooooo LA. Rooftop bar and pool attracts all varieties of social barnacles. Mobbed on weekends with tan people in bold striped shirts and expensive denim. Spacious suites with balconies, DVD players and Ono room service (though view of Pastis may beckon). $270-2400

Hotel on Rivington 107 Rivington St. (Ludlow & Essex Sts.) (212) 475-2600 New kid on the LES block. Sets itself as design-fueled destination amid this hood's booming restaurant scene and rock nightlife. Stylish and slick, with glass walls and Moby endorsement. Definitely a place to use the upgrade. Rooftop dream of a penthouse boasts whirlpool on deck. "Regular" rooms offer the "feel of old New York." Think tenements, folks. $235-5000 ☆

The Inn at Irving Place 56 Irving Pl. (17th & 18th Sts.) (212) 533-4600 Possibly the calmest in the city. Disappear behind unmarked door into rose-tinted haze on one of New York's quietest blocks. Very Edith Wharton. Take tea at the dainty Lady Mendl's tea salon or quaff blackberry cosmos at Cibar. Four-post beds and antiques abound. Window box seats. $325-500

The Maritime Hotel 363 W. 16th St. (8th & 9th Aves.) (212) 242-4300 Hope you brought your sea legs to Eric Goode's behemoth nautical playground. Studded with porthole windows, stuffed with an upscale Japanese and a rustic Italian restaurant, a sweeping patio, a palmy cocktail deck, a booming nightclub, as well as assorted scenesters, preps, and barely legal Russian tennis phenoms. Be thankful for the distractions, because rooms are cabin-sized. $345

The Mercer 147 Mercer St. (Prince St.) (212) 966-6060 Sets standard for SoHo dolce vita. 75 high-ceilinged mini-lofts feature FACE Stockholm products, exquisite linens, and Dean & Deluca minibar. 24-hour room service from Mercer Kitchen. Stops from Prada, Marc Jacobs, etc. Celeb scene in the lobby is almost always frighteningly A-List. $410-2300 **BlackBook**

Off Soho Suites 11 Rivington St. (Chrystie St. & Bowery) (212) 979-9808 Low rates rock on a block littered with crazies trying to get off the rock. Rooms clean and not too tight, limited but genial service. Comfortable downtown value for Henry Rollins, students and hostel-weary wanderers who don't need a designer label but dig proximity to Soho and the LES. $170-230

The Ritz-Carlton Battery Park 2 West St. (Battery Pl.) (212) 344-0800 Luxurious downtown waterfront rooms fit with a telescope, chilling in comfort beside historic military park and bustling financial district. Lady Liberty looks on as you're pampered with the amenities you'd expect from the Ritz, plus special care for families and tycoons who need to keep Street cred. Teddy bears for the kids, real Ross Bleckners for the parents. $249-4500

60 Thompson 60 Thompson St. (Broome & Spring Sts.) (212) 431-0400 Off the hectic main drags of SoHo, rocking custom designer furniture. Understated, elegant, trendy without being obnoxious. Beautiful rooms quite snug, but the spacious standup shower leaves room for mutual scrubbing. Kittichai is a fine dish downstairs and A 60's rooftop drinks offer unparalleled views. $325-3500

Soho Grand Hotel 310 W. Broadway (Grand & Canal Sts.) (212) 965-3000 Trendsetting, trendy pioneer boutique flawlessly merges SoHo's industrial hulk with its fashionista ways. Buff headset-bustin' staff navigates a steady stream of bold-faced head-turners who flood the hot Grand Bar. Prive's spa can make you one of them too. Unwind in The Yard as legions of dolled up lovelies idle past. $300-1700

Soho House 29 9th Ave. (13th St.) (212) 627-9800 Brit-style members-only club and hotel has lost some of its hype, but we wager that's when the fun really begins. Non-members can get into the mix via the hotel rooms that boast mix of antique and modern furniture, luxurious pillows and bedding. Endless celeb-spotting, prime hammock-testing and supreme views of the Hudson River. $200-825

Tribeca Grand Hotel 2 6th Ave. (White & Walker Sts.) (212) 519-6600 Sensual, pulsing, hot décor, beautiful tri-state trendies and in-the-know trippers cram Church Lounge and more exclusive inner Sanctum. Downtown via Vegas. White hot during the Tribeca Film Festival. Check the basement for discreet screenings in the comfy theater with the rising Hollywood starlet of your choice. $300-1700

Washington Square Hotel 103 Waverly Pl. (MacDougal St. & 6th Ave.) (212) 777-9515 Recently-renovated, the "deluxe" rooms have old Hollywood glamour shots and minimalist design. Other rooms are just minimalist. Quaint in feel with '30s lobby. As close to the famed park as one can get. Parents visiting NYU? This is the chance to meet the your daughter's weed dealer. $110-170

The Algonquin Hotel 59 W. 44th St. (5th & 6th Aves.) (212) 840-6800 The rapier wit from Miss Parker's Round Table has dulled a bit over the years. But you can sift through the evidence of their loose gaiety amidst the retouched marble and ironwork-infused study of a lobby. Homey and muted rooms, plus liquor-fueled high-kickin' intelligentsia history for dramatic breaths of the past. $250-420

Bryant Park Hotel 40 W. 40th St. (5th & 6th Aves.) (212) 869-0100 Style, ease and polish on display at this never stuck-up star hotel. Cellar Bar's a sophisticated rager. Rooms gorgeous, spacious, comfortably modern and quiet with treetop park views. Sublime stay, solid scene, always mighty. Go during Fashion Week for utter madness or in the summer for movies in the park. $350-3000

The Carlyle 35 E. 76th St. (Park & Madison Aves.) (212) 744-1600 Wow. Adopt unrecognizable accent, put on tuxedo and eye patch, and get ready to take over the world. Deluxe, dutiful, discreet. So classy it's sleazy. Diane von Furstenburg swaps Botox tips with Baron von Shittenstuff, under dense air of archaic formalities, international intrigue and mural by Madeline author Ludwig Bemelman. Spacious rooms, aristocratic décor. Over 23 grand pianos on the premises. 550-5000

City Club Hotel 55 W. 44th St. (5th & 6th Aves.) (212) 921-5500 Sublime quarters from party boy Jeff Klein, hosting boutique digs ideal for theater access. Intimate, private, well-designed with modern flourish. The baths alone are worth it. Snack on truffle burgers at ultra-cool DB Bistro Moderne, which is also reserved exclusively for guests at breakfast. $300-700 **BlackBook**

Dylan 52 E. 41st St. (Madison & Park Aves.) (212) 338-0500 Beaux-Arts building with 107 sexy rooms sporting dark walnut furnishings and electric candlelight. Alchemy suite is a vaulted Gothic chamber perfect for seduction. Business and tech savvy for those that need to check on the interweb. House restaurant Chemist Club has several prescriptions for self-medicating needs. $260-460

Four Seasons Hotel 57 E. 57th St. (Park & Madison Aves.) (212) 758-5700 Like living within plush confines of a Faberge egg. Vast rooms, celestial style, service nearing perfection. Catch Eminem breezing through the impressive grand lobby. Have an expensive dram at 57 57 and keep your eyes open for world-class beauties, Asian power brokers, and assorted moguls. Sophisticated excellence! $600-800

The Gershwin Hotel 7 E. 27th St. (Madison & 5th Aves.) (212) 545-8000 If Warhol's Factory ran a hostel. Starck design, pop murals, swirling fun. Good recreation for cool out-of-town friends, worth visiting them later to get hammered and naked on the nutty rooftop. Pretend you're going to one of the multiple art galleries located within, when in fact you beeline for the model-only floor $90-150

Hotel Elysée 60 E. 54th St. (Park & Madison Aves.) (212) 753-1066 Since 1926, one of NY's best. Fun hanging upside down at the Monkey Bar. Site of many Broadway bacchanals, upwardly mobiles gone wild. European sense and charm, mellow yet attentive staff. Rooms indulge both comfort and taste. Channel Tennessee Williams in the PH, or get romantic in the Club Room. $225-775

Hotel Giraffe 365 Park Ave. So. (26th) (212) 685-7700 Located on a reservation for the non-endangered Young-Affluent-White-Chicks-Who-Work-In-PR species. Glitzy boutique from the peeps behind the Library, Elysée and Casablanca. Not cheap, rooms a tad tiny, but you're close to Union Square and right next to a bunch of cool restaurants like Sushi Samba. Free breakfast adds compliment to comfort. $265-525

Hotel QT 125 W, 45th. St. (6th & 7th Aves.) (212) 354-2323 Swedish sauna culture meets Japanese love hotel. Andre Balazs' low-rent hustle right off Times Square. Check in at the ticket booth, pass tiny dip pool in the lobby and head to possibly the smallest rooms in the city (quite the feat in New York). Like living in a hip efficiency apartment. Those under 25 get reduced rates. $95-285 ★

Hudson Hotel 356 W. 58th St. (8th & 9th Aves.) (212) 554-6000 Schraeger and Starck's west side claim. Psychedelic garden, art show reception, crammed to the gills with trendy nightcrawlers lubricating at Hudson Bar. Pounding beats everywhere, even in the Library Bar. Rooms are small but serviceable. Zippy energy feels like you're entering another world. $150-400

Jazz on the Park Hostel 36 W. 106th St. (Park Ave.) (212) 932-1600 Represent uptown! Coolest city hostel works hard to keep you busy for less than forty bones: breakfast, towels, coffee bar, barbecues, outside terraces, Yankee games, walking tours and hard bebop. Alcohol use tolerated and appreciated. And no curfew, thank God. Just don't be surprised if the manager parties harder than you. $26-36

Library Hotel 299 Madison Ave. (41st St.) (212) 983-4500 Sedate, luxury boutique a tad close to Grand Central madness, yet remarkably serene. We'll be in the Erotic Literature room, brushing up on our de Sade. Try not to get stuck on the Science floor, though we have heard that synapses are sexy these days. Dewey Decimal never lived so large. Great fast-breaking upstairs on the terrace. $195-375

The Mansfield 12 W. 44th St. (5th & 6th Aves.) (212) 944-6050 Small, exquisitely appointed, copper façade, meticulous old-time craftsmanship. Gorgeous inside and out. Some nice rates to be found at this busty boutique. Includes every comfort possible. Stylish individual interiors in every room, mellow tones, jacuzzi and fireplace suites. 24-hour espresso machine if midtown activity isn't enough to wake you up. $190-350

The Mark Hotel 25 E. 77th St. (Madison & 5th Ave.) (212) 744-4300 One of the coolest uptown, so cool Johnny Depp had to go apeshit on one of the 57 beautiful suites. Surroundings are formal but there is a casual vibe. Excellent jewel-box bar loaded with bisexual Euros and straight-shooting Texans. Complimentary cell phones for guests and discreet, subtle service. $550-2500 **BlackBook**

Morgans Hotel 237 Madison Ave. (37th & 38th Sts.) (212) 686-0300 Classic city boutique still satisfies. Asia De Cuba seems a tad less ingenious since the world ran wild with its concept, but it's still a tight, popular noodle. Rooms are modern and stylish though a bit too wee to justify existence at times, but you'll be too busy canoodling downstairs with the hot scenery to mind. Randy Mapplethorpe prints provide wall inspiration for naughtier guests. $250-3000

The Muse 130 W. 46th St. (6th & 7th Aves.) (877) 692-6873 Theater-centric hotel offers spacious rooms and attention to details. Check out the customized business cards with your temporary address and phone number. They come in handy when meeting and greeting at in house District, lavishly designed by Rockwell. In house spa and gymnasium. Elegant lobby, huggable staff. $270-470

The New York Palace 455 Madison Ave. (50th & 51st Sts.) 1-800-NYPALACE Exquisite palatial digs owned by the Sultan of Brunei himself, with all the overwrought gaudiness you'd expect. Caligula-esque quality to the décor, but it can look mind-numbingly ornate and incredibly lavish. Try not to get lured to the Sultan's real palace overseas for quality time in his renowned "discotheque." $600-1500

Novotel 226 W. 52nd St. (Broadway) (212) 315-0100 Skying high above the great white way with postcard views of classic New York vistas. From the giant marquee to its position smack in the heart of Broadway, it's a theater-lover's luxury dream come true. Towering 33 floors of casual sophistication, well-trod by the business set, who can even rent laptops from the hotel. $275-450

Paramount Hotel 235 W. 46th St. (Broadway & 8th Ave.) (212) 764-5500 Hard to find anything this reasonably priced in Times Square that doesn't come from a Senegalese dude's briefcase. Fresh flowers for everyone. Uncomfortably tiny rooms a letdown after sweeping dramatic lobby. 24-hour gym to work off the Whiskey Bar hangover. $150-400

Parker Meridien 118 W 57th St (6th & 7th Aves.) (212) 245-5000 Stride like 50 Cent and Ashton through stately, grand columns and indulge all power trip perversions in pampering environs. Midtown's favorite brunch commanded at Norma's including a $1,000 omelette. Cheaper (and maybe better eats at hidden roadhouse Burger Joint. Rooftop pool, champagne and croissants in bed with a rose. $370-3,000

The Pierre 2 E. 61st St. (Madison & 5th Aves.) (212) 838-8000 Nursing home for Boardwalk/Park Place holders. Even the hookers haunting the bar are old. Elegant flowers n' antiques, generous, noble, basically perfect. We'd kick some life into this majestic site of the notorious 1972 jewel heist, but like a disguised Dashiell Hammett in 1932, we'd have to run out on the tab. $425-1000

Plaza Athénée 37 E. 64th St. (Park & Madison Aves.) (212) 734-9100 On blessed tree-lined block just off the otherworldly Madison Avenue scene. Within, you'll find Parisian polish, Parisian services, and regal extras. The floral arrangements are ornate, rich and lavish – much like the hotel guests themselves. It's quite awesome for those who can afford Louis XIV ridiculousness and a staff who'll do anything to please. $350-3600

The Ritz-Carlton Central Park 50 Central Park South (6th Ave.) (212) 308-9100 No matter what one asks for, it is always the staff's pleasure to assist. Dodge Lamborghini stopping on dime out front. 33-story five-star lodging replete with lobby harp. Frédéric Fekkai amenities, marble baths and Bang & Olufson electronics. Many of the rooms have Central Park views, but proximity to handsome cabstand leaves heavy air of manure at entrance. $600-2900

Royalton 44 W. 44th St. (5th & 6th Aves.) (212) 869-4400 Velvet and mahogany elegance, Dean & Deluca goodies, and more well-coiffed MILFs than you can shake an apple martini at. Still a ridiculous scene during fashion week, when the industry rubs shoulders in nipped and tucked lobby or doesn't eat at 44. Haute monde magnet perfect for batting outta one's league, or preying on the bountiful Conde Nasties. $200-700

Shoreham 33 W. 55th St. (5th Ave.) (212) 247-6700 Old school boutique vibe in the very heart of Midtown, a stone/telephone throw from Central Park. Stellar, sleek lobby, luxe beds, beautifully designed accents throughout, great see-thru bathrooms in the rooms, and complimentary breaking of the fast. Basically a sophisticated urban oasis. $269 and up

Sofitel 45 W. 44th St. (5th & 6th Aves.) (212) 354-8844 Very elegant, very French hospitality on the pulse of 5th Ave. in hot, rounded glass tower. The Frenchosity stops on the non-smoking floors, however. Gorgeous lush rooms and incredible suites, fine European bath products, city views to stop time and a delicious Pan-Gallic bite at Gaby's. $195-799

The St. Regis 2 E. 55th St (5th Ave.) (212) 753-4500 Marble, gold, crystal, tremendous bouquets and white-gloved butler service. King Cole might have scared off a few too many bar patrons with his offensive antics, but the attractive couples and stray packs of singles who do show up at disputed home of the Bloody Mary have grace. You couldn't be doing much better unless you had the dough to buy the joint. Hats off to GM Gunter Richter for another job perfectly done! $600-1300

Swissôtel New York·The Drake 440 Park Ave. (56th St.) (212) 421-0900 Shout-out from Fat Joe. Wooden wonderland in Midtown with polished ski-lodge vibe. Warm staff, excellent eats. Luxurious pleasures. Expansive suites might make you hide from check out. The spa heals, builds and soothes. Great stay. Runs smooth like an expertly crafted watch or a certain neutral government we admire. $225-1300

Time Hotel 224 W. 49th St (Broadway & 8th Ave.) (212) 246-5252 What time it is? Nineteen floors of boutique charm and modern, elegant digs. Chromatically-inspired boutique, down to the walls, jellybeans and perfumes meant to evoke certain colors. Fun lounge and fitness center, and pretty close to everything up here. Cocco Pazzo is a delicious treat below. $150-500

W New York 541 Lexington Ave. (49th and 50th Sts.) (212) 755-1200
W Times Square 1567 Broadway (47th St.) (212) 930-7400
W The Court 130 E. 39th St. (Lexington & Park Aves.) (212) 685-1100
W The Tuscany 120 E. 39th St. (Lexington & Park Aves.) (212) 686-1600
W Union Square 201 Park Ave. So. (17th St.) (212) 253-9119
You know you can always trust the W for glitz, quality and fun times. Union Square and Times Square are the coolest bets at the titans of fashionista boutiquery. The lobbies are always a guaranteed lounge scene worthy of the hippest cats. Restaurants like Icon, Blue Fin and Olive's offer diverse range of fresh, hip fare. Midtown rooms are comfy, but Union Square offers prime location and stunning looks. $220-950

HOTELS

The Waldorf·Astoria 301 Park Ave. (49th & 50th Sts.) (212) 355-3000 Where the president sleeps, rumored to have own subway exit in case of emergencies. Feel roaring vibes of '20s jazz ghosts and tycoon champagne orgies at New York's landmark behemoth hotel with three bars and four restaurants. Business travel focus leaves us a bit bummed that it's no longer the most epic place to party, but stokes us when we needs to get down to bidness. Impressive and gorgeous. $200-875

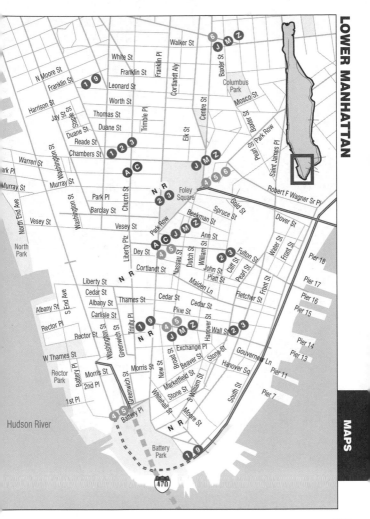

LOWER MANHATTAN

MAPS

BLACKBOOKMAG.COM 189

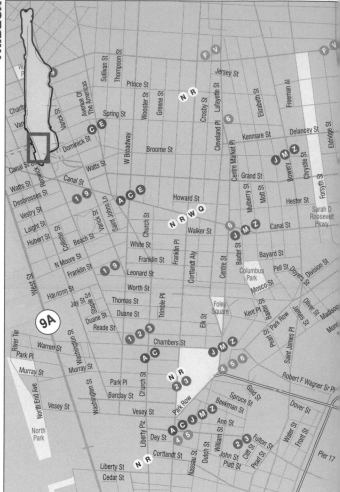

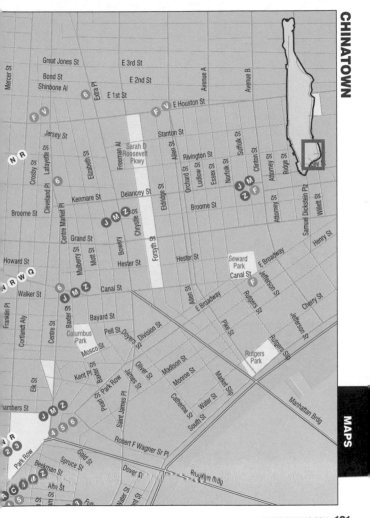

Mercer St
Great Jones St
Bond St
Shinbone Al
Edra Pl
E 3rd St
E 2nd St
E 1st St
Avenue A
Avenue B

F V
F V E Houston St

Jersey St
Stanton St

N R
Lafayette St
Crosby St
Freeman Al
Sarah D Roosevelt Pkwy
Allen St
Orchard St
Ludlow St
Essex St
Norfolk St
Suffolk St
Clinton St
Attorney St
Ridge St

6
Elizabeth St
Rivington St

Cleveland Pl
Kenmare St
Delancey St

Centre Market Pl
Eldridge St
Broome St

J M Z
Attorney St
Samuel Dickstein Plz
Willett St

Bev

J M Z F

Broome St

Mulberry St
Mott St
Bowery
Chrystie St
Forsyth St
Grand St

Howard St

N R W Q
Walker St

Hester St
Hester St

Seward Park
Canal St

E Broadway
Henry St

6 J M Z
Canal St

F

Baxter St
Bayard St

Centre St
Pell St
Doyers St
Division St
Allen St
E Broadway
Rutgers St
Jefferson St
Cherry St

Columbus Park
Mosco St

Franklin Pl
Cortlandt Aly

Elk St
Kent Pl
Baxter St
Pearl St
Park Row
Oliver St
James St
Madison St
Monroe St
Catherine St
Water St
South St
Market Slip
Rutgers Slip
Jefferson St
Rutgers Park

hambers St

J M Z
Saint James Pl
Robert F Wagner Sr Pl
Manhattan Brdg

N R
2 3
4 5 6
Park Row
Gold St
Spruce St
Beekman St
Dover St
Brooklyn Brdg

A C
J M Z
Ann St
Water St
Fult

5
am St
Ful

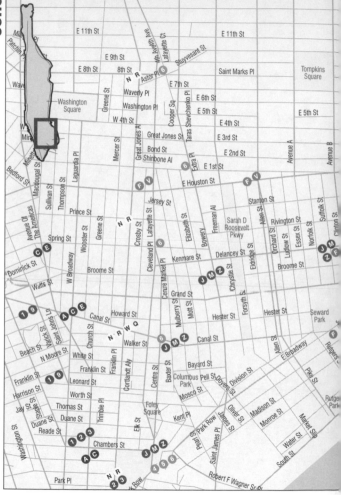

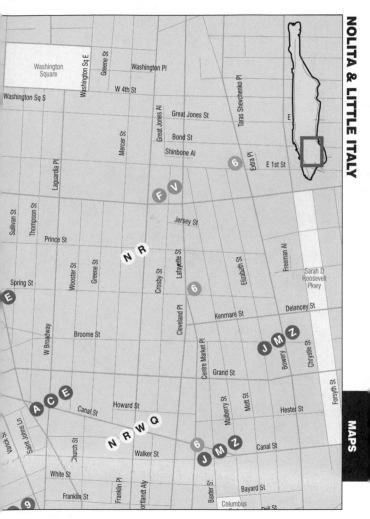

MAPS

LOWER EAST SIDE

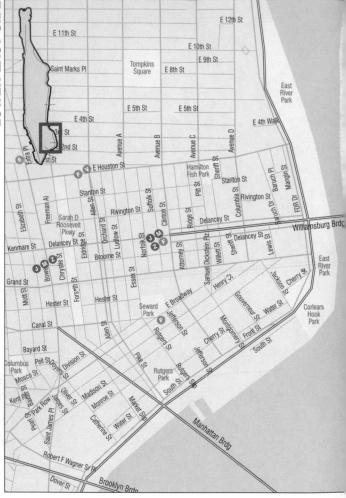

E 11th St

E 12th St

Saint Marks Pl

E 10th St

E 9th St

Tompkins
Square

E 8th St

E 5th St

E 5th St

East
River
Park

E 4th St

E 4th Walk

3rd St

Avenue A

Avenue B

Avenue C

Avenue D

2nd St

1st St

Extra Pl

E Houston St

Hamilton
Fish Park

Stanton St

Stanton St

Freeman Al

Sarah D
Roosevelt
Pkwy

Allen St

Orchard St

Rivington St

Suffolk St

Clinton St

Pitt St

Sheriff St

Rivington St

Columbia St

Baruch Pl

Mangin St

FDR Dr

Williamsburg Brdg

Elizabeth St

Ridge St

Delancey St

Kenmare St

Eldridge St

Ludlow St

Norfolk St

Attorney St

Willett St

Sheriff St

Lewis St

Delancey St

Bowery

Chrystie St

Delancey St

Broome St

Samuel Dickstein Plz

East
River
Park

Grand St

Forsyth St

Essex St

Mott St

Henry St

Jackson St

Cherry St

Hester St

Hester St

E Broadway

Gouverneur St

Montgomery St

Front St

Water St

Corlears
Hook
Park

Canal St

Seward
Park

Jefferson St

Cherry St

South St

Bayard St

Rutgers St

Pike St

Allen St

Columbus
Park

Pell St

Division St

Rutgers
Park

South St

Mosco St

Doyers St

Madison St

Jefferson St

Rutgers St

Manhattan Brdg

Kent Pl

Baxter St

Oliver St

James St

Monroe St

Catherine St

Market Slip

Water St

South St

Pearl St

Park Row

Saint James Pl

Robert F Wagner Sr Pl

Dover St

Brooklyn Brdg

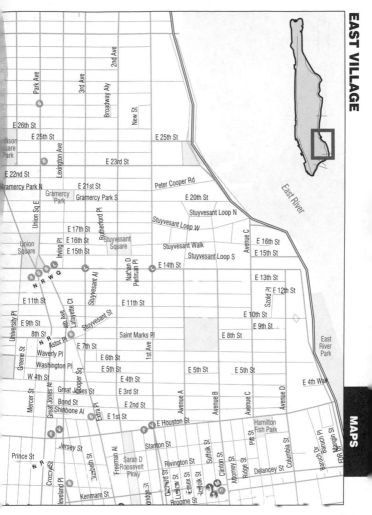

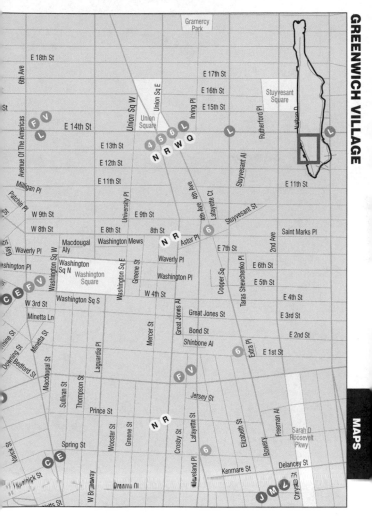

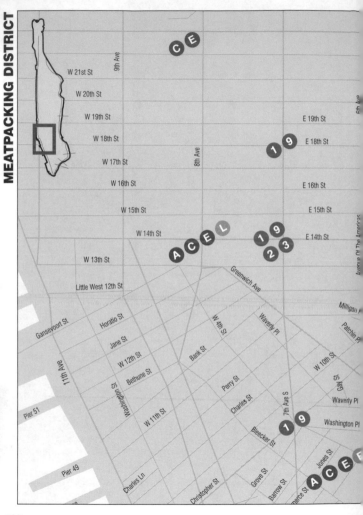

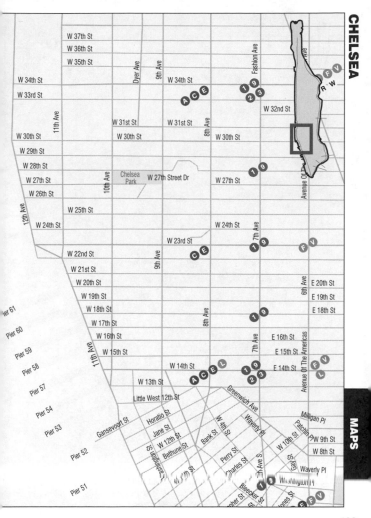

FLATIRON, UNION SQUARE & GRAMERCY

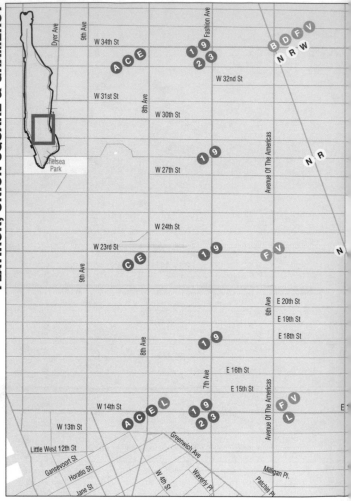

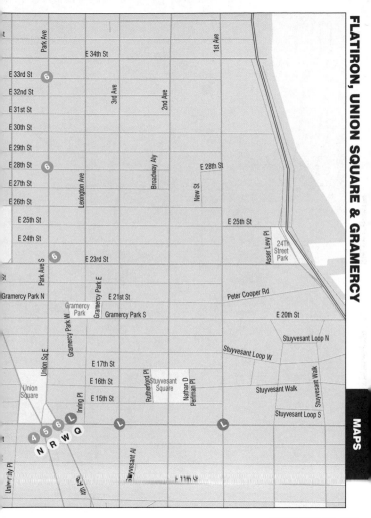

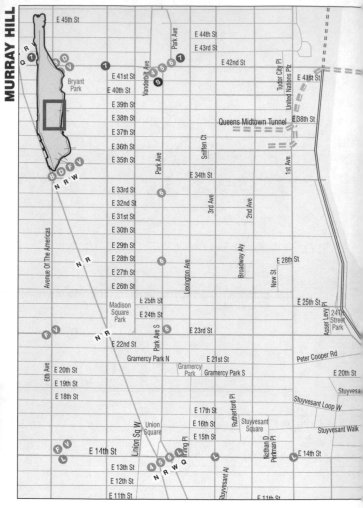

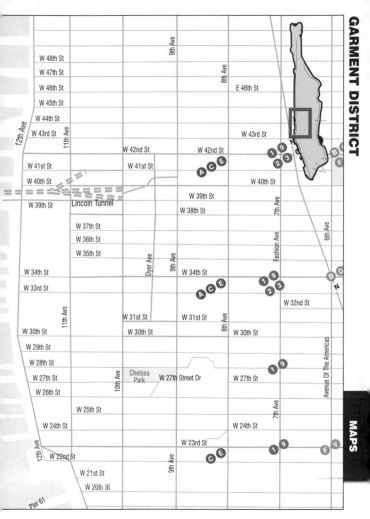

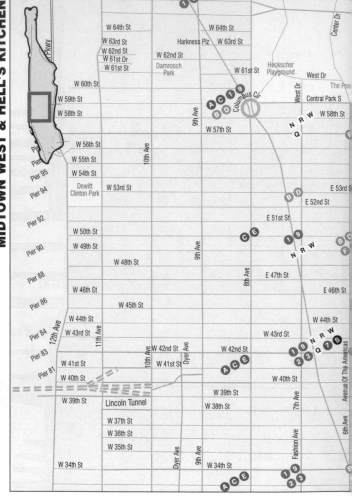

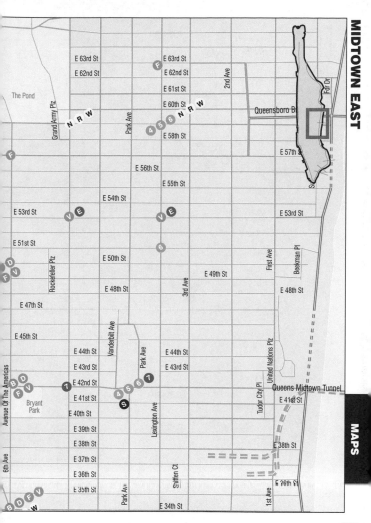

MAPS

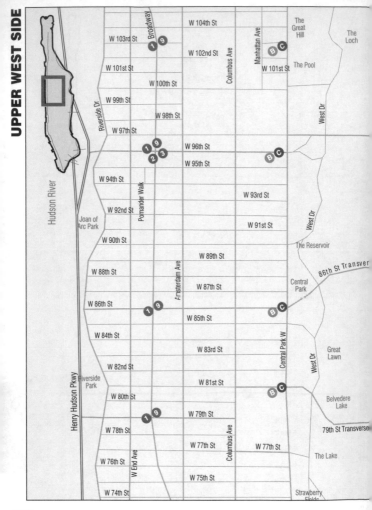

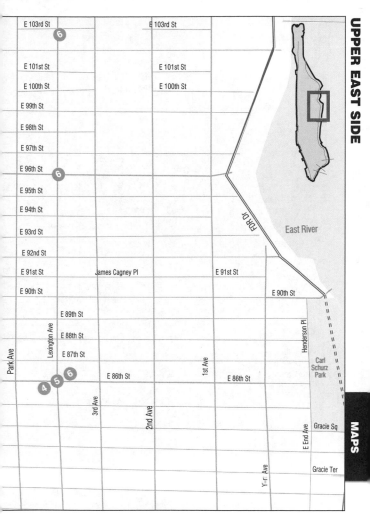

E 103rd St

6

E 103rd St

E 101st St

E 101st St

E 100th St

E 100th St

E 99th St

E 98th St

E 97th St

E 96th St

6

E 95th St

E 94th St

E 93rd St

E 92nd St

E 91st St

James Cagney Pl

E 91st St

E 90th St

E 90th St

E 89th St

E 88th St

E 87th St

E 86th St

E 86th St

E 103rd St

FDR Dr

East River

Henderson Pl

Carl Schurz Park

Park Ave

Lexington Ave

1st Ave

3rd Ave

2nd Ave

Y__r Ave

E End Ave

Gracie Sq

Gracie Ter

4 5 6

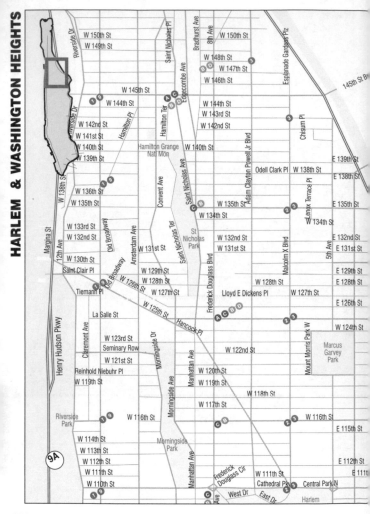

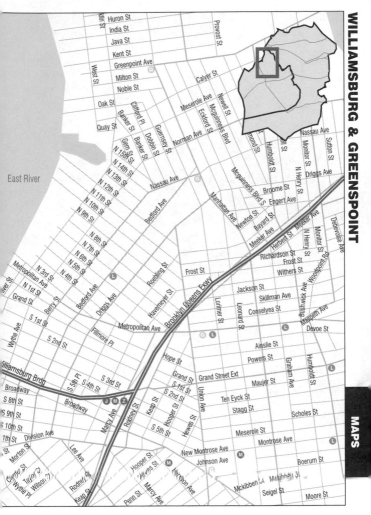

East River

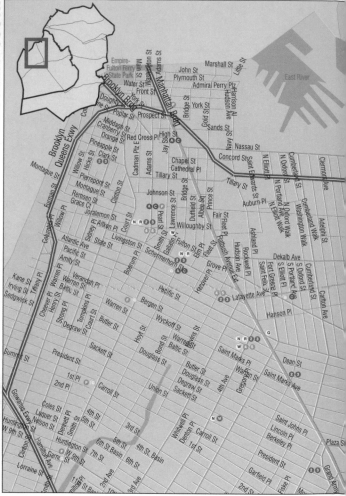

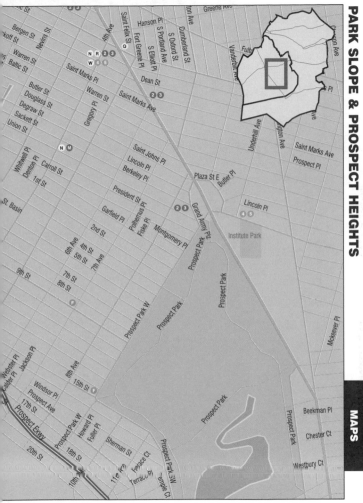

John Ericson Dr
Road Park
Owls Head Park
Owls Head Ct
68th St
70th St
Bliss Ter
Louise Ter
Mackay Pl
Ridge Crest
Bay Cliff Ter
Sedgwick Pl
Bergen Pl
Wakeman Pl
67th St
Senator St
68th St
Madeline Ct
Perry Ter
Bay Ridge Pl
72nd Ct
71st St
72nd St
73rd St
74th St
Narrows Ave
Colonial Rd
Ridge Ct
Barnett Ct
Ovington Ave
Bay Ridge Ave
Senator St
Vista Pl
62nd St
63rd St
64th St
65th St
62nd St
63rd St
64th St
3rd Ave
4th Ave
5th Ave
6th Ave
N R
66th St
Shore Road Dr
67th St
78th St
77th St
76th St
Shore Rd
80th St
Colonial Ct
Harbor Ln
Harbor View Ter
79th St
Ridge Blvd
78th St
80th St
81st St
82nd St
83rd St
Shore Road Ln
84th St
85th St
R
Bay Ridge Pkwy
7th Ave
71st St
72nd St
73rd St
74th St
Gowanus Expwy
Narrows Ave
Shore Ct
07th St
88th St
Ridge Blvd
3rd Ave
Colonial Gdns
91st St
90th St
92nd St
87th St
88th St
89th St
90th St
Forest
R
86th St
Fort Hamilton Pkwy
Dyker Pl
7th Ave
8th Ave
Oliver St
93rd St
94th St
Marine Ave
93rd St
94th St
95th St
96th St
93rd St
Lafayette Walk
Hamilton Walk
Wogan Ter
Gelston Ave
Fort Hamilton Pkwy
Gatling Pl
Dahlgren Pl
Battery Ave
Parrott Pl
90th St
95th St
96th St
97th St
Barwell Ter
98th St
97th St 97th St
R
95th St
Oliver St
99th St
Harbor Ct
99th St
100th St
101st St
Jackson Ct
Fort Hill Pl
Dahlgren Pl
Gowanus Expwy

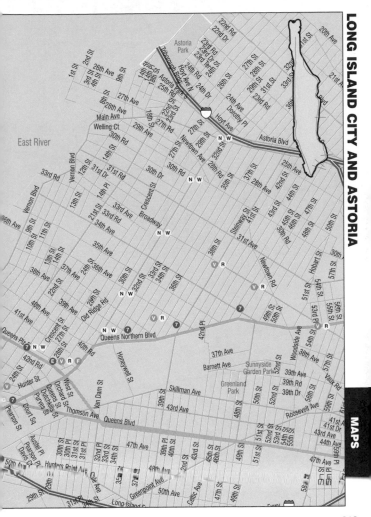

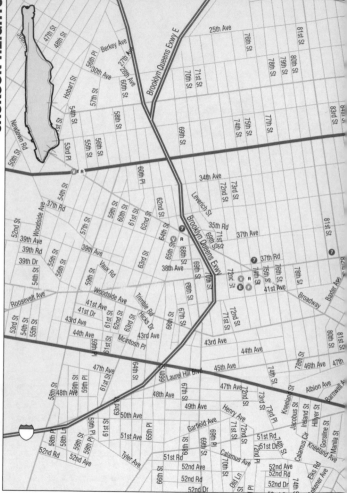

JACKSON HEIGHTS

"New York is a city of conversations overheard, of people at the next restaurant table

(micrometers away) checking your watch, of people reading the stories

in your newspaper on the subway train." —William E. Geist

INDEX

INDEX

T